Ninja Foodi
2-Basket Air Fryer

Cookbook for Beginners

Simple & Delicious Ninja 2-Basket Air Fryer Recipes

for Your Ninja Foodi Dual Zone Air Fryer

Doris Cason

Table of Contents

Introduction

Life is too busy today, and there is no time to cook for a long day. If you want to eat delicious and healthy meals, the Ninja Foodi 2-Basket Air Fryer solves your problem. The Ninja Foodi 2-Basket Air Fryer is a new arrival amongst diversified air fryers. Now, you can cook a large amount of food because it has two baskets. You can cook two different food items with two same or different settings. It is different from a single basket air fryer. This appliance targets people who want to enjoy delicious and healthy but less fatty meals with a crispy texture. The Ninja Foodi 2-Basket Air Fryer is an excellent appliance to fulfill all the cooking needs. You can create excellent restaurant-style meals in your kitchen with Ninja Foodi 2-Basket Air Fryer.

No doubt, the Ninja Foodi 2-Basket Air Fryer plays a vital role in making healthy and delicious foods. You don't need to stand in your kitchen cooking food for a long time. The benefits of this appliance are that it is easily washable and requires less oil to cook food.

The Ninja Foodi 2-Basket Air Fryer works on dual zone technology. It allows you to prepare double dishes at the same time with two different cooking baskets and temperatures. If you have a big family, then you can cook food for them at the same time. The cooking zones have a separate temperature controller and cyclonic fan that spread heat evenly into the cooking baskets.

The Ninja Foodi 2-Basket Air Fryer cooks your favorite food in less oil. It gives you crispy food without changing the taste and texture. You can create different dishes for any occasion or picnic. The Ninja Foodi 2-Basket Air Fryer has useful cooking functions, such as max crisp, air fry, and roasts, reheat, dehydrate, and bake. All valuable functions are present in one appliance. You don't need to purchasing separate appliances for baking or dehydrating food. You can roast chicken, beef, and fish using this appliance—Bake the cake, muffins, cupcakes, pancakes using bake cooking functions.

It is pretty simple to use. Once you understand Ninja Foodi 2-Basket Air Fryer, you can prepare delicious food for your family and friends without any hesitation. Cook food with The Ninja Foodi 2-Basket Air Fryer.

What is Ninja Foodi 2-Basket Air Fryer?

The Ninja Foodi 2-Basket Air Fryer works on dual zone technology. You can prepare multiple dishes at the same time with two different cooking temperatures in two different baskets. The Ninja Foodi 2-Basket Air Fryer has six useful cooking functions: max crisp, air fry, roast,

reheat, dehydrate and bake. It has a MATCH button with which one can cook food by copying the setting across both zones. It has a capacity large enough for a whole and big family up to four pounds. The two zones have separate cooking baskets that can cook food quickly using cyclonic fans.

The Ninja Foodi 2-Basket Air Fryer is easy to wash. You will find details of cleaning and maintenance tips for Ninja Foodi 2-Basket Air Fryer in the book.

It includes a smart finish feature cooking system so that you can cook food at the same time with two different settings. If you are looking to cut down your cooking in half, you can prepare same meals in two different baskets or different meals in two different baskets. You can set both zones same settings and cook the same meals in double portions without spending a lot of time; then, you need the Ninja Foodi 2-Basket Air Fryer. The method of using this appliance is pretty simple.

Main Functions

The Ninja Foodi 2-Basket Air Fryer has six cooking functions: max crisp, air fry, roast, reheat, dehydrate and bake. This appliance has a large capacity. You can prepare food for your big family. If you want to bake a cake with the Ninja Foodi 2-Basket Air Fryer, you can select "bake"

cooking mode.

MAX CRISP:

This cooking function is perfect for frozen foods such as chicken nuggets and French fries etc. Using this function, you will get crispy and tender food. With less time, you will get crispy and tender food.

AIR FRY:

This cooking function will allow you to cook food with less oil and fat than other cooking methods. Using this function, you will get crunchy and crispy food from the outside and juicy and tender food from the inside. You can prepare chicken, beef, lamb, pork, and seafood using this cooking option.

ROAST:

Now, you didn't need an oven to roast food. The Ninja Foodi 2-Basket Air Fryer has useful cooking function, "roast". With this function, you can roast chicken, lamb, seafood, and vegetable dishes. It is one of the dry cooking methods that give you a nice brown texture to the food and increase the flavor of your foods.

REHEAT:

The reheat function can quickly warm your food without changing its texture and flavor if you have leftover food. Now, you didn't need to place food onto the stovetop for reheating.

DEHYDRATE:

This cooking function is used to dehydrate fruits, meat, and vegetables. Using this cooking method, you can preserve food for a long time. It takes hours to dehydrate the food but gives you a delicious and crispy texture.

BAKE:

This cooking method allows you to bake cakes, muffins, cupcakes, and any other dessert on any occasion or regular day. You didn't need an oven to bake the food. The Ninja

Foodi 2-Basket Air Fryer has a baking option for baking your food with delicious texture.

Buttons and User Guide of Ninja Foodi 2-Basket Air Fryer

With the cooking function, the next thing you should focus on is operating buttons. The Ninja Foodi 2-Basket Air Fryer has effective features. Let's discuss!

ZONE 1: Control the output for the drawer on the left

ZONE 2: Control the output for the drawer on the right

SYNC button:

The function is used to sync the cooking time automatically and ensure that both cooking zones finish their cooking simultaneously, even if there is a difference between the cooking times.

TIME arrows:

Using these buttons, you can adjust cooking time according to recipe instructions.

TEMP arrows:

Using these buttons, you can adjust temperature according to recipe instructions.

MATCH button:

The function is used to match the cooking zone 2 settings with the cooking zone 1 settings on an enormous amount of different or same food cooking at the same time, temperature and function.

START/STOP button:

When you select the time and temperature for cooking food, then press the START/STOP button.

Power button:

The power button is used to turn the unit on or off and stops all cooking functions.

HOLD MODE:

This function will appear on the unit while in sync mode. When food is cooked in zone 1, then it holds zone 2 until times sync together.

STANDBY MODE:

After ten minutes with no interaction with the control panel, the unit will enter standby mode.

Cleaning and Maintenance

The interior parts of the Ninja Foodi 2-Basket Air Fryer are made of non-stick coating, so you can easily clean it. Here is how to clean and maintain your Ninja Foodi 2-Basket Air Fryer after cooking:

Unplug your appliance before cleaning it and allow it to cool completely.

Remove the air fryer baskets from the unit and let them cool.

When cooled, remove their crispier plates and wash them in the dishwasher.

Clean the baskets with soapy water and but don't use hard scrubbing; otherwise, it will damage the surface.

Wipe the main unit with a clean piece of cloth or damp cloth.

When all parts of the air fryer dried, return to the unit.

Now, you can use it again for cooking

4-Week Diet Plan

Week 1

Day 1:
Breakfast: Pumpkin Muffins
Lunch: Stuffed Tomatoes
Snack: Cheddar Quiche
Dinner: Salmon with Coconut
Dessert: Fried Oreos

Day 2:
Breakfast: Egg with Baby Spinach
Lunch: Zucchini with Stuffing
Snack: Peppered Asparagus
Dinner: Air Fryer Meatloaves
Dessert: Pumpkin Muffins with Cinnamon

Day 3:
Breakfast: Air Fried Bacon and Eggs
Lunch: Mixed Air Fry Veggies
Snack: Stuffed Bell Peppers
Dinner: Chili Chicken Wings
Dessert: Walnuts Fritters

Day 4:
Breakfast: Morning Egg Rolls
Lunch: Curly Fries
Snack: Tater Tots
Dinner: Seafood Shrimp Omelet
Dessert: Air Fried Beignets

Day 5:
Breakfast: Breakfast Bacon
Lunch: Buffalo Bites
Snack: Cauliflower Gnocchi
Dinner: Beef & Broccoli
Dessert: Apple Nutmeg Flautas

Day 6:
Breakfast: Breakfast Casserole
Lunch: Garlic-Herb Fried Squash
Snack: Onion Rings
Dinner: Chicken & Broccoli
Dessert: Cinnamon Sugar Dessert Fries

Day 7:
Breakfast: Bacon and Egg Omelet
Lunch: Fried Artichoke Hearts
Snack: Chicken Stuffed Mushrooms
Dinner: Breaded Scallops
Dessert: Mini Strawberry and Cream Pies

Week 2

Day 1:
Breakfast: Bacon and Eggs for Breakfast
Lunch: Quinoa Patties
Snack: Grill Cheese Sandwich
Dinner: Beef Cheeseburgers
Dessert: Chocolate Chip Muffins

Day 2:
Breakfast: Egg White Muffins
Lunch: Brussels Sprouts
Snack: Zucchini Chips
Dinner: Chicken Drumettes
Dessert: Bread Pudding

Day 3:
Breakfast: Banana Muffins
Lunch: Kale and Spinach Chips
Snack: Crispy Chickpeas
Dinner: Salmon with Green Beans
Dessert: Chocolate Chip Cake

Day 4:
Breakfast: Air Fried Sausage
Lunch: Air Fried Okra
Snack: Fried Pickles
Dinner: Ham Burger Patties
Dessert: Biscuit Doughnuts

Day 5:
Breakfast: Crispy Hash Browns
Lunch: Mushroom Roll-Ups
Snack: Potato Tater Tots
Dinner: Balsamic Duck Breast
Dessert: Air Fryer Sweet Twists

Day 6:
Breakfast: Sausage with Eggs
Lunch: Stuffed Sweet Potatoes
Snack: Parmesan Crush Chicken
Dinner: Garlic Butter Salmon
Dessert: Apple Crisp

Day 7:
Breakfast: Sweet Potatoes Hash
Lunch: Zucchini Cakes
Snack: Parmesan French Fries
Dinner: Breaded Pork Chops
Dessert: Churros

Week 3

Day 1:
Breakfast: Cinnamon Toasts
Lunch: Lime Glazed Tofu
Snack: Spicy Chicken Tenders
Dinner: Chicken Leg Piece
Dessert: Strawberry Nutella Hand Pies

Day 2:
Breakfast: Banana and Raisins Muffins
Lunch: Hasselback Potatoes
Snack: Crispy Tortilla Chips
Dinner: Glazed Scallops
Dessert: Fried Oreos

Day 3:
Breakfast: Air Fryer Sausage Patties
Lunch: Fried Olives
Snack: Ravioli
Dinner: Korean BBQ Beef
Dessert: Jelly Donuts

Day 4:
Breakfast: Hash Browns
Lunch: Green Beans with Baked Potatoes
Snack: Dijon Cheese Sandwich
Dinner: Dijon Chicken Wings
Dessert: Lava Cake

Day 5:
Breakfast: Bagels
Lunch: Pepper Poppers
Snack: Crispy Plantain Chips
Dinner: Honey Sriracha Mahi Mahi
Dessert: Apple Fritters

Day 6:
Breakfast: Spinach Egg Muffins
Lunch: Fried Avocado Tacos
Snack: Chicken Crescent Wraps
Dinner: Chipotle Beef
Dessert: Mini Blueberry Pies

Day 7:
Breakfast: Perfect Cinnamon Toast
Lunch: Fresh Mix Veggies in Air Fryer
Snack: Sweet Bites
Dinner: Chicken Breast Strips
Dessert: Apple Hand Pies

Week 4

Day 1:
Breakfast: Pepper Egg Cups
Lunch: Saucy Carrots
Snack: Stuffed Mushrooms
Dinner: Two-Way Salmon
Dessert: Zesty Cranberry Scones

Day 2:
Breakfast: Breakfast Sausage Omelet
Lunch: Fried Asparagus
Snack: Chicken Tenders
Dinner: Pork Chops
Dessert: Baked Apples

Day 3:
Breakfast: Yellow Potatoes with Eggs
Lunch: Herb and Lemon Cauliflower
Snack: Garlic Bread
Dinner: Cornish Hen with Asparagus
Dessert: Fudge Brownies

Day 4:
Breakfast: Sweet Potato Sausage Hash
Lunch: Garlic Potato Wedges in Air Fryer
Snack: Jalapeño Popper Chicken
Dinner: Crispy Ranch Nuggets
Dessert: Lemony Sweet Twists

Day 5:
Breakfast: Biscuit Balls
Lunch: Falafel
Snack: Fried Halloumi Cheese
Dinner: Crispy Catfish
Dessert: Air Fried Bananas

Day 6:
Breakfast: Morning Patties
Lunch: Cheesy Potatoes with Asparagus
Snack: Mac and Cheese Balls
Dinner: Glazed Steak Recipe
Dessert: Oreo Rolls

Day 7:
Breakfast: Donuts
Lunch: Garlic Herbed Baked Potatoes
Snack: Mozzarella Sticks
Dinner: Chicken Wings
Dessert: Grilled Peaches

Chapter 1 Breakfast Recipes

Morning Patties

Prep Time: 15 minutes | Cook Time: 13 minutes | Serves: 4

Ingredients:

1 lb. minced pork
1 lb. minced turkey
2 teaspoons dry rubbed sage

2 teaspoons fennel seeds
2 teaspoons garlic powder
1 teaspoon paprika

1 teaspoon of sea salt
1 teaspoon dried thyme

Preparation:

1. In a mixing bowl, add turkey and pork, then mix them together. 2. Mix sage, fennel, paprika, salt, thyme, and garlic powder in a small bowl. 3. Drizzle this mixture over the meat mixture and mix well. 4. Take 2 tablespoons of this mixture at a time and roll it into thick patties. 5. Place half of the patties in Zone 1, and the other half in Zone 2, then spray them all with cooking oil. 6. Return the crisper plate to the Ninja Foodi Dual Zone Air Fryer. 7. Choose the Air Fry mode for Zone 1 and set the temperature to 390 degrees F/200 degrees C and the time to 13 minutes. 8. Select the "MATCH" button to copy the settings for Zone 2. 9. Initiate cooking by pressing the START/STOP button. 10. Flip the patties in the drawers once cooked halfway through. 11. Serve warm and fresh.

Serving Suggestion: Serve the patties with toasted bread slices.

Variation Tip: Ground chicken or beef can also be used instead of ground pork and turkey.

Nutritional Information Per Serving: Calories 305 | Fat 25g | Sodium 532mg | Carbs 2.3g | Fiber 0.4g | Sugar 2g | Protein 18.3g

Crispy Hash Browns

Prep Time: 10 minutes | Cook Time: 13 minutes | Serves: 4

Ingredients:

3 russet potatoes
¼ cup chopped green peppers
¼ cup chopped red peppers

¼ cup chopped onions
2 garlic cloves chopped
1 teaspoon paprika

Salt and black pepper, to taste
2 teaspoons olive oil

Preparation:

1. Peel and grate all the potatoes with the help of a cheese grater. 2. Add potato shreds to a bowl filled with cold water and leave it soaked for 25 minutes. 3. Drain the water and place the potato shreds on a plate lined with a paper towel. 4. Transfer the shreds to a dry bowl and add olive oil, paprika, garlic, and black pepper. 5. Make four flat patties out of the potato mixture and place two into each of the crisper plate. 6. Return the crisper plate to the Ninja Foodi Dual Zone Air Fryer. 7. Choose the Air Fry mode for Zone 1 and set the temperature to 390 degrees F/200 degrees C and set the time to 13 minutes. 8. Select the "MATCH" button to copy the settings for Zone 2. 9. Initiate cooking by pressing the START/STOP button. 10. Flip the potato hash browns once cooked halfway through, then resume cooking. 11. Once done, serve warm.

Serving Suggestion: Serve the hash with toasted bread slices and crispy bacon.

Variation Tip: Add herbed cream on top of the hash browns.

Nutritional Information Per Serving: Calories 190 | Fat 18g | Sodium 150mg | Carbs 0.6g | Fiber 0.4g | Sugar 0.4g | Protein 7.2g

Air Fried Sausage

Prep Time: 10 minutes | Cook Time: 13 minutes | Serves: 4

Ingredients:

4 sausage links, raw and uncooked

Preparation:

1. Divide the sausages in the two crisper plates. 2. Return the crisper plate to the Ninja Foodi Dual Zone Air Fryer. 3. Choose the Air Fry mode for Zone 1 and set the temperature to 390 degrees F/200 degrees C and set the time to 13 minutes. 4. Select the "MATCH" button to copy the settings for Zone 2. 5. Initiate cooking by pressing the START/STOP button. 6. Serve warm and fresh.

Serving Suggestion: Serve the sausages with toasted bread and eggs.

Variation Tip: Add black pepper and salt for seasoning.

Nutritional Information Per Serving: Calories 267 | Fat 12g | Sodium 165mg | Carbs 39g | Fiber 1.4g | Sugar 22g | Protein 3.3g

Pepper Egg Cups

Prep Time: 15 minutes | Cook Time: 18 minutes | Serves: 4

Ingredients:

2 halved bell pepper, seeds removed
4 eggs

1 teaspoon olive oil
1 pinch salt and black pepper

1 pinch sriracha flakes

Preparation:

1. Slice the bell peppers in half, lengthwise, and remove their seeds and the inner portion to get a cup-like shape. 2. Rub olive oil on the edges of the bell peppers. 3. Place them in the two crisper plates with their cut side up and crack 1 egg in each half of bell pepper. 4. Drizzle salt, black pepper, and sriracha flakes on top of the eggs. 5. Return the crisper plates to the Ninja Foodi Dual Zone Air Fryer. 6. Choose the Air Fry mode for Zone 1 and set the temperature to 390 degrees F/200 degrees C and the time to 18 minutes. 7. Select the "MATCH" button to copy the settings for Zone 2. 8. Initiate cooking by pressing the START/STOP button. 9. Serve warm and fresh.

Serving Suggestion: Serve the cups with toasted bread slices and crispy bacon.

Variation Tip: Broil the cups with mozzarella cheese on top.

Nutritional Information Per Serving: Calories 183 | Fat 15g | Sodium 402mg | Carbs 2.5g | Fiber 0.4g | Sugar 1.1g | Protein 10g

Morning Egg Rolls

Prep Time: 15 minutes | Cook Time: 13 minutes | Serves: 6

Ingredients:

2 eggs
2 tablespoons milk
Salt, to taste

Black pepper, to taste
½ cup shredded cheddar cheese
2 sausage patties

6 egg roll wrappers
1 tablespoon olive oil
1 cup water

Preparation:

1. Grease a small skillet with some olive oil and place it over medium heat. 2. Add sausage patties and cook them until brown. 3. Chop the cooked patties into small pieces. Beat eggs with salt, black pepper, and milk in a mixing bowl. 4. Grease the same skillet with 1 teaspoon of olive oil and pour the egg mixture into it. 5. Stir cook to make scrambled eggs. 6. Add sausage, mix well and remove the skillet from the heat. 7. Spread an egg roll wrapper on the working surface in a diamond shape position. 8. Add a tablespoon of cheese at the bottom third of the roll wrapper. 9. Top the cheese with egg mixture and wet the edges of the wrapper with water. 10. Fold the two corners of the wrapper and roll it, then seal the edges. 11. Repeat the same steps and divide the rolls in the two crisper plates. 12. Return the crisper plates to the Ninja Foodi Dual Zone Air Fryer. 13. Choose the Air Fry mode for Zone 1 and set the temperature to 375 degrees F/190 degrees C and the time to 13 minutes. 14. Select the "MATCH" button to copy the settings for Zone 2. 15. Initiate cooking by pressing the START/STOP button. 16. Flip the rolls after 8 minutes and continue cooking for another 5 minutes. 17. Serve warm and fresh.

Serving Suggestion: Serve the rolls with your favorite hot sauce or cheese dip.

Variation Tip: Add crispy bacon to the filling.

Nutritional Information Per Serving: Calories 282 | Fat 15g | Sodium 526mg | Carbs 20g | Fiber 0.6g | Sugar 3.3g | Protein 16g

Spinach Egg Muffins

Prep Time: 10 minutes | Cook Time: 13 minutes | Serves: 4

Ingredients:

4 tablespoons milk
4 tablespoons frozen spinach, thawed
4 large eggs

8 teaspoons grated cheese
Salt, to taste
Black pepper, to taste

Cooking Spray

Preparation:

1. Grease four small-sized ramekin with cooking spray. 2. Add egg, cheese, spinach, and milk to a bowl and beat well. 3. Divide the mixture into the four small ramekins and top them with salt and black pepper. 4. Place the two ramekins in each of the two crisper plate. 5. Return the crisper plate to the Ninja Foodi Dual Zone Air Fryer. 6. Choose the Air Fry mode for Zone 1 and set the temperature to 390 degrees F/200 degrees C and the time to 13 minutes. 7. Select the "MATCH" button to copy the settings for Zone 2. 8. Initiate cooking by pressing the START/STOP button. 9. Serve warm.

Serving Suggestion: Serve the muffins with toasted bread slices and crispy bacon.

Variation Tip: Add sliced bell peppers to the muffins.

Nutritional Information Per Serving: Calories 237 | Fat 19g | Sodium 518mg | Carbs 7g | Fiber 1.5g | Sugar 3.4g | Protein 12g

Biscuit Balls

Prep Time: 10 minutes | Cook Time: 18 minutes | Serves: 6

Ingredients:

1 tablespoon butter
2 eggs, beaten
¼ teaspoon pepper

1 can (10.2-oz) Pillsbury Buttermilk biscuits
2 ounces cheddar cheese, diced into ten cubes
Cooking spray

Egg Wash
1 egg
1 tablespoon water

Preparation:

1. Place a suitable non-stick skillet over medium-high heat and cook the bacon until crispy, then place it on a plate lined with a paper towel. 2. Melt butter in the same skillet over medium heat. Beat eggs with pepper in a bowl and pour them into the skillet. 3. Stir cook for 5 minutes, then remove it from the heat. 4. Add bacon and mix well. 5. Divide the dough into 5 biscuits and slice each into 2 layers. 6. Press each biscuit into 4-inch round. 7. Add a tablespoon of the egg mixture at the center of each round and top it with a piece of cheese. 8. Carefully fold the biscuit dough around the filling and pinch the edges to seal. 9. Whisk egg with water in a small bowl and brush the egg wash over the biscuits. 10. Place half of the biscuit bombs in each of the crisper plate and spray them with cooking oil. 11. Return the crisper plate to the Ninja Foodi Dual Zone Air Fryer. 12. Choose the Air Fry mode for Zone 1 and set the temperature to 375 degrees F/190 degrees C and the time to 14 minutes. 13. Select the "MATCH" button to copy the settings for Zone 2. 14. Initiate cooking by pressing the START/STOP button. 15. Flip the egg bombs when cooked halfway through, then resume cooking. 16. Serve warm.

Serving Suggestion: Serve the eggs balls with crispy bacon.
Variation Tip: Add dried herbs to the egg filling.
Nutritional Information Per Serving: Calories 102 | Fat 7.6g | Sodium 545mg | Carbs 1.5g | Fiber 0.4g | Sugar 0.7g | Protein 7.1g

Breakfast Bacon

Prep Time: 10 minutes | Cook Time: 14 minutes | Serves: 4

Ingredients:

½ lb. bacon slices

Preparation:

1. Spread half of the bacon slices in each of the crisper plate evenly in a single layer. 2. Return the crisper plate to the Ninja Foodi Dual Zone Air Fryer. 3. Choose the Air Fry mode for Zone 1 and set the temperature to 390 degrees F/200 degrees C and the time to 14 minutes. 4. Select the "MATCH" button to copy the settings for Zone 2. 5. Initiate cooking by pressing the START/STOP button. 6. Flip the crispy bacon once cooked halfway through, then resume cooking. 7. Serve.

Serving Suggestion: Serve the bacon with eggs and bread slices.
Variation Tip: Add salt and black pepper for seasoning.
Nutritional Information Per Serving: Calories 273 | Fat 22g | Sodium 517mg | Carbs 3.3g | Fiber 0.2g | Sugar 1.4g | Protein 16.1g

Sausage with Eggs

Prep Time: 10 Minutes | Cook Time: 13 Minutes | Serves: 2

Ingredients:

4 sausage links, raw and uncooked
4 eggs, uncooked
1 tablespoon green onion

2 tablespoons chopped tomatoes
Salt and black pepper, to taste
2 tablespoons milk, dairy

Oil spray, for greasing

Preparation:

1. Take a bowl and whisk eggs in it. 2. Then pour milk, and add the onions and tomatoes. 3. Whisk it all well. 4. Now season it with salt and black pepper. 5. Take one cake pan that fits inside the air fryer and grease it with oil spray. 6. Pour the omelet into the greased cake pan. 7. Put the cake pan inside zone 1 of the Ninja Foodie 2-Basket Air Fryer. 8. Now place the sausage link into the zone 2 basket. 9. Select BAKE for zone 1 basket and set the timer to 8-10 minutes at 300 degrees F/150 degrees C. 10. For zone 2, select the AIR FRY button and set the timer to 12 minutes at 390 degrees F/200 degrees C. 11. Once the cooking cycle is complete, serve by transferring it to plates. 12. Chop the sausage or cut it in round chunks and then mix it with the egg. 13. Enjoy hot as a delicious breakfast.

Serving Suggestion: Serve it with toasted bread slices
Variation Tip: Use almond milk if you like non-dairy milk
Nutritional Information Per Serving: Calories 240 | Fat 18.4g | Sodium 396mg | Carbs 2.8g | Fiber 0.2g | Sugar 2g | Protein 15.6g

Cinnamon Toasts

Prep Time: 15 minutes | Cook Time: 8 minutes | Serves: 4

Ingredients:

4 pieces of bread
2 tablespoons butter
2 eggs, beaten

1 pinch salt
1 pinch cinnamon ground
1 pinch nutmeg ground

1 pinch ground clove
1 teaspoon icing sugar

Preparation:

1. Add two eggs to a mixing bowl and stir cinnamon, nutmeg, ground cloves, and salt, then whisk well. 2. Spread butter on both sides of the bread slices and cut them into thick strips. 3. Dip the breadsticks in the egg mixture and place them in the two crisper plates. 4. Return the crisper plates to the Ninja Foodi Dual Zone Air Fryer. 5. Choose the Air Fry mode for Zone 1 and set the temperature to 390 degrees F/200 degrees C and the time to 8 minutes. 6. Select the "MATCH" button to copy the settings for Zone 2. 7. Initiate cooking by pressing the START/STOP button. 8. Flip the French toast sticks when cooked halfway through. 9. Serve.

Serving Suggestion: Serve the toasted with chocolate syrup or Nutella spread.

Variation Tip: Use crushed cornflakes for breading to have extra crispiness.

Nutritional Information Per Serving: Calories 199 | Fat 11.1g | Sodium 297mg | Carbs 14.9g | Fiber 1g | Sugar 2.5g | Protein 9.9g

Breakfast Casserole

Prep Time: 5 Minutes | Cook Time: 10 Minutes | Serves: 4

Ingredients:

1 pound beef sausage, grounded
¼ cup diced white onion
1 diced green bell pepper

8 whole eggs, beaten
½ cup Colby Jack cheese, shredded
¼ teaspoon garlic salt

Oil spray, for greasing

Preparation:

1. Take a bowl and add the grounded sausage to it. 2. Add in the diced onions, bell peppers, eggs and whisk it well. 3. Then season it with garlic salt. 4. Spray both the baskets of the air fryer with oil spray. 5. Divide this mixture among the baskets; remember to remove the crisper plates. 6. Top the mixture with cheese. 7. Now, turn ON the Ninja Foodie 2-Basket Air Fryer zone 1 and select AIR FRY mode and set the time to 10 minutes at 390 degrees F/200 degrees C. 8. Select the MATCH button for zone 2 baskets, and hit START/STOP button. 9. Once the cooking cycle is complete, take out, and serve. 10. Serve and enjoy.

Serving Suggestion: Serve it with sour cream

Variation Tip: Use turkey sausages instead of beef sausages

Nutritional Information Per Serving: Calories 699 | Fat 59.1g | Sodium 1217 mg | Carbs 6.8g | Fiber 0.6g | Sugar 2.5g | Protein 33.1 g

Breakfast Sausage Omelet

Prep Time: 10 Minutes | Cook Time: 8 Minutes | Serves: 2

Ingredients:

¼ pound breakfast sausage, cooked and crumbled
4 eggs, beaten

½ cup pepper Jack cheese blend
2 tablespoons green bell pepper, sliced
1 green onion, chopped

1 pinch cayenne pepper
Cooking spray

Preparation:

1. Take a bowl and whisk eggs in it along with crumbled sausage, pepper Jack cheese, green onions, red bell pepper, and cayenne pepper. 2. Mix it all well. 3. Take two cake pans that fit inside the air fryer and grease it with oil spray. 4. Divide the omelet mixture between two cake pans. 5. Put the cake pans inside both of the Ninja Foodie 2-Basket Air Fryer baskets. 6. Turn on the BAKE function of the zone 1 basket and let it cook for 15-20 minutes at 310 degrees F/155 degrees F. 7. Select MATCH button for zone 2 basket. 8. Once the cooking cycle is complete, take out, and serve hot as a delicious breakfast.

Serving Suggestion: Serve it with ketchup

Variation Tip: Use Parmesan cheese instead of Pepper Jack cheese

Nutritional Information Per Serving: Calories 691 | Fat 52.4g | Sodium 1122 mg | Carbs 13.3g | Fiber 1.8g | Sugar 7g | Protein 42g

Pumpkin Muffins

Prep Time: 15 minutes | Cook Time: 13 minutes | Serves: 8

½ cup pumpkin puree
1 cup gluten-free oats
¼ cup honey

1 medium egg beaten
½ teaspoon coconut butter
½ tablespoon cocoa nib

½ tablespoon vanilla essence
Cooking spray
½ teaspoon nutmeg

Preparation:

1. Add oats, honey, eggs, pumpkin puree, coconut butter, cocoa nibs, vanilla essence, and nutmeg to a bowl and mix well until smooth. 2. Divide the batter into two 4-cup muffin trays, greased with cooking spray. 3. Place one mini muffin tray in each of the two crisper plates. 4. Return the crisper plates to the Ninja Foodi Dual Zone Air Fryer. 5. Choose the Air Fry mode for Zone 1 and set the temperature to 375 degrees F/190 degrees C and the time to 13 minutes. 6. Select the "MATCH" button to copy the settings for Zone 2. 7. Initiate cooking by pressing the START/STOP button. 8. Allow the muffins to cool, then serve.

Serving Suggestion: Serve the muffins with a hot coffee.

Variation Tip: Add raisins and nuts to the batter before baking.

Nutritional Information Per Serving: Calories 209 | Fat 7.5g | Sodium 321mg | Carbs 34.1g | Fiber 4g | Sugar 3.8g | Protein 4.3g

Egg and Avocado in The Ninja Foodi

Prep Time: 10 Minutes | Cook Time: 12 Minutes | Serves: 2

Ingredients:

2 avocados, pitted and cut in half
Garlic salt, to taste
Cooking oil for greasing

4 eggs
¼ teaspoon Paprika powder for sprinkling
⅓ cup Parmesan cheese, crumbled

6 bacon strips, raw

Preparation:

1. First, cut the avocado in half and pit it. 2. Now scoop out the flesh from the avocado and keep aside 3. Crack one egg in each hole of the avocado and sprinkle paprika and garlic salt. 4. Sprinkle it with cheese at the end. 5. Now put it into tin foils and then put it in the air fryer zone basket 1. 6. Put bacon strips in zone 2 basket. 7. Now for zone 1, set it to AIR FRY mode at 350 degrees F/175 degrees C for 10 minutes. 8. Place the bacon in zone 2, set it to 400 degrees F/200 degrees C for 12 minutes on AIR FRY mode. 9. Press the Sync button and press START/STOP button so it will finish at the same time. 10. Once done, serve and enjoy.

Serving Suggestion: Serve it with bread slices

Variation Tip: Use butter for greasing

Nutritional Information Per Serving: Calories 609 | Fat 53.2g | Sodium 335mg | Carbs 18.1g | Fiber 13.5g | Sugar 1.7g | Protein 21.3g

Sweet Potatoes Hash

Prep Time: 15 Minutes | Cook Time: 25 Minutes | Serves: 2

Ingredients:

450 grams sweet potatoes
½ white onion, diced
3 tablespoons olive oil

1 teaspoon smoked Paprika
¼ teaspoon cumin
⅓ teaspoon ground turmeric

¼ teaspoon garlic salt
1 cup guacamole

Preparation:

1. Peel and cut the potatoes into cubes. 2. Transfer the potatoes to a bowl and add oil, white onions, cumin, Paprika, turmeric, and garlic salt. 3. Put this mixture between both the baskets of the Ninja Foodie 2-Basket Air Fryer. 4. Set zone 1 to AIR FRY mode for 10 minutes at 390 degrees F/200 degrees C. 5. Press the MATCH button for zone 2. 6. Take out the baskets and shake them well. 7. Set the timer to 15 minutes at 390 degrees F/200 degrees C and AIR FRY again and MATCH for zone 2. 8. Once done, serve it with guacamole.

Serving Suggestion: Serve it with ketchup and omelet

Variation Tip: Use canola oil instead of olive oil

Nutritional Information Per Serving: Calories 691 | Fat 49.7g | Sodium 596mg | Carbs 64g | Fiber15g | Sugar 19g | Protein 8.1g

Bacon and Egg Omelet

Prep Time: 12 Minutes | Cook Time: 10 Minutes | Serves: 2

Ingredients:

2 eggs, whisked
½ teaspoon chopped tomatoes
Sea salt and black pepper, to taste

2 teaspoons almond milk
1 teaspoon cilantro, chopped
1 small green chili, chopped

4 strips bacon

Preparation:

1. Take a bowl and whisk the eggs in it. 2. Then add the green chili, salt, black pepper, cilantro, almond milk, and chopped tomatoes. 3. Grease the ramekins with. 4. Pour this into ramekins. 5. Put the bacon in the zone 1 basket and ramekins in zone 2 basket of the Ninja Foodi2-Basket Air Fryer. 6. Now for zone 1, set it to AIR FRY mode at 400 degrees F/200 degrees C for 10 minutes. 7. For zone 2, set it to 350 degrees F/175 degrees C or 10 minutes in AIR FRY mode. 8. Press theSync button and press START/STOP button so thatit will finish both at the same time. 9. Once done, serve and enjoy.

Serving Suggestion: Serve it with bread slices and ketchup
Variation Tip: Use garlic salt instead of sea salt
Nutritional Information Per Serving: Calories 285 | Fat 21.5g | Sodium 1000 mg | Carbs 2.2g | Fiber 0.1g | Sugar 1g | Protein 19.7g

Yellow Potatoes with Eggs

Prep Time: 10 Minutes | Cook Time: 35 Minutes | Serves: 2

Ingredients:

1 pound of Dutch yellow potatoes, quartered
1 red bell pepper, chopped
Salt and black pepper, to taste

1 green bell pepper, chopped
2 teaspoons olive oil
2 teaspoons garlic powder

1 teaspoon onion powder
1 egg
¼ teaspoon butter

Preparation:

1. Toss together diced potatoes, green pepper, red pepper, salt, black pepper, and olive oil along with garlic powder and onion powder. 2. Put the potatoes in the zone 1 basket of the air fryer. 3. Take a ramekin and grease it with oil spray. 4. Whisk the egg in a bowl and add salt and pepper along with ½ teaspoon of butter. 5. Pour the egg into the ramekin and place it in the zone 2 basket. 6. Set the timer for zone 1 basket to 30-35 minutes at 400 degrees F/200 degrees C at AIR FRY mode. 7. Now for zone 2, set it to AIR FRY mode at 350 degrees F/175 degrees C for 8-10 minutes. 8. Press the Sync button and press START/STOP button so both will finish at the same time. 9. Once done, serve and enjoy.

Serving Suggestion: Serve it with sourdough toasted bread slices
Variation Tip: Use white potatoes instead of yellow Dutch potatoes
Nutritional Information Per Serving: Calories 252 | Fat 7.5g | Sodium 37mg | Carbs 40g | Fiber 3.9g | Sugar 7g | Protein 6.7g

Egg with Baby Spinach

Prep Time: 12 Minutes | Cook Time: 12 Minutes | Serves: 4

Ingredients:

Nonstick spray, for greasing ramekins
2 tablespoons olive oil
6 ounces baby spinach

2 garlic cloves, minced
⅓ teaspoon kosher salt
6-8 large eggs

½ cup half and half
Salt and black pepper, to taste
8 Sourdough bread slices, toasted

Preparation:

1. Grease 4 ramekins with oil spray and set them aside for further use. 2. Take a skillet and heat oil in it. 3. Cook spinach for 2 minutes and add the garlic, salt and black pepper. 4. Let it simmer for 2 more minutes. 5. Once the spinach is wilted, transfer it to a plate. 6. Whisk the eggs in a small bowl. 7. Add in the spinach. 8. Whisk it well and then pour in the half and half. 9. Divide this mixture between 4 ramekins and remember not to overfill it to the top. 10. Put the ramekins in zone 1 and zone 2 baskets of the Ninja Foodie 2-Basket Air Fryer. 11. Press START/STOP button and set zone 1 to AIR FRY at 350 degrees F/175 degrees C for 8-12 minutes. 12. Press the MATCH button for zone 2. 13. Once it's cooked and eggs are done, serve with sourdough bread slices.

Serving Suggestion: Serve it with cream cheese topping
Variation Tip: Use plain bread slices instead of sourdough bread slices
Nutritional Information Per Serving: Calories 404 | Fat 19.6g | Sodium 761mg | Carbs 40.1g | Fiber 2.5g | Sugar 2.5g | Protein 19.2g

Banana and Raisins Muffins

Prep Time: 20 Minutes | Cook Time: 16 Minutes | Serves: 2

Ingredients:

Salt, pinch
2 eggs, whisked
⅓ cup butter, melted

4 tablespoons almond milk
¼ teaspoon vanilla extract
½ teaspoon baking powder

1-½ cup all-purpose flour
1 cup mashed bananas
2 tablespoons raisins

Preparation:

1. Take about 4 large (one-cup sized) ramekins and layer them with muffin papers. 2. Crack the eggs in a large bowl, and whisk it all well and addvanilla extract, almond milk, baking powder, and melted butter. 3. Whisk the ingredients in very well. 4. Take a separate bowl and add the all-purpose flour and salt. 5. Combine the dry ingredients with the wet ingredients. 6. Pour mashed bananas and raisins into the batter. 7. Mix it well to make a batter for the muffins. 8. Pour the batter into the four ramekins and divide the ramekins into the air fryer zones. 9. Set the timer for zone 1 to 16 minutes at 350 degrees F/175 degrees C on AIR FRY mode. 10. Select the MATCH button for the zone 2 basket. 11. Check and if not done, and let it AIR FRY for one more minute. 12. Once it is done, serve.

Serving Suggestion: None
Variation Tip: None
Nutritional Information Per Serving: Calories 727 | Fat 43.1g | Sodium 366 mg | Carbs 74.4g | Fiber 4.7g | Sugar 16.1g | Protein 14.1g

Bacon and Eggs for Breakfast

Prep Time: 12 Minutes | Cook Time: 12 Minutes | Serves: 1

Ingredients:

4 strips of thick-sliced bacon
2 small eggs

Salt and black pepper, to taste
Oil spray for greasing ramekins

Preparation:

1. Take 2 ramekins and grease them with oil spray. 2. Crack eggs into a bowl and season with salt and black pepper. 3. Divide the egg mixture between the two ramekins. 4. Put the bacon slices into the Ninja Foodie 2-Basket Air Fryer zone 1 basket, and the ramekins in zone 2 basket. 5. Now for zone 1 set it to AIR FRY mode at 400 degrees F/200 degrees C for 12 minutes. 6. For zone 2 set it to 350 degrees F/175 degrees C for 8 minutes using AIR FRY mode. 7. Press the Syncbutton and press START/STOP button so they both finish at the same time. 8. Once done, serve and enjoy.

Serving Suggestion: None
Variation Tip: Use butter for greasing the ramekins
Nutritional Information Per Serving: Calories 131 | Fat 10g | Sodium 187mg | Carbs 0.6 g | Fiber 0g | Sugar 0.6g | Protein 10.7

Air Fried Bacon and Eggs

Prep Time: 5 minutes | Cook Time: 10 minutes | Serves: 1

Ingredients:

2 eggs

2 slices bacon

Preparation:

1. Grease a ramekin using cooking spray. 2. Install the crisper plate in the zone 1 drawer and place the bacon inside it. Insert the drawer into the unit. 3. Crack the eggs and add them to the greased ramekin. 4. Install the crisper plate in the zone 2 drawer and place the ramekin inside it. Insert the drawer into the unit. 5. Select zone 1 to AIR FRY for 9–11 minutes at 400 degrees F/200 degrees C. Select zone 2 to AIR FRY for 8–9 minutes at 350 degrees F/175 degrees C. Press SYNC. 6. Press START/STOP to begin cooking. 7. Enjoy!

Serving Suggestion: Serve with slices of toast.
Variation Tip: You can use ham instead.
Nutritional Information Per Serving: Calories 331 | Fat 24.5g | Sodium 1001mg | Carbs 1.2g | Fiber 0g | Sugar 0.7g | Protein 25.3g

Sweet Potato Sausage Hash

Prep Time: 10 minutes | Cook Time: 20 minutes | Serves: 4

Ingredients:

1½ pounds sweet potato, peeled and diced into ½-inch pieces
1 tablespoon minced garlic
1 teaspoon kosher salt plus more, as desired
Ground black pepper, as desired

2 tablespoons canola oil
1 tablespoon dried sage
1-pound uncooked mild ground breakfast sausage
½ large onion, peeled and diced

½ teaspoon ground cinnamon
1 teaspoon chili powder
4 large eggs, poached or fried (optional)

Preparation:

1. Toss the sweet potatoes with the garlic, salt, pepper, and canola oil in a mixing bowl. 2. Install the crisper plate in the zone 1 drawer, fill it with the sweet potato mixture, and insert the drawer in the unit. 3. Place the ground sausage in the zone 2 drawer (without the crisper plate) and place it in the unit. 4. Select zone 1, then AIR FRY, and set the temperature to 400 degrees F/200 degrees C with a 30-minute timer. 5. Select zone 2, then ROAST, then set the temperature to 400 degrees F/200 degrees C with a 20-minute timer. SYNC is the option to choose. To begin cooking, press the START/STOP button. 6. When the zone 1 and zone 2 times have reached 10 minutes, press START/STOP and remove the drawers from the unit. Shake each for 10 seconds. 7. Half of the sage should be added to the zone 1 drawer. 8. Add the onion to the zone 2 drawer and mix to incorporate. To continue cooking, press START/STOP and reinsert the drawers. 9. Remove both drawers from the unit once the cooking is finished and add the potatoes to the sausage mixture. Mix in the cinnamon, sage, chili powder, and salt until thoroughly combined. 10. When the hash is done, stir it and serve it right away with a poached or fried egg on top, if desired.

Serving Suggestion: Serve with slices of toast.

Variation Tip: You can use other kinds of potatoes.

Nutritional Information Per Serving: Calories 491 | Fat 19.5g | Sodium 736mg | Carbs 51g | Fiber 8g | Sugar 2g | Protein 26.3

Air Fryer Sausage Patties

Prep Time: 5 minutes | Cook Time: 10 minutes | Serves: 12

Ingredients:

1-pound pork sausage or ready-made patties   Fennel seeds or preferred seasonings

Preparation:

1. Prepare the sausage by slicing it into patties, then flavor it with fennel seed or your favorite seasonings. 2. Install a crisper plate in both drawers. Place half the patties in zone 1 and half in zone 2, then insert the drawers into the unit. 3. Select zone 1, select AIR FRY, set temperature to 390 degrees F/200 degrees C, and set time to 10 minutes. 4. Select MATCH to match zone 2 settings to zone 1. 5. Press the START/STOP button to begin cooking. 6. When cooking is complete, remove the patties from the unit and serve with sauce or make a burger.

Serving Suggestion: Serve in a burger bun.

Variation Tip: You can use chicken sausage instead.

Nutritional Information Per Serving: Calories 130 | Fat 10.5g | Sodium 284mg | Carbs 0.3g | Fiber 0.2g | Sugar 0g | Protein 7.4g

Hash Browns

Prep Time: 5 minutes | Cook Time: 5 minutes | Serves: 4

Ingredients:

4 frozen hash browns patties   Cooking oil spray of choice

Preparation:

1. Install a crisper plate in both drawers. Place half the hash browns in zone 1 and half in zone 2, then insert the drawers into the unit. Spray the hash browns with some cooking oil. 2. Select zone 1, select AIR FRY, set temperature to 390 degrees F/200 degrees C, and set time to 5 minutes. 3. Select MATCH to match zone 2 settings to zone 1. Press the START/STOP button to begin cooking. 4. When cooking is complete, remove the hash browns and serve.

Serving Suggestion: Serve with ketchup or any condiment of your choice.

Variation Tip: You can use coconut oil.

Nutritional Information Per Serving: Calories 130 | Fat 7g | Sodium 300mg | Carbs 15g | Fiber 2g | Sugar 0g | Protein 1g

Bagels

Prep Time: 10 minutes | Cook Time: 15 minutes | Serves: 8

Ingredients:

2 cups self-rising flour
2 cups non-fat plain Greek yogurt

2 beaten eggs for egg wash (optional)
½ cup sesame seeds (optional)

Preparation:

1. In a medium mixing bowl, combine the self-rising flour and Greek yogurt using a wooden spoon. 2. Knead the dough for about 5 minutes on a lightly floured board. 3. Divide the dough into four equal pieces and roll each into a thin rope, securing the ends to form a bagel shape. 4. Install a crisper plate in both drawers. Place 4 bagels in a single layer in each drawer. Insert the drawers into the unit. 5. Select zone 1, select AIR FRY, set temperature to 360 degrees F/180 degrees C, and set time to 15 minutes. Select MATCH to match zone 2 settings to zone 1. Select START/STOP to begin. 6. Once the timer has finished, remove the bagels from the units. 7. Serve and enjoy!

Serving Suggestion: Serve with cream cheese.
Variation Tip: You can use all-purpose flour.
Nutritional Information Per Serving: Calories 202 | Fat 4.5g | Sodium 55mg | Carbs 31.3g | Fiber 2.7g | Sugar 4.7g | Protein 8.7g

Banana Muffins

Prep Time: 5 minutes | Cook Time: 15 minutes | Serves: 10

Ingredients:

2 very ripe bananas
⅓ cup olive oil
1 egg

½ cup brown sugar
1 teaspoon vanilla extract
1 teaspoon cinnamon

¾ cup self-rising flour

Preparation:

1. In a large mixing bowl, mash the bananas, then add the egg, brown sugar, olive oil, and vanilla. To blend, stir everything together thoroughly. 2. Fold in the flour and cinnamon until everything is just blended. 3. Fill muffin molds evenly with the mixture (silicone or paper). 4. Install a crisper plate in both drawers. Place the muffin molds in a single layer in each drawer. Insert the drawers into the unit. 5. Select zone 1, select AIR FRY, set temperature to 360 degrees F/180 degrees C, and set time to 15 minutes. Select MATCH to match zone 2 settings to zone 1. Select START/STOP to begin. 6. Once the timer has finished, remove the muffins from the drawers. 7. Serve and enjoy!

Serving Suggestion: Serve with a smoothie.
Variation Tip: You can use almond flour.
Nutritional Information Per Serving: Calories 148 | Fat 7.3g | Sodium 9mg | Carbs 19.8g | Fiber 1g | Sugar 10g | Protein 1.8g

Donuts

Prep Time: 5 minutes | Cook Time: 15 minutes | Serves: 6

Ingredients:

1 cup granulated sugar
2 tablespoons ground cinnamon

1 can refrigerated flaky buttermilk biscuits
¼ cup unsalted butter, melted

Preparation:

1. Combine the sugar and cinnamon in a small shallow bowl and set aside. 2. Remove the biscuits from the can and put them on a chopping board, separated. Cut holes in the center of each biscuit with a 1-inch round biscuit cutter (or a similarly sized bottle cap). 3. Place a crisper plate in each drawer. In each drawer, place 4 biscuits in a single layer. Insert the drawers into the unit. 4. Select zone 1, then AIR FRY, then set the temperature to 360 degrees F/180 degrees C with a 10-minute timer. To match zone 2 settings to zone 1, choose MATCH. To begin cooking, select START/STOP. 5. Remove the donuts from the drawers after the timer has finished.

Serving Suggestion: Serve the donuts with tea.
Variation Tip: You can add some ground nutmeg.
Nutritional Information Per Serving: Calories 223 | Fat 8g | Sodium 150mg | Carbs 40g | Fiber 1.4g | Sugar 34.2g | Protein 0.8g

Egg White Muffins

Prep Time: 15 minutes | Cook Time: 10 minutes | Serves: 8

Ingredients:

4 slices center-cut bacon, cut into strips
4 ounces baby bella mushrooms, roughly chopped
2 ounces sun-dried tomatoes

2 tablespoon sliced black olives
2 tablespoons grated or shredded parmesan
2 tablespoons shredded mozzarella
¼ teaspoon black pepper

¾ cup liquid egg whites
2 tablespoons liquid egg whites

Preparation:

1. Heat a saucepan with a little oil, add the bacon and mushrooms and cook until fully cooked and crispy, about 6–8 minutes. 2. While the bacon and mushrooms cook, mix the ¾ cup liquid egg whites, sun-dried tomato, olives, parmesan, mozzarella, and black pepper together in a large bowl. 3. Add the cooked bacon and mushrooms to the tomato and olive mixture, stirring everything together. 4. Spoon the mixture into muffin molds, followed by 2 tablespoons of egg whites over the top. 5. Place half the muffins mold in zone 1 and half in zone 2, then insert the drawers into the unit. 6. Select zone 1, select AIR FRY, set temperature to 390 degrees F/200 degrees C, and set time to 22 minutes. 7. Select MATCH to match zone 2 settings to zone 1. Press the START/STOP button to begin cooking. 8. When cooking is complete, remove the molds and enjoy!

Serving Suggestion: Serve the muffins with a sauce of your choice.

Variation Tip: You can also add shredded zucchini.

Nutritional Information Per Serving: Calories 104 | Fat 5.6g | Sodium 269mg | Carbs 3.5g | Fiber 0.8g | Sugar 0.3g | Protein 10.3g

Perfect Cinnamon Toast

Prep Time: 5 minutes | Cook Time: 10 minutes | Serves: 6

Ingredients:

12 slices whole-wheat bread
1 stick butter, room temperature
½ cup white sugar

1½ teaspoons ground cinnamon
1½ teaspoons pure vanilla extract
1 pinch kosher salt

2 pinches freshly ground black pepper (optional)

Preparation:

1. Mash the softened butter with a fork or the back of a spoon in a bowl. Add the sugar, cinnamon, vanilla, and salt. Stir until everything is well combined. 2. Spread one-sixth of the mixture onto each slice of bread, making sure to cover the entire surface. 3. Install a crisper plate in both drawers. Place half the bread sliced in the zone 1 drawer and half in the zone 2 drawer, then insert the drawers into the unit. 4. Select zone 1, select AIR FRY, set temperature to 400 degrees F/200 degrees C, and set time to 5 minutes. Select MATCH to match zone 2 settings to zone 1. Press theSTART/STOP button to begin cooking 5. When cooking is complete, remove the slices and cut them diagonally. 6. Serve immediately.

Serving Suggestion: Serve with maple syrup.

Variation Tip: You can use honey.

Nutritional Information Per Serving: Calories 322 | Fat 16.5g | Sodium 249mg | Carbs 39.3g | Fiber 4.2g | Sugar 18.2g | Protein 8.2g

Chapter 2 Snacks and Appetizers Recipes

Chicken Stuffed Mushrooms

Prep Time: 15 minutes | Cook Time: 15 minutes | Serves: 6

Ingredients:

6 large fresh mushrooms, stems removed

Stuffing:

½ cup chicken meat, cubed
1 (4 ounces) package cream cheese, softened
¼ lb. imitation crabmeat, flaked

1 cup butter
1 garlic clove, peeled and minced
Black pepper and salt to taste

Garlic powder to taste
Crushed red pepper to taste

Preparation:

1. Melt and heat butter in a skillet over medium heat. 2. Add chicken and sauté for 5 minutes. 3. Add in all the remaining ingredients for the stuffing. 4. Cook for 5 minutes, then turn off the heat. 5. Allow the mixture to cool. Stuff each mushroom with a tablespoon of this mixture. 6. Divide the stuffed mushrooms in the two crisper plates. 7. Return the crisper plate to the Ninja Foodi Dual Zone Air Fryer. 8. Choose the Air Fry mode for Zone 1 and set the temperature to 375 degrees F/190 degrees C and the time to 15 minutes. 9. Select the "MATCH" button to copy the settings for Zone 2. 10. Initiate cooking by pressing the START/STOP button. 11. Serve warm.
Serving Suggestion: Serve with mayonnaise or cream cheese dip.
Variation Tip: Use crushed cornflakes for breading to have extra crispiness.
Nutritional Information Per Serving: Calories 180 | Fat 3.2g | Sodium 133mg | Carbs 32g | Fiber 1.1g | Sugar 1.8g | Protein 9g

Chicken Crescent Wraps

Prep Time: 10 minutes | Cook Time: 12 minutes | Serves: 6

Ingredients:

3 tablespoons chopped onion
3 garlic cloves, peeled and minced
¾ (8 ounces) package cream cheese

6 tablespoons butter
2 boneless chicken breasts, cubed, cooked
3 (10 ounces) cans refrigerated crescent roll

dough

Preparation:

1. Heat oil in a skillet and add onion and garlic to sauté until soft. 2. Add cooked chicken, sautéed veggies, butter, and cream cheese to a blender. 3. Blend well until smooth. Spread the crescent dough over a flat surface. 4. Slice the dough into 12 rectangles. 5. Spoon the chicken mixture at the center of each rectangle. 6. Roll the dough to wrap the mixture and form a ball. 7. Divide these balls into the two crisper plate. 8. Return the crisper plate to the Ninja Foodi Dual Zone Air Fryer. 9. Choose the Air Fry mode for Zone 1 and set the temperature to 390 degrees F/200 degrees C and the time to 12 minutes. 10. Select the "MATCH" button to copy the settings for Zone 2. 11. Initiate cooking by pressing the START/STOP button. 12. Serve warm.
Serving Suggestion: Serve with tomato sauce or cream cheese dip.
Variation Tip: You can also prepare the filling using leftover turkey or pork.
Nutritional Information Per Serving: Calories 100 | Fat 2g | Sodium 480mg | Carbs 4g | Fiber 2g | Sugar 0g | Protein 18g

Onion Rings

Prep Time: 10 minutes | Cook Time: 22 minutes | Serves: 4

Ingredients:

¾ cup all-purpose flour
1 teaspoon salt
1 large onion, cut into rings
½ cup cornstarch

2 teaspoons baking powder
1 cup low-fat milk
1 egg
1 cup bread crumbs

⅙ teaspoons paprika
Cooking spray
⅙ teaspoons garlic powder

Preparation:

1. Mix flour with baking powder, cornstarch, and salt in a small bowl. 2. First, coat the onion rings with flour mixture; set them aside. 3. Beat milk with egg, then add the remaining flour mixture into the egg. 4. Mix them well together to make a thick batter. 5. Now dip the floured onion rings into the prepared batter and coat them well. 6. Place the rings on a wire rack for 10 minutes. 7. Spread bread crumbs in a shallow bowl. 8. Coat the onion rings with breadcrumbs and shake off the excess. 9. Set the coated onion rings in the two crisper plates. 10. Spray all the rings with the cooking spray. 11. Return the crisper plate to the Ninja Foodi Dual Zone Air Fryer. 12. Choose the Air Fry mode for Zone 1 and set the temperature to 375 degrees F/190 degrees C and the time to 22 minutes. 13. Select the "MATCH" button to copy the settings for Zone 2. 14. Initiate cooking by pressing the START/STOP button. 15. Flip once cooked halfway through, then resume cooking 16. Season the air fried onion rings with garlic powder and paprika. 17. Serve.
Serving Suggestion: Serve with tomato sauce or cream cheese dip.

Variation Tip: Use crushed cornflakes for breading to have extra crispiness.
Nutritional Information Per Serving: Calories 229 | Fat 1.9 | Sodium 567mg | Carbs 1.9g | Fiber 0.4g | Sugar 0.6g | Protein 11.8g

Potato Tater Tots

Prep Time: 10 minutes | Cook Time: 27 minutes | Serves: 4

Ingredients:

2 potatoes, peeled
½ teaspoon Cajun seasoning

Olive oil cooking spray
Sea salt to taste

Preparation:

1. Boil water in a cooking pot and cook potatoes in it for 15 minutes. 2. Drain and leave the potatoes to cool in a bowl. 3. Grate these potatoes and toss them with Cajun seasoning. 4. Make small tater tots out of this mixture. 5. Divide them into the two crisper plates and spray them with cooking oil. 6. Return the crisper plates to the Ninja Foodi Dual Zone Air Fryer. 7. Choose the Air Fry mode for Zone 1 and set the temperature to 375 degrees F/190 degrees C and the time to 27 minutes. 8. Select the "MATCH" button to copy the settings for Zone 2. 9. Initiate cooking by pressing the START/STOP button. 10. Flip them once cooked halfway through, and resume cooking. 11. Serve warm.

Serving Suggestion: Serve with ketchup, mayonnaise, or cream cheese dip.

Variation Tip: Use crushed cornflakes for breading to have extra crispiness.

Nutritional Information Per Serving: Calories 185 | Fat 11g | Sodium 355mg | Carbs 21g | Fiber 5.8g | Sugar 3g | Protein 4.7g

Spicy Chicken Tenders

Prep Time: 15 Minutes | Cook Time: 12 Minutes | Serves: 2

Ingredients:

2 large eggs, whisked
2 tablespoons lemon juice
Salt and black pepper
1 pound chicken tenders

1 cup Panko bread crumbs
½ cup Italian bread crumbs
1 teaspoon smoked Paprika
¼ teaspoon garlic powder

¼ teaspoon onion powder
½ cup fresh grated Parmesan cheese

Preparation:

1. Take a bowl and whisk the eggs and set aside. 2. In a large bowl, add lemon juice, Paprika, salt, black pepper, garlic powder, onion powder 3. In a separate bowl, mix Panko bread crumbs, Italian bread crumbs, and Parmesan cheese. 4. Dip the chicken tenders in the spice mixture and coat well. 5. Let the tenders sit for 1 hour. 6. Dip each tender into the egg mixture and then into the bread crumbs. 7. Line both the baskets of the air fryer with parchment paper. 8. Divide the tenders between the baskets. 9. Set zone 1 basket to AIR FRY mode at 350 degrees F/175 degrees C for 12 minutes. 10. Select the MATCH button for the zone 2 basket. 11. Once it's done, serve.

Serving Suggestion: Serve it with ketchup

Variation Tip: Use mild Paprika instead of smoked Paprika

Nutritional Information Per Serving: Calories 836 | Fat 36g | Sodium 1307 mg | Carbs 31.3g | Fiber 2.5g | Sugar 3.3 g | Protein 95.3g

Peppered Asparagus

Prep Time: 10 minutes | Cook Time: 16 minutes | Serves: 6

Ingredients:

1 bunch of asparagus, trimmed
Avocado or Olive Oil

Himalayan salt, to taste
Black pepper, to taste

Preparation:

1. Divide the asparagus in the two crisper plate. 2. Toss the asparagus with salt, black pepper, and oil. 3. Return the crisper plate to the Ninja Foodi Dual Zone Air Fryer. 4. Choose the Air Fry mode for Zone 1 and set the temperature to 390 degrees F/200 degrees C and the time to 16 minutes. 5. Select the "MATCH" button to copy the settings for Zone 2. 6. Initiate cooking by pressing the START/STOP button. 7. Serve warm.

Serving Suggestion: Serve with mayonnaise or cream cheese dip.

Variation Tip: Use panko crumbs for breading to have extra crispiness.

Nutritional Information Per Serving: Calories 163 | Fat 11.5g | Sodium 918mg | Carbs 8.3g | Fiber 4.2g | Sugar 0.2g | Protein 7.4g

Cauliflower Gnocchi

Prep Time: 15 minutes | Cook Time: 17 minutes | Serves: 5

Ingredients:

1 bag frozen cauliflower gnocchi
1½ tablespoons olive oil
1 teaspoon garlic powder

3 tablespoons parmesan, grated
½ teaspoon dried basil
Salt to taste

Fresh chopped parsley for topping

Preparation:

1. Toss gnocchi with olive oil, garlic powder, 1 tablespoon of parmesan, salt, and basil in a bowl. 2. Divide the gnocchi in the two crisper plate. 3. Return the crisper plate to the Ninja Foodi Dual Zone Air Fryer. 4. Choose the Air Fry mode for Zone 1 and set the temperature to 400 degrees F/200 degrees C and the time to 10 minutes. 5. Select the "MATCH" button to copy the settings for Zone 2. 6. Initiate cooking by pressing the START/STOP button. 7. Toss the gnocchi once cooked halfway through, then resume cooking. 8. Drizzle the remaining parmesan on top of the gnocchi and cook again for 7 minutes. 9. Serve warm.

Serving Suggestion: Serve with tomato or sweet chili sauce.

Variation Tip: Use crushed cornflakes for breading to have extra crispiness.

Nutritional Information Per Serving: Calories 134 | Fat 5.9g | Sodium 343mg | Carbs 9.5g | Fiber 0.5g | Sugar 1.1g | Protein 10.4g

Crispy Plantain Chips

Prep Time: 15 minutes | Cook Time: 20 minutes | Serves: 4

Ingredients:

1 green plantain

1 teaspoon canola oil

½ teaspoon sea salt

Preparation:

1. Peel and cut the plantains into long strips using a mandolin slicer. 2. Grease the crisper plates with ½ teaspoon of canola oil. 3. Toss the plantains with salt and remaining canola oil. 4. Divide these plantains in the two crisper plates. 5. Return the crisper plate to the Ninja Foodi Dual Zone Air Fryer. 6. Choose the Air Fry mode for Zone 1 and set the temperature to 350 degrees F/175 degrees C and the time to 20 minutes. 7. Select the "MATCH" button to copy the settings for Zone 2. 8. Initiate cooking by pressing the START/STOP button. 9. Toss the plantains after 10 minutes and resume cooking. 10. Serve warm.

Serving Suggestion: Serve with cream cheese dip and celery sticks.

Variation Tip: Use black pepper to season the chips.

Nutritional Information Per Serving: Calories 122 | Fat 1.8g | Sodium 794mg | Carbs 17g | Fiber 8.9g | Sugar 1.6g | Protein 14.9g

Crispy Tortilla Chips

Prep Time: 15 minutes | Cook Time: 13 minutes | Serves: 8

Ingredients:

4 (6-inch) corn tortillas
1 tablespoon Avocado Oil

Sea salt to taste
Cooking spray

Preparation:

1. Spread the corn tortillas on the working surface. 2. Slice them into bite-sized triangles. 3. Toss them with salt and cooking oil. 4. Divide the triangles in the two crisper plates into a single layer. 5. Return the crisper plates to the Ninja Foodi Dual Zone Air Fryer. 6. Choose the Air Fry mode for Zone 1 and set the temperature to 390 degrees F/200 degrees C and the time to 13 minutes. 7. Select the "MATCH" button to copy the settings for Zone 2. 8. Initiate cooking by pressing the START/STOP button. 9. Toss the chips once cooked halfway through, then resume cooking. 10. Serve and enjoy.

Serving Suggestion: Serve with guacamole, mayonnaise, or cream cheese dip.

Variation Tip: Drizzle parmesan cheese on top before Air Frying.

Nutritional Information Per Serving: Calories 103 | Fat 8.4g | Sodium 117mg | Carbs 3.5g | Fiber 0.9g | Sugar 1.5g | Protein 5.1g

Parmesan French Fries

Prep Time: 10 minutes | Cook Time: 20 minutes | Serves: 6

Ingredients:

3 medium russet potatoes
2 tablespoons parmesan cheese

2 tablespoons fresh parsley, chopped
1 tablespoon olive oil

Salt, to taste

Preparation:

1. Wash the potatoes and pass them through the fries' cutter to get ¼-inch-thick fries. 2. Place the fries in a colander and drizzle salt on top. 3. Leave these fries for 10 minutes, then rinse. 4. Toss the potatoes with parmesan cheese, oil, salt, and parsley in a bowl. 5. Divide the potatoes into the two crisper plates. 6. Return the crisper plates to the Ninja Foodi Dual Zone Air Fryer. 7. Choose the Air Fry mode for Zone 1 and set the temperature to 360 degrees F/180 degrees C and the time to 20 minutes. 8. Select the "MATCH" button to copy the settings for Zone 2. 9. Initiate cooking by pressing the START/STOP button. 10. Toss the chips once cooked halfway through, then resume cooking. 11. Serve warm.
Serving Suggestion: Serve with tomato ketchup, Asian coleslaw, or creamed cabbage.
Variation Tip: Toss fries with black pepper for change of taste.
Nutritional Information Per Serving: Calories 307 | Fat 8.6g | Sodium 510mg | Carbs 22.2g | Fiber 1.4g | Sugar 13g | Protein 33.6g

Blueberries Muffins

Prep Time: 15 Minutes | Cook Time: 15 Minutes | Serves: 2

Ingredients:

Salt, 1 pinch
2 eggs
⅓ cup sugar
⅓ cup vegetable oil

4 tablespoons water
1 teaspoon lemon zest
¼ teaspoon vanilla extract
½ teaspoon baking powder

1 cup all-purpose flour
1 cup blueberries

Preparation:

1. Take 4 ramekins that are oven safe and layer them with muffin papers. 2. Take a bowl and whisk the egg, sugar, oil, water, vanilla extract, and lemon zest in. 3. Whisk it all very well. 4. In a separate bowl, mix the flour, baking powder, and salt. 5. Add the dry ingredients slowly to the wet ingredients. 6. Pour the batter into the ramekins and top with blueberries. 7. Divide them between both zones of the Ninja Foodi 2-Basket Air Fryer. 8. Set the time for zone 1 to 15 minutes at 350 degrees F/175 degrees C on AIR FRY mode. 9. Select the MATCH button for the zone 2 basket. 10. Check if not done, and let it AIR FRY for one more minute. 11. Once it is done, serve.
Serving Suggestion: Serve it with whipped cream topping
Variation Tip: Use butter instead of vegetable oil
Nutritional Information Per Serving: Calories 781 | Fat 41.6g | Sodium 143mg | Carbs 92.7g | Fiber 3.5g | Sugar41.2 g | Protein 0g

Strawberries and Walnuts Muffins

Prep Time: 15 Minutes | Cook Time: 15 Minutes | Serves: 2

Ingredients:

Salt, pinch
2 eggs, whisked
⅓ cup maple syrup
⅓ cup coconut oil

4 tablespoons water
1 teaspoon orange zest
¼ teaspoon vanilla extract
½ teaspoon baking powder

1 cup all-purpose flour
1 cup strawberries, finely chopped
⅓ cup walnuts, chopped and roasted

Preparation:

1. Layer 4 ramekins with muffin paper. 2. Add egg, maple syrup, oil, water, vanilla extract, and orange zest to a bowl and mix well. 3. In a separate bowl, mix flour, baking powder, and salt. 4. Add the dry ingredients slowly to the wet ingredients. 5. Pour the batter into the ramekins and top with strawberries and walnuts. 6. Divide the ramekins into both zones. For zone 1, set to AIR FRY mode at 350 degrees F/175 degrees C for 15 minutes. 7. Select the MATCH button for the zone 2 basket. 8. Check and if not done, let it AIR FRY for one more minute. 9. Once done, serve.
Serving Suggestion: Serve it with coffee
Variation Tip: Use vegetable oil instead of coconut oil
Nutritional Information Per Serving: Calories 897 | Fat 53.9g | Sodium 148mg | Carbs 92g | Fiber 4.7g | Sugar 35.6 g | Protein 17.5g

Cheddar Quiche

Prep Time: 10 Minutes | Cook Time: 12 Minutes | Serves: 2

Ingredients:

4 eggs, organic
1¼ cup heavy cream

Salt, pinch
½ cup broccoli florets

½ cup Cheddar cheese, shredded and for sprinkling

Preparation:

1. Take a Pyrex pitcher and crack two eggs into it. 2. Fill it with heavy cream, about half the way up. 3. Add in the salt and then the broccoli. 4. Pour the mixture into two quiche dishes, and top it with shredded Cheddar cheese. 5. Divide it into both zones of the baskets. 6. For zone 1, set the time to 10-12 minutes at 325 degrees F/160 degrees C on AIR FRY mode. 7. Select the MATCH button for the zone 2 basket. 8. Once done, serve hot.

Serving Suggestion: Serve with herbs as a topping
Variation Tip: Use spinach instead of broccoli florets
Nutritional Information Per Serving: Calories 454 | Fat 40g | Sodium 406mg | Carbs 4.2g | Fiber 0.6g | Sugar 1.3 g | Protein 20g

Chicken Tenders

Prep Time: 15 Minutes | Cook Time: 12 Minutes | Serves: 3

Ingredients:

1 pound chicken tenders
Salt and black pepper, to taste
1 cup Panko bread crumbs

2 cups Italian bread crumbs
1 cup Parmesan cheese
2 eggs

Oil spray, for greasing

Preparation:

1. Sprinkle the tenders with salt and black pepper. 2. In a medium bowl mix the Panko bread crumbs with Italian bread crumbs. 3. Add salt, pepper, and Parmesan cheese. 4. Crack two eggs into a bowl. 5. Dip the chicken tenders into the eggs and then into the bread crumbs and spray with oil spray. 6. Line both of the baskets of the air fryer with parchment paper. 7. Divide the tenders between the baskets of Ninja Foodi 2-Basket Air Fryer. 8. Set zone 1 basket to AIR FRY mode at 350 degrees F/175 degrees C for 12 minutes. 9. Select the MATCH button for the zone 2 basket. 10. Once it's done, serve.

Serving Suggestion: Serve it with ranch or ketchup
Variation Tip: Use Italian seasoning instead of Italian bread crumbs
Nutritional Information Per Serving: Calories 558 | Fat 23.8g | Sodium 872mg | Carbs 20.9g | Fiber 1.7 g | Sugar 2.2 g | Protein 63.5g

Grill Cheese Sandwich

Prep Time: 15 Minutes | Cook Time: 10 Minutes | Serves: 2

Ingredients:

4 white bread slices
2 tablespoons butter, melted

2 slices sharp Cheddar
2 slices Swiss cheese

2 slices Mozzarella cheese

Preparation:

1. Brush melted butter on one side of all the bread slices and then top the 2 bread slices with Cheddar, Swiss, and mozzarella. 2. Top it with the other slice to make a sandwich. 3. Divide it between the two baskets of the air fryer. 4. Turn toAIR FRY mode for zone 1 basket at 350 degrees F/175 degrees C for 10 minutes. 5. Use the MATCH button for zone 2. 6. Once done, serve.

Serving Suggestion: Serve with tomato soup
Variation Tip: Use oil spray instead of butter
Nutritional Information Per Serving: Calories 577 | Fat 38g | Sodium 1466mg | Carbs 30.5g | Fiber 1.1g | Sugar 6.5g | Protein 27.6g

Dijon Cheese Sandwich

Prep Time: 10 Minutes | Cook Time: 10 Minutes | Serves: 2

Ingredients:

4 large slices sourdough, whole grain
4 tablespoons Dijon mustard

1½ cup grated sharp Cheddar cheese
2 teaspoons green onion, green part chopped off

2 tablespoons butter melted

Preparation:

1. Brush the melted butter on one side of all the bread slices. 2. Spread Dijon mustard on the other side of the slices. 3. Top the 2 bread slices with Cheddar cheese and top it with green onions. 4. Cover with the remaining two slices to make two sandwiches. 5. Place one sandwich in each basket of the air fryer. 6. Turn to AIR FRY mode for zone 1 basket at 350 degrees F/175 degrees C for 10 minutes. 7. Use the MATCH button for zone 2. 8. Once it's done, serve.

Serving Suggestion: Serve with tomato soup
Variation Tip: Use oil spray instead of butter
Nutritional Information Per Serving: Calories 617 | Fat 38g | Sodium 1213mg | Carbs 40.8g | Fiber 5g | Sugar 5.6g | Protein 29.5g

Jalapeño Popper Chicken

Prep Time: 20 minutes | Cook Time: 50 minutes | Serves: 4

Ingredients:

2 ounces cream cheese, softened
¼ cup shredded cheddar cheese
¼ cup shredded mozzarella cheese
¼ teaspoon garlic powder

4 small jalapeño peppers, seeds removed and diced
Kosher salt, as desired
Ground black pepper, as desired

4 organic boneless, skinless chicken breasts
8 slices bacon

Preparation:

1. Cream together the cream cheese, cheddar cheese, mozzarella cheese, garlic powder, and jalapeño in a mixing bowl. Add salt and pepper to taste. 2. Make a deep pocket in the center of each chicken breast, but be cautious not to cut all the way through. 3. Fill each chicken breast's pocket with the cream cheese mixture. 4. Wrap two strips of bacon around each chicken breast and attach them with toothpicks. 5. Place a crisper plate in each drawer. Put the chicken breasts in the drawers. Place both drawers in the unit. 6. Select zone 1, then AIR FRY, and set the temperature to 350 degrees F/175 degrees C with a 30-minute timer. To match zone 2 and zone 1 settings, select MATCH. To begin cooking, press the START/STOP button. 7. When cooking is complete, remove the chicken breasts and allow them to rest for 5 minutes before serving

Serving Suggestion: Serve with a dipping sauce of your choice.
Variation Tip: You can use turkey breasts instead.
Nutritional Information Per Serving: Calories 507 | Fat 27.5g | Sodium 1432mg | Carbs 2.3g | Fiber 0.6g | Sugar 0.6g | Protein 58.2g

Ravioli

Prep Time: 5 minutes | Cook Time: 6 minutes | Serves: 2

Ingredients:

12 frozen portions of ravioli

½ cup buttermilk

½ cup Italian breadcrumbs

Preparation:

1. Place two bowls side by side. Put the buttermilk in one and breadcrumbs in the other. 2. Dip each piece of ravioli into the buttermilk then breadcrumbs, making sure to coat them as best as possible. 3. Place a crisper plate in both drawers. In each drawer, put four breaded ravioli pieces in a single layer. Insert the drawers into the unit. 4. Select zone 1, then AIR FRY, then set the temperature to 360 degrees F/180 degrees C with a 6-minute timer. To match zone 2 settings to zone 1, choose MATCH. To begin, select START/STOP. 5. Remove the ravioli from the drawers after the timer has finished.

Serving Suggestion: Serve with your favorite pasta sauce.
Variation Tip: You can use panko breadcrumbs.
Nutritional Information Per Serving: Calories 481 | Fat 20g | Sodium 1162mg | Carbs 56g | Fiber 4g | Sugar 9g | Protein 19g

Sweet Bites

Prep Time: 25 Minutes | Cook Time: 12 Minutes | Serves: 4

Ingredients:

10 sheets Phyllo dough, (filo dough)
2 tablespoons melted butter

1 cup walnuts, chopped
2 teaspoons honey

1 Pinch of cinnamon
1 teaspoon orange zest

Preparation:

1. First, layer together 10 Phyllo dough sheets on a flat surface. 2. Then cut it into 4 *4-inch squares. 3. Coat the squares with butter then drizzle some honey, orange zest, walnuts, and cinnamon on top. 4. Bring all 4 corners together and press the corners to make a little purse like design. 5. Divide them into both the air fryer baskets and select zone 1 to AIR FRY mode, and set it for 7 minutes at 375 degrees F/190 degrees C. 6. Select the MATCH button for the zone 2 basket. 7. Once done, take out and serve.

Serving Suggestion: Serve with a topping of nuts

Variation Tip: None

Nutritional Information Per Serving: Calories 397 | Fat 27.1 g | Sodium 271mg | Carbs 31.2 g | Fiber 3.2g | Sugar 3.3g | Protein 11g

Parmesan Crush Chicken

Prep Time: 20 Minutes | Cook Time: 18 Minutes | Serves: 4

Ingredients:

4 chicken breasts
1 cup Parmesan cheese

1 cup bread crumbs
2 eggs, whisked

Salt, to taste
Oil spray, for greasing

Preparation:

1. Whisk the eggs in a large bowl and set aside. 2. Season the chicken breasts with salt and then dip them in the egg wash. 3. Next, dredge them with the breadcrumbs then Parmesan cheese. 4. Line both the baskets of the air fryer with parchment paper. 5. Divide the breasts between the baskets, and oil spray the breast pieces. 6. Set zone 1 basket to AIR FRY mode at 350 degrees F/175 degrees C for 18 minutes. 7. Select the MATCH button for the zone 2 basket. 8. Once it's done, serve.

Serving Suggestion: Serve them with ketchup

Variation Tip: Use Cheddar cheese instead of Parmesan

Nutritional Information Per Serving: Calories 574 | Fat 25g | Sodium 848mg | Carbs 21.4g | Fiber 1.2g | Sugar 1.8g | Protein 64.4g

Stuffed Bell Peppers

Prep Time: 25 Minutes | Cook Time: 16 Minutes | Serves: 3

Ingredients:

6 large bell peppers

1½ cups cooked rice

2 cups Cheddar cheese

Preparation:

1. Cut the bell peppers in half lengthwise and remove all the seeds. 2. Fill the cavity of each bell pepper with cooked rice. 3. Divide the bell peppers into the two zones of the air fryer baskets. 4. Set the time for zone 1 for 200 degrees F/95 degrees C for 10 minutes on AIR FRY mode. 5. Select MATCH button of zone 2 basket. 6. Take out the baskets and sprinkle cheese on top. 7. Set the time for zone 1 for 200 degrees F/95 degrees C for 6 more minutes on AIR FRY. 8. Select MATCH button of zone 2 basket. 9. Once it's done, serve.

Serving Suggestion: Serve it mashed potatoes

Variation Tip: You can use any cheese you like

Nutritional Information Per Serving: Calories 605 | Fat 26g | Sodium 477mg | Carbs 68.3g | Fiber 4g | Sugar 12.5g | Protein 25.6 g

Zucchini Chips

Prep Time: 10 minutes | Cook Time: 15 minutes | Serves: 4

Ingredients:

1 medium-sized zucchini
½ cup panko breadcrumbs

½ teaspoon garlic powder
¼ teaspoon onion powder

1 egg
3 tablespoons flour

Preparation:

1. Slice the zucchini into thin slices, about ¼-inch thick. 2. In a mixing bowl, combine the panko breadcrumbs, garlic powder, and onion powder. 3. The egg should be whisked in a different bowl, while the flour should be placed in a third bowl. 4. Dip the zucchini slices in the flour, then in the egg, and finally in the breadcrumbs. 5. Place a crisper plate in each drawer. Put the zucchini slices into each drawer in a single layer. Insert the drawers into the unit. 6. Select zone 1, then AIR FRY, then set the temperature to 360 degrees F/180 degrees C with a 6-minute timer. To match zone 2 settings to zone 1, choose MATCH. To begin, select START/STOP. 7. Remove the zucchini from the drawers after the timer has finished.

Serving Suggestion: Serve the chips with mayo.

Variation Tip: You can use coconut flour if you prefer.

Nutritional Information Per Serving: Calories 82 | Fat 1.5g | Sodium 89mg | Carbs 14.1g | Fiber 1.7g | Sugar 1.2g | Protein 3.9g

Garlic Bread

Prep Time: 7 minutes | Cook Time: 10 minutes | Serves: 4

Ingredients:

½ loaf of bread
3 tablespoons butter, softened

3 garlic cloves, minced
½ teaspoon Italian seasoning

Small pinch of red pepper flakes

Optional

¼ cup shredded mozzarella cheese

Freshly grated parmesan cheese

Chopped fresh parsley for serving/topping

Preparation:

1. Slice the bread in half horizontally or as appropriate to fit inside the air fryer. 2. Combine the softened butter, garlic, Italian seasoning, and red pepper flakes in a mixing bowl. 3. Brush the garlic butter mixture evenly over the bread. 4. Place a crisper plate in each drawer. Place the bread pieces into each drawer. Insert the drawers into the unit. 5. Select zone 1, then AIR FRY, then set the temperature to 360 degrees F/180 degrees C with a 6-minute timer. To match zone 2 settings to zone 1, choose MATCH. To begin, select START/STOP. 6. Remove the garlic bread from your air fryer, slice, and serve!

Serving Suggestion: Serve with a sauce of your choice.

Variation Tip: You can use garlic salt for seasoning.

Nutritional Information Per Serving: Calories 150 | Fat 8.2g | Sodium 208mg | Carbs 14.3g | Fiber 2.3g | Sugar 1.2g | Protein 4.9g

Tater Tots

Prep Time: 10 minutes | Cook Time: 8 minutes | Serves: 4

Ingredients:

16 ounces tater tots
½ cup shredded cheddar cheese

1½ teaspoons bacon bits
2 green onions, chopped

Sour cream (optional)

Preparation:

1. Place a crisper plate in each drawer. Put the tater tots into the drawers in a single layer. Insert the drawers into the unit. 2. Select zone 1, then AIR FRY, then set the temperature to 360 degrees F/180 degrees C with a 6-minute timer. To match zone 2 settings to zone 1, choose MATCH. To begin, select START/STOP. 3. When the cooking time is over, add the shredded cheddar cheese, bacon bits, and green onions over the tater tots. Select zone 1, AIR FRY, 360 degrees F/180 degrees C, for 4 minutes. Select MATCH. Press START/STOP. 4. Drizzle sour cream over the top before serving. 5. Enjoy!

Serving Suggestion: Serve sprinkled with some chopped parsley.

Variation Tip: You can use scallions.

Nutritional Information Per Serving: Calories 335 | Fat 19.1g | Sodium 761mg | Carbs 34.1g | Fiber 3g | Sugar 0.6g | Protein 8.9g

Stuffed Mushrooms

Prep Time: 7 minutes | Cook Time: 8 minutes | Serves: 5

Ingredients:

8 ounces fresh mushrooms (I used Monterey)
4 ounces cream cheese
¼ cup shredded parmesan cheese

⅛cup shredded sharp cheddar cheese
⅛ cup shredded white cheddar cheese
1 teaspoon Worcestershire sauce

2 garlic cloves, minced
Salt and pepper, to taste

Preparation:

1. To prepare the mushrooms for stuffing, remove their stems. Make a circle cut around the area where the stem used to be. Continue to cut until all of the superfluous mushroom is removed. 2. To soften the cream cheese, microwave it for 15 seconds. 3. Combine the cream cheese, shredded cheeses, salt, pepper, garlic, and Worcestershire sauce in a medium mixing bowl. To blend, stir everything together. 4. Stuff the mushrooms with the cheese mixture. 5. Place a crisper plate in each drawer. Put the stuffed mushrooms in a single layer in each drawer. Insert the drawers into the unit. 6. Select zone 1, then AIR FRY, then set the temperature to 360 degrees F/180 degrees C with an 8-minute timer. To match zone 2 settings to zone 1, choose MATCH. To begin, select START/STOP. 7. Serve and enjoy!

Serving Suggestion: Serve with a green salad.

Variation Tip: You can use soy sauce instead of Worcestershire.

Nutritional Information Per Serving: Calories 230 | Fat 9.5g | Sodium 105mg | Carbs 35.5g | Fiber 5.1g | Sugar 0.1g | Protein 7.1g

Crispy Chickpeas

Prep Time: 10 minutes | Cook Time: 15 minutes | Serves: 4

Ingredients:

1 (15-ounce) can unsalted chickpeas, rinsed and drained
1½ tablespoons toasted sesame oil

¼ teaspoon smoked paprika
¼ teaspoon crushed red pepper
⅛ teaspoon salt

Cooking spray
2 lime wedges

Preparation:

1. The chickpeas should be spread out over multiple layers of paper towels. Roll the chickpeas under the paper towels to dry both sides, then top with more paper towels and pat until completely dry. 2. In a medium mixing bowl, combine the chickpeas and oil. Add the paprika, crushed red pepper, and salt to taste. 3. Place a crisper plate in each drawer. Put the chickpeas in a single layer in each drawer. Insert the drawers into the unit. 4. Select zone 1, then ROAST, then set the temperature to 400 degrees F/200 degrees C with a 15-minute timer. To match zone 2 settings to zone 1, choose MATCH. To begin, select START/STOP.

Serving Suggestion: Serve with roasted veggies.

Variation Tip: You can use garlic powder.

Nutritional Information Per Serving: Calories 169 | Fat 5g | Sodium 357mg | Carbs 27.3g | Fiber 5.7g | Sugar 0.6g | Protein 5.9g

Mozzarella Sticks

Prep Time: 1 hour 10 minutes | Cook Time: 1 hour 15 minutes | Serves: 8

Ingredients:

8 mozzarella sticks
¼ cup all-purpose flour

1 egg, whisked
1 cup panko breadcrumbs

½ teaspoon each onion powder, garlic powder, smoked paprika, salt

Preparation:

1. Freeze the mozzarella sticks for 30 minutes after placing them on a parchment-lined plate. 2. In the meantime, set up your "breading station": Fill a Ziploc bag halfway with flour. In a small dish, whisk the egg. In a separate shallow bowl, combine the panko and spices. 3. To bread your mozzarella sticks: Toss the sticks into the bag of flour, seal it, and shake to coat the cheese evenly. Take out the sticks and dip them in the egg, then in the panko, one at a time. Put the coated sticks back on the plate and put them in the freezer for another 30 minutes. 4. Place a crisper plate in each drawer, then add the mozzarella sticks in a single layer to each. Insert the drawers into the unit. 5. Select zone 1, then AIR FRY, then set the temperature to 400 degrees F/200 degrees C with a 15-minute timer. To match zone 2 settings to zone 1, choose MATCH. To begin, select START/STOP.

Serving Suggestion: Serve with a sauce of your choice.

Variation Tip: You can use coconut flour if you prefer.

Nutritional Information Per Serving: Calories 131 | Fat 5.3g | Sodium 243mg | Carbs 11.3g | Fiber 1.1g | Sugar 0.3g | Protein 9.9g

Mac and Cheese Balls

Prep Time: 15 minutes | Cook Time: 20 minutes | Serves: 4

Ingredients:

1 cup panko breadcrumbs
4 cups prepared macaroni and cheese, refrigerated
3 tablespoons flour

1 teaspoon salt, divided
1 teaspoon ground black pepper, divided
1 teaspoon smoked paprika, divided
½ teaspoon garlic powder, divided

2 eggs
1 tablespoon milk
¼ cup ranch dressing, garlic aioli, or chipotle mayo, for dipping (optional)

Preparation:

1. Preheat a conventional oven to 400 degrees F/200 degrees C. 2. Shake the breadcrumbs onto a baking sheet so that they're evenly distributed. Bake in the oven for 3 minutes, then shake and bake for an additional 1 to 2 minutes, or until toasted. 3. Form the chilled macaroni and cheese into golf ball-sized balls and set them aside. 4. Combine the flour, ½ teaspoon salt, ½ teaspoon black pepper, ½ teaspoon smoked paprika, and ¼ teaspoon garlic powder in a large mixing bowl. 5. In a small bowl, whisk together the eggs and milk. 6. Combine the breadcrumbs, remaining salt, pepper, paprika, and garlic powder in a mixing bowl. 7. To coat the macaroni and cheese balls, roll them in the flour mixture, then the egg mixture, and then the breadcrumb mixture. 8. Place a crisper plate in each drawer. Put the cheese balls in a single layer in each drawer. Insert the drawers into the unit. 9. Select zone 1, then AIR FRY, then set the temperature to 360 degrees F/180 degrees C with an 8-minute timer. To match zone 2 settings to zone 1, choose MATCH. To begin, select START/STOP. 10. Serve and enjoy!

Serving Suggestion: Serve with a dipping sauce of your choice.
Variation Tip: You can use whole-wheat or Italian seasoned breadcrumbs.
Nutritional Information Per Serving: Calories 489 | Fat 15.9g | Sodium 1402mg | Carbs 69.7g | Fiber 2.5g | Sugar 4g | Protein 16.9g

Fried Halloumi Cheese

Prep Time: 10 minutes | Cook Time: 12 minutes | Serves: 6

Ingredients:

1 block of halloumi cheese, sliced

2 teaspoons olive oil

Preparation:

1. Divide the halloumi cheese slices in the crisper plate. 2. Drizzle olive oil over the cheese slices. 3. Return the crisper plate to the Ninja Foodi Dual Zone Air Fryer. 4. Choose the Air Fry mode for Zone 1 and set the temperature to 360 degrees F/180 degrees C and the time to 12 minutes. 5. Flip the cheese slices once cooked halfway through. 6. Serve.

Serving Suggestion: Serve with fresh yogurt dip or cucumber salad.
Variation Tip: Add black pepper and salt for seasoning.
Nutritional Information Per Serving: Calories 186 | Fat 3g | Sodium 223mg | Carbs 31g | Fiber 8.7g | Sugar 5.5g | Protein 9.7g

Fried Pickles

Prep Time: 10 minutes | Cook Time: 15 minutes | Serves: 4

Ingredients:

2 cups sliced dill pickles
1 cup flour

1 tablespoon garlic powder
1 tablespoon Cajun spice

½ tablespoon cayenne pepper
Olive Oil or cooking spray

Preparation:

1. Mix together the flour and spices in a bowl. 2. Coat the sliced pickles with the flour mixture. 3. Place a crisper plate in each drawer. Put the pickles in a single layer in each drawer. Insert the drawers into the unit. 4. Select zone 1, then AIR FRY, then set the temperature to 400 degrees F/200 degrees C with a 15-minute timer. To match zone 2 settings to zone 1, choose MATCH. To begin, select START/STOP.

Serving Suggestion: Serve with a dipping sauce of your choice.
Variation Tip: You can use coconut flour.
Nutritional Information Per Serving: Calories 161 | Fat 4.1g | Sodium 975mg | Carbs 27.5g | Fiber 2.2g | Sugar 1.5g | Protein 4g

Chapter 3 Vegetables and Sides Recipes

Lime Glazed Tofu

Prep Time: 10 minutes | Cook Time: 14 minutes | Serves: 6

Ingredients:

⅔ cup coconut aminos
2 (14-oz) packages extra-firm, water-packed

tofu, drained
6 tablespoons toasted sesame oil

⅔ cup lime juice

Preparation:

1. Pat dry the tofu bars and slice into half-inch cubes. 2. Toss all the remaining ingredients in a small bowl. 3. Marinate for 4 hours in the refrigerator. Drain off the excess water. 4. Divide the tofu cubes in the two crisper plates. 5. Return the crisper plates to the Ninja Foodi Dual Zone Air Fryer. 6. Choose the Air Fry mode for Zone 1 and set the temperature to 400 degrees F/200 degrees C and the time to 14 minutes. 7. Select the "MATCH" button to copy the settings for Zone 2. 8. Initiate cooking by pressing the START/STOP button. 9. Toss the tofu once cooked halfway through, then resume cooking. 10. Serve warm.

Serving Suggestion: Serve with sautéed green vegetables.
Variation Tip: Add sautéed onion and carrot to the tofu cubes.
Nutritional Information Per Serving: Calories 284 | Fat 7.9g | Sodium 704mg | Carbs 38.1g | Fiber 1.9g | Sugar 1.9g | Protein 14.8g

Saucy Carrots

Prep Time: 15 minutes | Cook Time: 25 minutes | Serves: 6

Ingredients:

1 lb. cup carrots, cut into chunks
1 tablespoon sesame oil
½ tablespoon ginger, minced

½ tablespoon soy sauce
½ teaspoon garlic, minced
½ tablespoon scallions, chopped, for garnish

½ teaspoon sesame seeds for garnish

Preparation:

1. Toss all the ginger carrots ingredients, except the sesame seeds and scallions, in a suitable bowl. 2. Divide the carrots in the two crisper plates in a single layer. 3. Return the crisper plates to the Ninja Foodi Dual Zone Air Fryer. 4. Choose the Air Fry mode for Zone 1 and set the temperature to 390 degrees F/200 degrees C and the time to 25 minutes. 5. Select the "MATCH" button to copy the settings for Zone 2. 6. Initiate cooking by pressing the START/STOP button. 7. Toss the carrots once cooked halfway through. 8. Garnish with sesame seeds and scallions. 9. Serve warm.

Serving Suggestion: Serve with mayo sauce or ketchup.
Variation Tip: Use some honey for a sweet taste.
Nutritional Information Per Serving: Calories 206 | Fat 3.4g | Sodium 174mg | Carbs 35g | Fiber 9.4g | Sugar 5.9g | Protein 10.6g

Falafel

Prep Time: 15 minutes | Cook Time: 14 minutes | Serves: 6

Ingredients:

1 (15.5-oz) can chickpeas, rinsed and drained
1 small yellow onion, cut into quarters
3 garlic cloves, chopped
⅓ cup parsley, chopped

⅓ cup cilantro, chopped
⅓ cup scallions, chopped
1 teaspoon cumin
½ teaspoons salt

⅛ teaspoons crushed red pepper flakes
1 teaspoon baking powder
4 tablespoons all-purpose flour
Olive oil spray

Preparation:

1. Dry the chickpeas on paper towels. 2. Add onions and garlic to a food processor and chop them. 3. Add the parsley, salt, cilantro, scallions, cumin, and red pepper flakes. 4. Press the pulse button for 60 seconds, then toss in chickpeas and blend for 3 times until it makes a chunky paste. 5. Stir in baking powder and flour and mix well. 6. Transfer the falafel mixture to a bowl and cover to refrigerate for 3 hours. 7. Make 12 balls out of the falafel mixture. 8. Place 6 falafels in each of the crisper plate and spray them with oil. 9. Return the crisper plate to the Ninja Foodi Dual Zone Air Fryer. 10. Choose the Air Fry mode for Zone 1 and set the temperature to 350 degrees F/175 degrees C and the time to 14 minutes. 11. Select the "MATCH" button to copy the settings for Zone 2. 12. Initiate cooking by pressing the START/STOP button. 13. Toss the falafel once cooked halfway through, and resume cooking. 14. Serve warm.

Serving Suggestion: Serve with yogurt dip and sautéed carrots.
Variation Tip: Use breadcrumbs for breading to have extra crispiness.
Nutritional Information Per Serving: Calories 113 | Fat 3g | Sodium 152mg | Carbs 20g | Fiber 3g | Sugar 1.1g | Protein 3.5g

Zucchini Cakes

Prep Time: 10 minutes | Cook Time: 32 minutes | Serves: 6

Ingredients:

2 medium zucchinis, grated

1 cup corn kernel

1 medium potato cooked

2 tablespoons chickpea flour

2 garlic minced

2 teaspoons olive oil

Salt and black pepper

For Serving:

Yogurt tahini sauce

Preparation:

1. Mix grated zucchini with a pinch of salt in a colander and leave them for 15 minutes. 2. Squeeze out their excess water. 3. Mash the cooked potato in a large-sized bowl with a fork. 4. Add zucchini, corn, garlic, chickpea flour, salt, and black pepper to the bowl. 5. Mix these fritters' ingredients together and make 2 tablespoons-sized balls out of this mixture and flatten them lightly. 6. Divide the fritters in the two crisper plates in a single layer and spray them with cooking. 7. Return the crisper plates to the Ninja Foodi Dual Zone Air Fryer. 8. Choose the Air Fry mode for Zone 1 and set the temperature to 390 degrees F/200 degrees C and the time to 17 minutes. 9. Select the "MATCH" button to copy the settings for Zone 2. 10. Initiate cooking by pressing the START/STOP button. 11. Flip the fritters once cooked halfway through, then resume cooking. 12. Serve.

Serving Suggestion: Serve with mayonnaise or cream cheese dip.

Variation Tip: Use crushed cornflakes for breading to have extra crispiness.

Nutritional Information Per Serving: Calories 270 | Fat 14.6g | Sodium 394mg | Carbs 31.3g | Fiber 7.5g | Sugar 9.7g | Protein 6.4g

Quinoa Patties

Prep Time: 15 minutes | Cook Time: 32 minutes | Serves: 4

Ingredients:

1 cup quinoa red

1½ cups water

1 teaspoon salt

black pepper, ground

1½ cups rolled oats

3 eggs beaten

¼ cup minced white onion

½ cup crumbled feta cheese

¼ cup chopped fresh chives

Salt and black pepper, to taste

Vegetable or canola oil

4 hamburger buns

4 arugulas

4 slices tomato sliced

Cucumber Yogurt Dill Sauce

1 cup cucumber, diced

1 cup Greek yogurt

2 teaspoons lemon juice

¼ teaspoon salt

Black pepper, ground

1 tablespoon chopped fresh dill

1 tablespoon olive oil

Preparation:

1. Add quinoa to a saucepan filled with cold water, salt, and black pepper, and place it over medium-high heat. 2. Cook the quinoa to a boil, then reduce the heat, cover, and cook for 20 minutes on a simmer. 3. Fluff and mix the cooked quinoa with a fork and remove it from the heat. 4. Spread the quinoa in a baking stay. 5. Mix eggs, oats, onion, herbs, cheese, salt, and black pepper. 6. Stir in quinoa, then mix well. Make 4 patties out of this quinoa cheese mixture. 7. Divide the patties in the two crisper plates and spray them with cooking oil. 8. Return the crisper plates to the Ninja Foodi Dual Zone Air Fryer. 9. Choose the Air Fry mode for Zone 1 and set the temperature to 390 degrees F/200 degrees C and the time to 13 minutes. 10. Select the "MATCH" button to copy the settings for Zone 2. 11. Initiate cooking by pressing the START/STOP button. 12. Flip the patties once cooked halfway through, and resume cooking. 13. Meanwhile, prepare the cucumber yogurt dill sauce by mixing all of its ingredients in a mixing bowl. 14. Place each quinoa patty in a burger bun along with arugula leaves. 15. Serve with yogurt dill sauce.

Serving Suggestion: Serve with yogurt dip.

Variation Tip: Use crushed cornflakes for breading to have extra crispiness.

Nutritional Information Per Serving: Calories 231 | Fat 9g | Sodium 271mg | Carbs 32.8g | Fiber 6.4g | Sugar 7g | Protein 6.3g

Air Fried Okra

Prep Time: 10 minutes | Cook Time: 13 minutes | Serves: 2

Ingredients:

½ lb. okra pods sliced
1 teaspoon olive oil

¼ teaspoon salt
⅛ teaspoon black pepper

Preparation:

1. Preheat the Ninja Foodi Dual Zone Air Fryer to 350 degrees F/175 degrees C. 2. Toss okra with olive oil, salt, and black pepper in a bowl. 3. Spread the okra in a single layer in the two crisper plates. 4. Return the crisper plate to the Ninja Foodi Dual Zone Air Fryer. 5. Choose the Air Fry mode for Zone 1 and set the temperature to 375 degrees F/190 degrees C and the time to 13 minutes. 6. Select the "MATCH" button to copy the settings for Zone 2. 7. Initiate cooking by pressing the START/STOP button. 8. Toss the okra once cooked halfway through, and resume cooking. 9. Serve warm.

Serving Suggestion: Serve with potato chips and bread slices.
Variation Tip: Sprinkle cornmeal before cooking for added crisp.
Nutritional Information Per Serving: Calories 208 | Fat 5g | Sodium 1205mg | Carbs 34.1g | Fiber 7.8g | Sugar 2.5g | Protein 5.9g

Garlic Potato Wedges in Air Fryer

Prep Time: 10 Minutes | Cook Time: 23 Minutes | Serves: 2

Ingredients:

4 medium potatoes, peeled and cut into wedges
4 tablespoons butter

1 teaspoon chopped cilantro
1 cup plain flour

1 teaspoon garlic, minced
Salt and black pepper, to taste

Preparation:

1. Soak the potato wedges in cold water for about 30 minutes. 2. Drain and pat dry with a paper towel. 3. Boil water in a large pot and boil the wedges for 3 minutes and place on a paper towel. 4. In a bowl, mix garlic, melted butter, salt, pepper, and cilantro. 5. Add the flour to a separate bowl along with the salt and black pepper. 6. Add water to the flour so it gets a runny in texture. 7. Coat the potatoes with the flour mixture and divide them into two foil tins. 8. Place the foil tins in each air fryer basket. 9. Set the zone 1 basket to AIR FRY mode at 390 degrees F/200 degrees C for 20 minutes. 10. Select the MATCH button for the zone 2 basket. 11. Once done, serve and enjoy.

Serving Suggestion: Serve with ketchup
Variation Tip: Use olive oil instead of butter
Nutritional Information Per Serving: Calories 727 | Fat 24.1g | Sodium 191mg | Carbs 115.1g | Fiber 12g | Sugar 5.1g | Protein 14g

Fresh Mix Veggies in Air Fryer

Prep Time: 15 Minutes | Cook Time: 12 Minutes | Serves: 4

Ingredients: :

1 cup cauliflower florets
1 cup carrots, peeled chopped
1 cup broccoli florets

2 tablespoons avocado oil
Salt, to taste
½ teaspoon chili powder

½ teaspoon garlic powder
½ teaspoon herbs de Provence
1 cup Parmesan cheese

Preparation:

1. Take a bowl, and add all the veggies to it. 2. Toss and then season the veggies with salt, chili powder, garlic powder, and herbs de Provence. 3. Toss it all well and then drizzle avocado oil. 4. Make sure the ingredients are coated well. 5. Distribute the veggies among both baskets of the air fryer. 6. Turn on the START/STOP button and set it to AIR FRY mode at 390 degrees F/200 degrees C for 10-12 minutes. 7. For the zone 2 basket setting, press the MATCH button. 8. After 8 minutes of cooking, press the START/STOP button and then take out the baskets and sprinkle Parmesan cheese on top of the veggies. 9. Then let the cooking cycle complete for the next 3-4 minutes. 10. Once done, serve.

Serving Suggestion: Serve the veggies with rice
Variation Tip: Use canola oil or butter instead of avocado oil
Nutritional Information Per Serving: Calories 161 | Fat 9.3g | Sodium 434mg | Carbs 7.7g | Fiber 2.4g | Sugar 2.5g | Protein 13.9

Mixed Air Fry Veggies

Prep Time: 15 Minutes | Cook Time: 25 Minutes | Serves: 4

Ingredients

2 cups carrots, cubed
2 cups potatoes, cubed
2 cups shallots, cubed

2 cups zucchini, diced
2 cups yellow squash, cubed
Salt and black pepper, to taste

1 tablespoon Italian seasoning
2 tablespoons ranch seasoning
4 tablespoons olive oil

Preparation:

1. Take a large bowl and add all the veggies to it. 2. Season the veggies with salt, pepper, Italian seasoning, ranch seasoning, and olive oil 3. Toss all the ingredients well. 4. Divide the veggies into both the baskets of the air fryer. 5. Set zone 1 basket to AIR FRY mode at 360 degrees F for 25 minutes. 6. Select the MATCH button for the zone 2 basket. 7. Once it is cooked and done, serve, and enjoy.

Serving Suggestion: Serve it with rice

Variation Tip: None

Nutritional Information Per Serving: Calories 275 | Fat 15.3g | Sodium 129 mg | Carbs 33g | Fiber 3.8g | Sugar 5g | Protein 4.4g

Hasselback Potatoes

Prep Time: 15 minutes | Cook Time: 15 minutes | Serves: 4

Ingredients:

4 medium Yukon Gold potatoes
3 tablespoons melted butter
1 tablespoon olive oil

3 garlic cloves, crushed
½ teaspoon ground paprika
Salt and black pepper ground, to taste

1 tablespoon chopped fresh parsley

Preparation:

1. Slice each potato from the top to make ¼-inch slices without cutting its ½-inch bottom, keeping the potato's bottom intact. 2. Mix butter with olive oil, garlic, and paprika in a small bowl. 3. Brush the garlic mixture on top of each potato and add the mixture into the slits. 4. Season them with salt and black pepper. 5. Place 2 seasoned potatoes in each of the crisper plate 6. Return the crisper plate to the Ninja Foodi Dual Zone Air Fryer. 7. Choose the Air Fry mode for Zone 1 and set the temperature to 375 degrees F/190 degrees C and the time to 25 minutes. 8. Select the "MATCH" button to copy the settings for Zone 2. 9. Initiate cooking by pressing the START/STOP button. 10. Brushing the potatoes again with butter mixture after 15 minutes, then resume cooking. 11. Garnish with parsley. 12. Serve warm.

Serving Suggestion: Serve with mayonnaise or cream cheese dip.

Variation Tip: Add tomato and cheese slices to the potato slits before air frying.

Nutritional Information Per Serving: Calories 350 | Fat 2.6g | Sodium 358mg | Carbs 64.6g | Fiber 14.4g | Sugar 3.3g | Protein 19.9g

Sweet Potatoes with Honey Butter

Prep Time: 15 minutes | Cook Time: 40 minutes | Serves: 4

Ingredients:

4 sweet potatoes, scrubbed

1 teaspoon oil

Honey Butter

4 tablespoons unsalted butter
1 tablespoon Honey

2 teaspoons hot sauce
¼ teaspoon salt

Preparation:

1. Rub the sweet potatoes with oil and place two potatoes in each crisper plate. 2. Return the crisper plate to the Ninja Foodi Dual Zone Air Fryer. 3. Choose the Air Fry mode for Zone 1 and set the temperature to 400 degrees F/200 degrees C and the time to 40 minutes. 4. Select the "MATCH" button to copy the settings for Zone 2. 5. Initiate cooking by pressing the START/STOP button. 6. Flip the potatoes once cooked halfway through, then resume cooking. 7. Mix butter with hot sauce, honey, and salt in a bowl. 8. When the potatoes are done, cut a slit on top and make a well with a spoon 9. Pour the honey butter in each potato jacket. 10. Serve.

Serving Suggestion: Serve with sautéed vegetables and salad.

Variation Tip: Sprinkle crumbled bacon and parsley on top.

Nutritional Information Per Serving: Calories 288 | Fat 6.9g | Sodium 761mg | Carbs 46g | Fiber 4g | Sugar 12g | Protein 9.6g

Curly Fries

Prep Time: 10 minutes | Cook Time: 20 minutes | Serves: 6

Ingredients:

2 spiralized zucchinis
1 cup flour
2 tablespoons paprika

1 teaspoon cayenne pepper
1 teaspoon garlic powder
1 teaspoon black pepper

1 teaspoon salt
2 eggs
Olive oil or cooking spray

Preparation:

1. Mix flour with paprika, cayenne pepper, garlic powder, black pepper, and salt in a bowl. 2. Beat eggs in another bowl and dip the zucchini in the eggs. 3. Coat the zucchini with the flour mixture and divide it into two crisper plates. 4. Spray the zucchini with cooking oil. 5. Return the crisper plate to the Ninja Foodi Dual Zone Air Fryer. 6. Choose the Air Fry mode for Zone 1 and set the temperature to 400 degrees F/200 degrees C and the time to 20 minutes. 7. Select the "MATCH" button to copy the settings for Zone 2. 8. Initiate cooking by pressing the START/STOP button. 9. Toss the zucchini once cooked halfway through, then resume cooking. 10. Serve warm.

Serving Suggestion: Serve with red chunky salsa or chili sauce.

Variation Tip: Use crushed cornflakes for breading to have extra crispiness.

Nutritional Information Per Serving: Calories 212 | Fat 11.8g | Sodium 321mg | Carbs 24.6g | Fiber 4.4g | Sugar 8g | Protein 7.3g

Green Beans with Baked Potatoes

Prep Time: 15 Minutes | Cook Time: 45 Minutes | Serves: 2

Ingredients:

2 cups green beans
2 large potatoes, cubed
3 tablespoons olive oil

1 teaspoon seasoned salt
½ teaspoon chili powder
⅙ teaspoon garlic powder

¼ teaspoon onion powder

Preparation:

1. Take a large bowl and pour olive oil into it. 2. Add all the seasoning in the olive oil and whisk it well. 3. Toss the green beans in and mix well and then transfer to zone 1 basket of the air fryer. 4. Season the potatoes with the oil seasoning and add them to the zone 2 basket. 5. Press the Sync button. 6. Once the cooking cycle is complete, take out and serve.

Serving Suggestion: Serve with rice

Variation Tip: Use canola oil instead of olive oil

Nutritional Information Per Serving: Calories 473 | Fat 21.6g | Sodium 796mg | Carbs 66.6g | Fiber 12.9g | Sugar 6g | Protein 8.4g

Fried Olives

Prep Time: 15 minutes | Cook Time: 9 minutes | Serves: 6

Ingredients:

2 cups blue cheese stuffed olives, drained
½ cup all-purpose flour

1 cup panko breadcrumbs
½ teaspoon garlic powder

1 pinch oregano
2 eggs

Preparation:

1. Mix flour with oregano and garlic powder in a bowl and beat two eggs in another bowl. 2. Spread panko breadcrumbs in a bowl. 3. Coat all the olives with the flour mixture, dip in the eggs and then coat with the panko breadcrumbs. 4. As you coat the olives, place them in the two crisper plates in a single layer, then spray them with cooking oil. 5. Return the crisper plates to the Ninja Foodi Dual Zone Air Fryer. 6. Choose the Air Fry mode for Zone 1 and set the temperature to 375 degrees F/190 degrees C and the time to 9 minutes. 7. Select the "MATCH" button to copy the settings for Zone 2. 8. Initiate cooking by pressing the START/STOP button. 9. Flip the olives once cooked halfway through, then resume cooking. 10. Serve.

Serving Suggestion: Serve with red chunky salsa or chili sauce.

Variation Tip: Use crushed cornflakes for breading to have extra crispiness.

Nutritional Information Per Serving: Calories 166 | Fat 3.2g | Sodium 437mg | Carbs 28.8g | Fiber 1.8g | Sugar 2.7g | Protein 5.8g

Cheesy Potatoes with Asparagus

Prep Time: 15 Minutes | Cook Time: 35 Minutes | Serves: 2

Ingredients:

1½ pounds russet potato, wedges or cut in half
2 teaspoons mixed herbs
2 teaspoons chili flakes
2 cups asparagus

1 cup chopped onion
1 tablespoon Dijon mustard
¼ cup fresh cream
1 teaspoon olive oil

2 tablespoons butter
½ teaspoon salt and black pepper
Water as required
½ cup Parmesan cheese

Preparation:

1. Take a bowl and add asparagus and sweet potato wedges to it. 2. Season it with salt, black pepper, and olive oil. 3. Add the potato wedges to the zone 1 air fryer basket and asparagus to the zone 2 basket. 4. Set zone 1 to AIR FRY mode at 390 degrees F/200 degrees C for 12 minutes. 5. Set the zone 2 basket to AIR FRY mode at 390 degrees F/200 degrees C for 30-35 minutes. Click Sync button. 6. Meanwhile, take a skillet and add butter and sauté the onion in it for a few minutes. 7. Then add salt and Dijon mustard and chili flakes, Parmesan cheese, and fresh cream. 8. Once the veggies are cooked take them out and drizzle the cream mixture on top.

Serving Suggestion: Serve with rice

Variation Tip: Use olive oil instead of butter

Nutritional Information Per Serving: Calories 251 | Fat 11g | Sodium 279mg | Carbs 31.1g | Fiber 5g | Sugar 4.1g | Protein 9g

Fried Artichoke Hearts

Prep Time: 15 minutes | Cook Time: 10 minutes | Serves: 6

Ingredients:

3 cans Quartered Artichokes, drained
½ cup mayonnaise

1 cup panko breadcrumbs
⅓ cup grated Parmesan

salt and black pepper to taste
Parsley for garnish

Preparation:

1. Mix mayonnaise with salt and black pepper and keep the sauce aside. 2. Spread panko breadcrumbs in a bowl. 3. Coat the artichoke pieces with the breadcrumbs. 4. As you coat the artichokes, place them in the two crisper plates in a single layer, then spray them with cooking oil. 5. Return the crisper plates to the Ninja Foodi Dual Zone Air Fryer. 6. Choose the Air Fry mode for Zone 1 and set the temperature to 375 degrees F/190 degrees C and the time to 10 minutes. 7. Select the "MATCH" button to copy the settings for Zone 2. 8. Initiate cooking by pressing the START/STOP button. 9. Flip the artichokes once cooked halfway through, then resume cooking. 10. Serve warm with mayo sauce.

Serving Suggestion: Serve with red chunky salsa or chili sauce.

Variation Tip: Use crushed cornflakes for breading to have extra crispiness.

Nutritional Information Per Serving: Calories 193 | Fat 1g | Sodium 395mg | Carbs 38.7g | Fiber 1.6g | Sugar 0.9g | Protein 6.6g

Zucchini with Stuffing

Prep Time: 12 Minutes | Cook Time: 20 Minutes | Serves: 3

Ingredients:

1 cup quinoa, rinsed
1 cup black olives
6 medium zucchinis, about 2 pounds
2 cups cannellini beans, drained

1 white onion, chopped
¼ cup almonds, chopped
4 cloves garlic, chopped
4 tablespoons olive oil

1 cup water
2 cups Parmesan cheese, for topping

Preparation:

1. First wash the zucchini and cut it lengthwise. 2. Take a skillet and heat oil in it 3. Sauté the onion in olive oil for a few minutes. 4. Then add the quinoa and water and let it cook for 8 minutes with the lid on top. 5. Transfer the quinoa to a bowl and add all the remaining ingredients, excluding zucchini and Parmesan cheese. 6. Scoop out the seeds of the zucchinis. 7. Fill the cavity of zucchinis with the quinoa mixture. 8. Top it with a handful of Parmesan cheese. 9. Arrange the zucchinis in both air fryer baskets. 10. Select zone 1 basket at AIR FRY mode for 20 minutes and temperature to 390 degrees F/200 degrees C. 11. Use the MATCH button to select the same setting for zone 2. 12. Serve and enjoy.

Serving Suggestion: Serve them with pasta

Variation Tip: None

Nutritional Information Per Serving: Calories 1171 | Fat 48.6g | Sodium 1747mg | Carbs 132.4g | Fiber 42.1g | Sugar 11.5g | Protein 65.7g

Garlic Herbed Baked Potatoes

Prep Time: 25 Minutes | Cook Time: 45 Minutes | Serves: 4

Ingredients:

4 large baking potatoes

Salt and black pepper, to taste

2 teaspoons avocado oil

Cheese Ingredients:

2 cups sour cream

1 teaspoon garlic clove, minced

1 teaspoon fresh dill

2 teaspoons chopped chives

Salt and black pepper, to taste

2 teaspoons Worcestershire sauce

Preparation:

1. Pierce the skin of the potatoes with a fork. 2. Season the potatoes with olive oil, salt, and black pepper. 3. Divide the potatoes into the air fryer baskets. 4. Now press 1 for zone 1 and set it to AIR FRY mode at 350 degrees F/175 degrees C, for 45 minutes. 5. Select the MATCH button for zone 2. 6. Meanwhile, take a bowl and mix all the cheese ingredients together. 7. Once the cooking cycle is complete, take out the potatoes and make a slit in-between each one. 8. Add the cheese mixture in the cavity and serve it hot.

Serving Suggestion: Serve with gravy

Variation Tip: None

Nutritional Information Per Serving: Calories 382 | Fat 24.6g | Sodium 107mg | Carbs 36.2g | Fiber 2.5g | Sugar 2g | Protein 7.3g

Brussels Sprouts

Prep Time: 15 Minutes | Cook Time: 20 Minutes | Serves: 2

Ingredients:

2 pounds Brussels sprouts

2 tablespoons avocado oil

Salt and pepper, to taste

1 cup pine nuts, roasted

Preparation:

1. Trim the bottom of the Brussels sprouts. 2. Take a bowl and combine the avocado oil, salt, and black pepper. 3. Toss the Brussels sprouts into the bowl and m ix well. 4. Divide the mixture into both air fryer baskets. 5. For zone 1 set to AIR FRY mode for 20 minutes at 390 degrees F/200 degrees C. 6. Select the MATCH button for the zone 2 basket. 7. Once the Brussels sprouts get crisp and tender, take out and serve.

Serving Suggestion: Serve with rice

Variation Tip: Use olive oil instead of avocado oil

Nutritional Information Per Serving: Calories 672 | Fat 50g | Sodium 115mg | Carbs 51g | Fiber 20.2g | Sugar 12.3g | Protein 25g

Kale and Spinach Chips

Prep Time: 12 Minutes | Cook Time: 6 Minutes | Serves: 2

Ingredients:

2 cups spinach, torn in pieces and stem removed

2 cups kale, torn in pieces, stems removed

1 tablespoon olive oil

Sea salt, to taste

⅓ cup Parmesan cheese

Preparation:

1. Take a bowl and add spinach to it. 2. Take another bowl and add kale to it. 3. Season both of them with olive oil and sea salt. 4. Add the kale to the zone 1 basket and spinach to the zone 2 basket. 5. Select AIR FRY mode for zone 1 at 350 degrees F/175 degrees C for 6 minutes. 6. Set zone 2 to AIR FRY mode at 350 degrees F/175 degrees C for 5 minutes. 7. Once done, take out the crispy chips and sprinkle Parmesan cheese on top. 8. Serve and Enjoy.

Serving Suggestion: Serve with baked potato

Variation Tip: Use canola oil instead of olive oil

Nutritional Information Per Serving: Calories 166 | Fat 11.1g | Sodium 355mg | Carbs 8.1g | Fiber 1.7 g | Sugar 0.1g | Protein 8.2g

Pepper Poppers

Prep Time: 15 minutes | Cook Time: 20 minutes | Serves: 24

Ingredients:

8 ounces cream cheese, softened
¾ cup shredded cheddar cheese
¾ cup shredded Monterey Jack cheese
6 bacon strips, cooked and crumbled
¼ teaspoon salt

¼ teaspoon garlic powder
¼ teaspoon chili powder
¼ teaspoon smoked paprika
1-pound fresh jalapeño peppers, halved
lengthwise and deseeded

½ cup dry breadcrumbs
Sour cream, French onion dip, or ranch salad
dressing (optional)

Preparation:

1. In a large bowl, combine the cheeses, bacon, and seasonings; mix well. Spoon 1½ to 2 tablespoons of the mixture into each pepper half. Roll them in the breadcrumbs. 2. Place a crisper plate in each drawer. Put the prepared peppers in a single layer in each drawer. Insert the drawers into the unit. 3. Select zone 1, then AIR FRY, then set the temperature to 360 degrees F/180 degrees C with a 20-minute timer. To match zone 2 settings to zone 1, choose MATCH. To begin, select START/STOP. 4. Remove the peppers from the drawers after the timer has finished.

Serving Suggestion: Serve with sour cream, French onion dip, or ranch dressing.

Variation Tip: You can use bell peppers instead.

Nutritional Information Per Serving: Calories 81 | Fat 6g | Sodium 145mg | Carbs 3g | Fiber 4g | Sugar 1g | Protein 3g

Stuffed Tomatoes

Prep Time: 12 Minutes | Cook Time: 8 Minutes | Serves: 2

Ingredients:

2 cups brown rice, cooked
1 cup tofu, grilled and chopped
4 large red tomatoes

4 tablespoons basil, chopped
¼ tablespoon olive oil
Salt and black pepper, to taste

2 tablespoons lemon juice
1 teaspoon red chili powder
½ cup Parmesan cheese

Preparation:

1. Take a large bowl and mix rice, tofu, basil, olive oil, salt, black pepper, lemon juice, and chili powder. 2. Core the center of the tomatoes. 3. Fill the cavity with the rice mixture. 4. Top them off with the cheese sprinkle. 5. Divide the tomatoes into two air fryer baskets. 6. Turn zone 1 to AIR FRY mode for 8 minutes at 400 degrees F/200 degrees C. 7. Select the MATCH button for zone 2. 8. Serve and enjoy.

Serving Suggestion: Serve it with Greek yogurt

Variation Tip: Use canola oil instead of olive oil

Nutritional Information Per Serving: Calories 1034 | Fat 24.2g | Sodium 527mg | Carbs 165g | Fiber 12.1g | Sugar 1.2g | Protein 43.9g

Fried Asparagus

Prep Time: 5 minutes | Cook Time: 6 minutes | Serves: 4

Ingredients:

¼ cup mayonnaise
4 teaspoons olive oil
1½ teaspoons grated lemon zest

1 garlic clove, minced
½ teaspoon pepper
¼ teaspoon seasoned salt

1-pound fresh asparagus, trimmed
2 tablespoons shredded parmesan cheese
Lemon wedges (optional)

Preparation:

1. In a large bowl, combine the first 6 ingredients. 2. Add the asparagus; toss to coat. 3. Put a crisper plate in both drawers. Put the asparagus in a single layer in each drawer. Top with the parmesan cheese. Place the drawers into the unit. 4. Select zone 1, then AIR FRY, then set the temperature to 375 degrees F/190 degrees C with a 6-minute timer. To match zone 2 settings to zone 1, choose MATCH. To begin, select START/STOP. 5. Remove the asparagus from the drawers after the timer has finished.

Serving Suggestion: Serve with lemon wedges.

Variation Tip: You can use green beans instead.

Nutritional Information Per Serving: Calories 156 | Fat 15g | Sodium 214mg | Carbs 3g | Fiber 1g | Sugar 1g | Protein 2g

Mushroom Roll-Ups

Prep Time: 30 minutes | Cook Time: 10 minutes | Serves: 10

Ingredients:

2 tablespoons extra virgin olive oil
8 ounces large portobello mushrooms (gills discarded), finely chopped
1 teaspoon dried oregano
1 teaspoon dried thyme
½ teaspoon crushed red pepper flakes
¼ teaspoon salt
8 ounces cream cheese, softened
4 ounces whole-milk ricotta cheese
10 flour tortillas (8-inch)
Cooking spray
Chutney, for serving (optional)

Preparation:

1. Heat the oil in a pan over medium heat. Add the mushrooms and cook for 4 minutes. Sauté until the mushrooms are browned, about 4-6 minutes, with the oregano, thyme, pepper flakes, and salt. Cool. 2. Combine the cheeses in a mixing bowl; fold in the mushrooms until thoroughly combined. 3. On the bottom center of each tortilla, spread 3 tablespoons of the mushroom mixture. Tightly roll up each tortilla and secure with toothpicks. 4. Place a crisper plate in each drawer. Put the roll-ups in a single layer in each. Insert the drawers into the unit. 5. Select zone 1, then AIR FRY, then set the temperature to 400 degrees F/200 degrees C with a 10-minute timer. To match zone 2 settings to zone 1, choose MATCH. To begin, select START/STOP. 6. Remove the roll-ups from the drawers after the timer has finished. When they have cooled enough to handle, discard the toothpicks. 7. Serve and enjoy!

Serving Suggestion: Serve the roll-ups with chutney.
Variation Tip: You can use gluten-free tortillas.
Nutritional Information Per Serving: Calories 291 | Fat 16g | Sodium 380mg | Carbs 31g | Fiber 2g | Sugar 2g | Protein 8g

Fried Avocado Tacos

Prep Time: 30 minutes | Cook Time: 10 minutes | Serves: 4

Ingredients:

For the Sauce:
2 cups shredded fresh kale or coleslaw mix
¼ cup minced fresh cilantro
¼ cup plain Greek yogurt
2 tablespoons lime juice
1 teaspoon honey
¼ teaspoon salt
¼ teaspoon ground chipotle pepper
¼ teaspoon pepper

For the Tacos:
1 large egg, beaten
¼ cup cornmeal
½ teaspoon salt
½ teaspoon garlic powder
½ teaspoon ground chipotle pepper
2 medium avocados, peeled and sliced
Cooking spray
8 flour tortillas or corn tortillas (6 inches), heated up
1 medium tomato, chopped
Crumbled queso fresco (optional)

Preparation:

1. Combine the first 8 ingredients in a bowl. Cover and refrigerate until serving. 2. Place the egg in a shallow bowl. In another shallow bowl, mix the cornmeal, salt, garlic powder, and chipotle pepper. 3. Dip the avocado slices in the egg, then into the cornmeal mixture, gently patting to help adhere. 4. Place a crisper plate in both drawers. Put the avocado slices in the drawers in a single layer. Insert the drawers into the unit. 5. Select zone 1, then AIR FRY, then set the temperature to 360 degrees F/180 degrees C with a 6-minute timer. To match zone 2 settings to zone 1, choose MATCH. To begin, select START/STOP. 6. Put the avocado slices, prepared sauce, tomato, and queso fresco in the tortillas and serve.

Serving Suggestion: Add some more chopped cilantro.
Variation Tip: You can use panko breadcrumbs instead of cornmeal.
Nutritional Information Per Serving: Calories 407 | Fat 21g | Sodium 738mg | Carbs 48g | Fiber 4g | Sugar 9g | Protein 9g

Buffalo Bites

Prep Time: 10 minutes | Cook Time: 30 minutes | Serves: 6

Ingredients:

For the Bites:

1 small cauliflower head, cut into florets

2 tablespoons olive oil

3 tablespoons buffalo wing sauce

3 tablespoons butter, melted

For the Dip:

1½ cups 2% cottage cheese

¼ cup fat-free plain Greek yogurt

¼ cup crumbled blue cheese

1 sachet ranch salad dressing mix

Celery sticks (optional)

Preparation:

1. In a large bowl, combine the cauliflower and oil; toss to coat. 2. Place a crisper plate in each drawer. Put the coated cauliflower florets in each drawer in a single layer. Place the drawers in the unit. 3. Select zone 1, then AIR FRY, then set the temperature to 360 degrees F/180 degrees C with a 15-minute timer. To match zone 2 settings to zone 1, choose MATCH. To begin, select START/STOP. 4. Remove the cauliflower from the drawers after the timer has finished. 5. Combine the buffalo sauce and melted butter in a large mixing bowl. Put in the cauliflower and toss to coat. Place on a serving dish and serve. 6. Combine the dip ingredients in a small bowl. Serve with the cauliflower and celery sticks, if desired.

Serving Suggestion: Serve with the dipping sauce.

Variation Tip: You can use buttermilk.

Nutritional Information Per Serving: Calories 203 | Fat 13g | Sodium 1470mg | Carbs 13g | Fiber 4g | Sugar 1g | Protein 9g

Garlic-Rosemary Brussels Sprouts

Prep Time: 5 minutes | Cook Time: 15 minutes | Serves: 4

Ingredients:

3 tablespoons olive oil

2 garlic cloves, minced

½ teaspoon salt

¼ teaspoon pepper

1-pound Brussels sprouts, trimmed and halved

½ cup panko breadcrumbs

1½ teaspoons minced fresh rosemary

Preparation:

1. Place the first 4 ingredients in a small microwave-safe bowl; microwave on high for 30 seconds. 2. Toss the Brussels sprouts in 2 tablespoons of the microwaved mixture. 3. Place a crisper plate in each drawer. Put the sprouts in a single layer in each drawer. Insert the drawers into the units. 4. Select zone 1, then AIR FRY, then set the temperature to 360 degrees F/180 degrees C with a 6-minute timer. To match zone 2 settings to zone 1, choose MATCH. To begin, select START/STOP. 5. Remove the sprouts from the drawers after the timer has finished. 6. Toss the breadcrumbs with the rosemary and remaining oil mixture; sprinkle over the sprouts. 7. Continue cooking (same settings) until the crumbs are browned, and the sprouts are tender (3 to 5 minutes). Serve immediately.

Serving Suggestion: Serve with a side salad.

Variation Tip: Use cracker crumbs instead of breadcrumbs.

Nutritional Information Per Serving: Calories 164 | Fat 11g | Sodium 342mg | Carbs 15g | Fiber 3g | Sugar 4g | Protein 5g

Herb and Lemon Cauliflower

Prep Time: 5 minutes | Cook Time: 10 minutes | Serves: 4

Ingredients:

1 medium cauliflower, cut into florets (about 6 cups)

4 tablespoons olive oil, divided

¼ cup minced fresh parsley

1 tablespoon minced fresh rosemary

1 tablespoon minced fresh thyme

1 teaspoon grated lemon zest

2 tablespoons lemon juice

½ teaspoon salt

¼ teaspoon crushed red pepper flakes

Preparation:

1. In a large bowl, combine the cauliflower florets and 2 tablespoons olive oil; toss to coat. 2. Put a crisper plate in both drawers, then put the cauliflower in a single layer in each. Insert the drawers into the unit. 3. Select zone 1, then AIR FRY, then set the temperature to 350 degrees F/175 degrees C with a 10-minute timer. To match zone 2 settings to zone 1, choose MATCH. To begin, select START/STOP. 4. Remove the cauliflower from the drawers after the timer has finished. 5. In a small bowl, combine the remaining ingredients. Stir in the remaining 2 tablespoons of oil. 6. Transfer the cauliflower to a large bowl and drizzle with the herb mixture. Toss to combine.

Serving Suggestion: Serve with a side salad.

Variation Tip: You can use broccoli instead.

Nutritional Information Per Serving: Calories 161 | Fat 14g | Sodium 342mg | Carbs 8g | Fiber 3g | Sugar 3g | Protein 3g

Garlic-Herb Fried Squash

Prep Time: 5 minutes | Cook Time: 15 minutes | Serves: 4

Ingredients:

5 cups halved small pattypan squash (about 1¼ pounds)

1 tablespoon olive oil

2 garlic cloves, minced

½ teaspoon salt

¼ teaspoon dried oregano

¼ teaspoon dried thyme

¼ teaspoon pepper

1 tablespoon minced fresh parsley, for serving

Preparation:

1. Place the squash in a large bowl. 2. Mix the oil, garlic, salt, oregano, thyme, and pepper; drizzle over the squash. Toss to coat. 3. Place a crisper plate in both drawers. Put the squash in a single layer in each drawer. Insert the drawers into the unit. 4. Select zone 1, then AIR FRY, then set the temperature to 360 degrees F/180 degrees C with a 6-minute timer. To match zone 2 settings to zone 1, choose MATCH. To begin, select START/STOP. 5. Remove the squash from the drawers after the timer has finished. Sprinkle with the parsley.

Serving Suggestion: Serve alongside soup.

Variation Tip: You can use garlic powder.

Nutritional Information Per Serving: Calories 58 | Fat 3g | Sodium 296mg | Carbs 6g | Fiber 2g | Sugar 3g | Protein 2g

Stuffed Sweet Potatoes

Prep Time: 20 minutes | Cook Time: 55 minutes | Serves: 4

Ingredients:

2 medium sweet potatoes
1 teaspoon olive oil
1 cup cooked chopped spinach, drained
1 cup shredded cheddar cheese, divided

2 cooked bacon strips, crumbled
1 green onion, chopped
¼ cup fresh cranberries, coarsely chopped
⅓ cup chopped pecans, toasted

2 tablespoons butter
¼ teaspoon kosher salt
¼ teaspoon pepper

Preparation:

1. Brush the sweet potatoes with the oil. 2. Place a crisper plate in both drawers. Add one sweet potato to each drawer. Place the drawers in the unit. 3. Select zone 1, then AIR FRY, then set the temperature to 360 degrees F/180 degrees C with a 40-minute timer. To match zone 2 settings to zone 1, choose MATCH. To begin, select START/STOP. 4. Remove the sweet potatoes from the drawers after the timer has finished. Cut them in half lengthwise. Scoop out the pulp, leaving a ¼-inch thick shell. 5. Put the pulp in a large bowl and stir in the spinach, ¾ cup of cheese, bacon, onion, pecans, cranberries, butter, salt, and pepper. 6. Spoon the mixture into the potato shells, mounding the mixture slightly. 7. Place a crisper plate in each drawer. Put one filled potato into each drawer and insert them into the unit. 8. Select zone 1, then AIR FRY, then set the temperature to 360 degrees F/180 degrees C with a 10-minute timer. To match zone 2 settings to zone 1, choose MATCH. To begin, select START/STOP. 9. Sprinkle with the remaining ¼ cup of cheese. Cook using the same settings until the cheese is melted (about 1 to 2 minutes).

Serving Suggestion: Serve with a side salad.

Variation Tip: Use kale instead of spinach.

Nutritional Information Per Serving: Calories 376 | Fat 25g | Sodium 489mg | Carbs 28g | Fiber 10g | Sugar 5g | Protein 12g

Beets With Orange Gremolata and Goat's Cheese

Time: 25 minutes | Cook Time: 45 minutes | Serves: 12

Ingredients:

3 medium fresh golden beets (about 1 pound)
3 medium fresh beets (about 1 pound)
2 tablespoons lime juice
2 tablespoons orange juice

½ teaspoon fine sea salt
1 tablespoon minced fresh parsley
1 tablespoon minced fresh sage
1 garlic clove, minced

1 teaspoon grated orange zest
3 tablespoons crumbled goat's cheese
2 tablespoons sunflower kernels

Preparation:

1. Scrub the beets and trim the tops by 1 inch. 2. Place the beets on a double thickness of heavy-duty foil (about 24 x 12 inches). Fold the foil around the beets, sealing tightly. 3. Place a crisper plate in both drawers. Put the beets in a single layer in each drawer. Insert the drawers into the unit. 4. Select zone 1, then AIR FRY, then set the temperature to 360 degrees F/180 degrees C with a 45-minute timer. To match zone 2 settings to zone 1, choose MATCH. To begin, select START/STOP. 5. Remove the beets from the drawers after the timer has finished. Peel, halve, and slice them when they're cool enough to handle. Place them in a serving bowl. 6. Toss in the lime juice, orange juice, and salt to coat. Sprinkle the beets with the parsley, sage, garlic, and orange zest. The sunflower kernels and goat's cheese go on top.

Serving Suggestion: Serve warm or cooled.

Variation Tip: You can use lemon zest.

Nutritional Information Per Serving: Calories 481 | Fat 20g | Sodium 1162mg | Carbs 56g | Fiber 4g | Sugar 9g | Protein 19g

Chapter 4 Fish and Seafood Recipes

Salmon Patties

Prep Time: 15 minutes | Cook Time: 18 minutes | Serves: 8

Ingredients:

1 lb. fresh Atlantic salmon side	1½ teaspoons yellow curry powder	2 brown eggs
¼ cup avocado, mashed	½ teaspoons sea salt	½ cup coconut flakes
¼ cup cilantro, diced	¼ cup, 4 teaspoons tapioca starch	Coconut oil, melted, for brushing

For the Greens:

2 teaspoons organic coconut oil, melted	6 cups arugula & spinach mix, tightly packed	Pinch of sea salt

Preparation:

1. Remove the fish skin and dice the flesh. 2. Place in a large bowl. Add cilantro, avocado, salt, and curry powder mix gently. 3. Add tapioca starch and mix well again. 4. Make 8 salmon patties out of this mixture, about a half-inch thick. 5. Place them on a baking sheet lined with wax paper and freeze them for 20 minutes. 6. Place ¼ cup tapioca starch and coconut flakes on a flat plate. 7. Dip the patties in the whisked egg, then coat the frozen patties in the starch and flakes. 8. Place half of the patties in each of the crisper plate and spray them with cooking oil 9. Return the crisper plate to the Ninja Foodi Dual Zone Air Fryer. 10. Choose the Air Fry mode for Zone 1 and set the temperature to 390 degrees F/200 degrees C and the time to 17 minutes. 11. Select the "MATCH" button to copy the settings for Zone 2. 12. Initiate cooking by pressing the START/STOP button. 13. Flip the patties once cooked halfway through, then resume cooking. 14. Sauté arugula with spinach in coconut oil in a pan for 30 seconds. 15. Serve the patties with sautéed greens mixture

Serving Suggestion: Serve with sautéed green beans or asparagus.

Variation Tip: Add lemon juice to the mixture before mixing.

Nutritional Information Per Serving: Calories 260 | Fat 16g | Sodium 585mg | Carbs 3.1g | Fiber 1.3g | Sugar 0.2g | Protein 25.5g

Scallops with Greens

Prep Time: 15 minutes | Cook Time: 13 minutes | Serves: 8

Ingredients:

¾ cup heavy whipping cream	1 teaspoon garlic, minced	12 ounces frozen spinach thawed
1 tablespoon tomato paste	½ teaspoons salt	8 jumbo sea scallops
1 tablespoon chopped fresh basil	½ teaspoons pepper	Vegetable oil to spray

Preparation:

1. Season the scallops with vegetable oil, salt, and pepper in a bowl 2. Mix cream with spinach, basil, garlic, salt, pepper, and tomato paste in a bowl. 3. Pour this mixture over the scallops and mix gently. 4. Divide the scallops in the Air Fryers Baskets without using the crisper plate. 5. Return the crisper plate to the Ninja Foodi Dual Zone Air Fryer. 6. Choose the Air Fry mode for Zone 1 and set the temperature to 390 degrees F/200 degrees C and the time to 13 minutes. 7. Select the "MATCH" button to copy the settings for Zone 2. 8. Initiate cooking by pressing the START/STOP button. 9. Serve right away.

Serving Suggestion: Serve with fresh cucumber salad.

Variation Tip: Use crushed cornflakes for breading to have extra crispiness.

Nutritional Information Per Serving: Calories 266 | Fat 6.3g | Sodium 193mg | Carbs 39.1g | Fiber 7.2g | Sugar 5.2g | Protein 14.8g

Fish Sandwich

Prep Time: 15 minutes | Cook Time: 22 minutes | Serves: 4

Ingredients:

4 small cod fillets, skinless	Spray oil	1 squeeze of lemon juice
Salt and black pepper, to taste	9 ounces of frozen peas	4 bread rolls, cut in halve
2 tablespoons flour	1 tablespoon creme fraiche	
¼ cup dried breadcrumbs	12 capers	

Preparation:

1. First, coat the cod fillets with flour, salt, and black pepper. 2. Then coat the fish with breadcrumbs. 3. Divide the coated codfish in the two crisper plates and spray them with cooking spray. 4. Return the crisper plate to the Ninja Foodi Dual Zone Air Fryer. 5. Choose the Air Fry mode for Zone 1 and set the temperature to 390 degrees F/200 degrees C and the time to 17 minutes. 6. Select the "MATCH" button to copy the settings for Zone 2. 7. Initiate cooking by pressing the START/STOP button. 8. Meanwhile, boil peas in hot water for 5 minutes until soft. 9. Then drain the peas and transfer them to the blender. 10. Add capers, lemon juice, and crème fraiche to the blender. 11. Blend until it makes a smooth mixture. 12. Spread the peas crème mixture on top of 2 lower halves of the bread roll, and place the fish fillets on it. 13. Place the remaining bread slices on top. 14. Serve fresh.

Serving Suggestion: Serve with sautéed or fresh greens with melted butter.

Variation Tip: Coat the fish with crushed cornflakes for extra crispiness.

Nutritional Information Per Serving: Calories 348 | Fat 30g | Sodium 660mg | Carbs 5g | Fiber 0g | Sugar 0g | Protein 14g

Crusted Shrimp

Prep Time: 20 minutes | Cook Time: 13 minutes | Serves: 4

Ingredients:

1 lb. shrimp
½ cup flour, all-purpose
1 teaspoon salt

½ teaspoon baking powder
⅔ cup water
2 cups coconut shred

½ cup bread crumbs

Preparation:

1. In a small bowl, whisk together flour, salt, water, and baking powder. Set aside for 5 minutes. 2. In another shallow bowl, toss bread crumbs with coconut shreds together. 3. Dredge shrimp in liquid, then coat in coconut mixture, making sure it's totally covered. 4. Repeat until all shrimp are coated. 5. Spread half of the shrimp in each crisper plate and spray them with cooking oil. 6. Return the crisper plates to the Ninja Foodi Dual Zone Air Fryer. 7. Choose the Air Fry mode for Zone 1 and set the temperature to 390 degrees F/200 degrees C and the time to 13 minutes. 8. Select the "MATCH" button to copy the settings for Zone 2. 9. Initiate cooking by pressing the START/STOP button. 10. Shake the baskets once cooked halfway, then resume cooking. 11. Serve with your favorite dip.
Serving Suggestion: Serve on top of mashed potato or mashed cauliflower.
Variation Tip: Use crushed cornflakes for breading to have extra crispiness.
Nutritional Information Per Serving: Calories 297 | Fat 1g | Sodium 291mg | Carbs 35g | Fiber 1g | Sugar 9g | Protein 29g

Salmon with Fennel Salad

Prep Time: 10 minutes | Cook Time: 17 minutes | Serves: 4

Ingredients:

2 teaspoons fresh parsley, chopped
1 teaspoon fresh thyme, chopped
1 teaspoon salt
4 (6-oz) skinless center-cut salmon fillets

2 tablespoons olive oil
4 cups fennel, sliced
⅔ cup Greek yogurt
1 garlic clove, grated

2 tablespoons orange juice
1 teaspoon lemon juice
2 tablespoons fresh dill, chopped

Preparation:

1. Preheat your Ninja Foodi Dual Zone Air Fryer to 200 degrees F/95 degrees C. 2. Mix ½ teaspoon of salt, thyme, and parsley in a small bowl. 3. Brush the salmon with oil first, then rub liberally rub the herb mixture. 4. Place 2 salmon fillets in each of the crisper plate. 5. Return the crisper plate to the Ninja Foodi Dual Zone Air Fryer. 6. Choose the Air Fry mode for Zone 1 and set the temperature to 390 degrees F/200 degrees C and the time to 17 minutes. 7. Select the "MATCH" button to copy the settings for Zone 2. 8. Initiate cooking by pressing the START/STOP button. 9. Meanwhile, mix fennel with garlic, yogurt, lemon juice, orange juice, remaining salt, and dill in a mixing bowl. 10. Serve the air fried salmon fillets with fennel salad. 11. Enjoy.
Serving Suggestion: Serve with melted butter on top.
Variation Tip: Rub the salmon with lemon juice before cooking.
Nutritional Information Per Serving: Calories 305 | Fat 15g | Sodium 482mg | Carbs 17g | Fiber 3g | Sugar 2g | Protein 35g

Fried Lobster Tails

Prep Time: 10 minutes | Cook Time: 18 minutes | Serves: 4

Ingredients:

4 (4-oz) lobster tails
8 tablespoons butter, melted
2 teaspoons lemon zest

2 garlic cloves, grated
Salt and black pepper, ground to taste
2 teaspoons fresh parsley, chopped

4 wedges lemon

Preparation:

1. Spread the lobster tails into Butterfly, slit the top to expose the lobster meat while keeping the tail intact. 2. Place two lobster tails in each of the crisper plate with their lobster meat facing up. 3. Mix melted butter with lemon zest and garlic in a bowl. 4. Brush the butter mixture on top of the lobster tails. 5. And drizzle salt and black pepper on top. 6. Return the crisper plate to the Ninja Foodi Dual Zone Air Fryer. 7. Choose the Air Fry mode for Zone 1 and set the temperature to 390 degrees F/200 degrees C and the time to 18 minutes. 8. Select the "MATCH" button to copy the settings for Zone 2. 9. Initiate cooking by pressing the START/STOP button. 10. Garnish with parsley and lemon wedges. 11. Serve warm.
Serving Suggestion: Serve on a bed of lettuce leaves.
Variation Tip: Drizzle crushed cornflakes on top to have extra crispiness.
Nutritional Information Per Serving: Calories 257 | Fat 10.4g | Sodium 431mg | Carbs 20g | Fiber 0g | Sugar 1.6g | Protein 21g

Savory Salmon Fillets

Prep Time: 10 minutes | Cook Time: 17 minutes | Serves: 4

Ingredients:

4 (6-oz) salmon fillets
Salt, to taste
Black pepper, to taste

4 teaspoons olive oil
4 tablespoons wholegrain mustard
2 tablespoons packed brown sugar

2 garlic cloves, minced
1 teaspoon thyme leaves

Preparation:

1. Rub the salmon with salt and black pepper first. 2. Whisk oil with sugar, thyme, garlic, and mustard in a small bowl. 3. Place two salmon fillets in each of the crisper plate and brush the thyme mixture on top of each fillet. 4. Return the crisper plates to the Ninja Foodi Dual Zone Air Fryer. 5. Choose the Air Fry mode for Zone 1 and set the temperature to 390 degrees F/200 degrees C and the time to 17 minutes. 6. Select the "MATCH" button to copy the settings for Zone 2. 7. Initiate cooking by pressing the START/STOP button. 8. Serve warm and fresh.

Serving Suggestion: Serve with parsley and melted butter on top.

Variation Tip: Rub the fish fillets with lemon juice before cooking.

Nutritional Information Per Serving: Calories 336 | Fat 6g | Sodium 181mg | Carbs 1.3g | Fiber 0.2g | Sugar 0.4g | Protein 69.2g

Buttered Mahi-Mahi

Prep Time: 15 minutes | Cook Time: 22 minutes | Serves: 4

Ingredients:

4 (6-oz) mahi-mahi fillets
Salt and black pepper ground to taste

Cooking spray
⅔ cup butter

Preparation:

1. Preheat your Ninja Foodi Dual Zone Air Fryer to 350 degrees F/175 degrees C. 2. Rub the mahi-mahi fillets with salt and black pepper. 3. Place two mahi-mahi fillets in each of the crisper plate. 4. Return the crisper plates to the Ninja Foodi Dual Zone Air Fryer. 5. Choose the Air Fry mode for Zone 1 and set the temperature to 390 degrees F/200 degrees C and the time to 17 minutes. 6. Select the "MATCH" button to copy the settings for Zone 2. 7. Initiate cooking by pressing the START/STOP button. 8. Add butter to a saucepan and cook for 5 minutes until slightly brown. 9. Remove the butter from the heat. 10. Drizzle butter over the fish and serve warm.

Serving Suggestion: Serve with pasta or fried rice.

Variation Tip: Drizzle parmesan cheese on top.

Nutritional Information Per Serving: Calories 399 | Fat 16g | Sodium 537mg | Carbs 28g | Fiber 3g | Sugar 10g | Protein 35g

Crusted Cod

Prep Time: 15 minutes | Cook Time: 13 minutes | Serves: 4

Ingredients:

2 lbs. cod fillets
Salt, to taste
Freshly black pepper, to taste

½ cup all-purpose flour
1 large egg, beaten
2 cups panko bread crumbs

1 teaspoon Old Bay seasoning
Lemon wedges, for serving
Tartar sauce, for serving

Preparation:

1. Rub the fish with salt and black pepper. 2. Add flour in one shallow bowl, beat eggs in another bowl, and mix panko with Old Bay in a shallow bowl. 3. First coat the fish with flour, then dip it in the eggs and finally coat it with the panko mixture. 4. Place half of the seasoned codfish in each crisper plate. 5. Return the crisper plates to the Ninja Foodi Dual Zone Air Fryer. 6. Choose the Air Fry mode for Zone 1 and set the temperature to 390 degrees F/200 degrees C and the time to 13 minutes. 7. Select the "MATCH" button to copy the settings for Zone 2. 8. Initiate cooking by pressing the START/STOP button. 9. Flip the fish once cooked halfway, then resume cooking. 10. Serve warm and fresh with tartar sauce and lemon wedges.

Serving Suggestion: Enjoy with creamy coleslaw on the side.

Variation Tip: Use crushed cornflakes for extra crispiness.

Nutritional Information Per Serving: Calories 155 | Fat 4.2g | Sodium 963mg | Carbs 21.5g | Fiber 0.8g | Sugar 5.7g | Protein 8.1g

Glazed Scallops

Prep Time: 15 minutes | Cook Time: 13 minutes | Serves: 6

Ingredients:

12 scallops	3 tablespoons olive oil	Black pepper and salt to taste

Preparation:

1. Rub the scallops with olive oil, black pepper, and salt. 2. Divide the scallops in the two crisper plates. 3. Return the crisper plate to the Ninja Foodi Dual Zone Air Fryer. 4. Choose the Air Fry mode for Zone 1 and set the temperature to 390 degrees F/200 degrees C and the time to 13 minutes. 5. Select the "MATCH" button to copy the settings for Zone 2. 6. Initiate cooking by pressing the START/STOP button. 7. Flip the scallops once cooked halfway through, and resume cooking. 8. Serve warm.

Serving Suggestion: Serve with melted butter on top.

Variation Tip: Drizzle breadcrumbs on top before air frying.

Nutritional Information Per Serving: Calories 308 | Fat 24g | Sodium 715mg | Carbs 0.8g | Fiber 0.1g | Sugar 0.1g | Protein 21.9g

Crusted Tilapia

Prep Time: 20 minutes | Cook Time: 17 minutes | Serves: 4

Ingredients:

¾ cup breadcrumbs	2 ½ tablespoons vegetable oil	4 tilapia fillets
1 packet dry ranch-style dressing	2 eggs beaten	Herbs and chilies to garnish

Preparation:

1. Thoroughly mix ranch dressing with panko in a bowl. 2. Whisk eggs in a shallow bowl. 3. Dip each fish fillet in the egg, then coat evenly with the panko mixture. 4. Set two coated fillets in each of the crisper plate. 5. Return the crisper plates to the Ninja Foodi Dual Zone Air Fryer. 6. Choose the Air Fry mode for Zone 1 and set the temperature to 390 degrees F/200 degrees C and the time to 17 minutes. 7. Select the "MATCH" button to copy the settings for Zone 2. 8. Initiate cooking by pressing the START/STOP button. 9. Serve warm with herbs and chilies.

Serving Suggestion: Serve with sautéed asparagus on the side.

Variation Tip: Coat the fish with crushed cornflakes for extra crispiness.

Nutritional Information Per Serving: Calories 196 | Fat 7.1g | Sodium 492mg | Carbs 21.6g | Fiber 2.9g | Sugar 0.8g | Protein 13.4g

Crispy Catfish

Prep Time: 15 minutes | Cook Time: 17 minutes | Serves: 4

Ingredients:

4 catfish fillets	1 tablespoon olive oil	1 lemon, sliced
¼ cup Louisiana Fish fry	1 tablespoon parsley, chopped	Fresh herbs, to garnish

Preparation:

1. Mix fish fry with olive oil, and parsley then liberally rub over the catfish. 2. Place two fillets in each of the crisper plate. 3. Return the crisper plates to the Ninja Foodi Dual Zone Air Fryer. 4. Choose the Air Fry mode for Zone 1 and set the temperature to 390 degrees F/200 degrees C and the time to 17 minutes. 5. Select the "MATCH" button to copy the settings for Zone 2. 6. Initiate cooking by pressing the START/STOP button. 7. Garnish with lemon slices and herbs. 8. Serve warm.

Serving Suggestion: Serve with creamy dip and crispy fries.

Variation Tip: Use crushed cornflakes for breading to have extra crispiness.

Nutritional Information Per Serving: Calories 275 | Fat 1.4g | Sodium 582mg | Carbs 31.5g | Fiber 1.1g | Sugar 0.1g | Protein 29.8g

Beer Battered Fish Fillet

Prep Time: 18 Minutes | Cook Time: 14 Minutes | Serves: 2

Ingredients:

1 cup all-purpose flour
4 tablespoons cornstarch
1 teaspoon baking soda
8 ounces beer

2 egg beaten
1 teaspoon smoked Paprika
1 teaspoon salt
¼ teaspoon freshly ground black pepper

¼ teaspoon cayenne pepper
2 cod fillets, 1½-inches thick, cut into 4 pieces
Oil spray, for greasing

Preparation:

1. Take a large bowl and combine 1 cup flour, baking soda, cornstarch, and salt. 2. In a separate bowl, beat the eggs along with the beer. 3. In a shallow dish, mix paprika, salt, pepper, and cayenne pepper. 4. Dry the codfish fillets with a paper towel. 5. Dip the fish into the eggs and coat them with the flour mixture. 6. Then dip it in the seasoning. 7. Grease the fillets with oil spray. 8. Divide the fillets between both zones. 9. Set zone 1 to AIR FRY mode at 400 degrees F/200 degrees C for 14 minutes. 10. Select MATCH button for zone 2 basket. 11. Press START/STOP button and let them cook. 12. Once the cooking is done, serve the fish. 13. Enjoy it hot.

Serving Suggestion: Serve it with rice

Variation Tip: Use mild Paprika instead of smoked Paprika

Nutritional Information Per Serving: Calories 1691 | Fat 6.1g | Sodium 3976mg | Carbs 105.1 g | Fiber 3.4g | Sugar 15.6 g | Protein 270g

Breaded Scallops

Prep Time: 15 minutes | Cook Time: 12 minutes | Serves: 4

Ingredients:

½ cup crushed buttery crackers
½ teaspoon garlic powder

½ teaspoon seafood seasoning
2 tablespoons butter, melted

1 pound sea scallops patted dry
cooking spray

Preparation:

1. Mix cracker crumbs, garlic powder, and seafood seasoning in a shallow bowl. Spread melted butter in another shallow bowl. 2. Dip each scallop in the melted butter and then roll in the breading to coat well. 3. Grease each Air fryer basket with cooking spray and place half of the scallops in each. 4. Return the crisper plate to the Ninja Foodi Dual Zone Air Fryer. 5. Select the Air Fry mode for Zone 1 and set the temperature to 390 degrees F/200 degrees C and the time to 12 minutes. 6. Press the "MATCH" button to copy the settings for Zone 2. 7. Initiate cooking by pressing the START/STOP button. 8. Flip the scallops with a spatula after 4 minutes and resume cooking. 9. Serve warm.

Serving Suggestion: Serve with creamy dip and crispy fries.

Variation Tip: Use crushed cornflakes for breading to have extra crispiness.

Nutritional Information Per Serving: Calories 275 | Fat 1.4g | Sodium 582mg | Carbs 31.5g | Fiber 1.1g | Sugar 0.1g | Protein 29.8g

Fish and Chips

Prep Time: 15 Minutes | Cook Time: 22 Minutes | Serves: 2

Ingredients:

1 pound potatoes, cut lengthwise
1 cup seasoned flour
2 eggs, organic

⅓ cup buttermilk
2 cups seafood fry mix
½ cup bread crumbs

2 codfish fillets, 6 ounces each
Oil spray, for greasing

Preparation:

1. Take a bowl and whisk the eggs in it along the buttermilk. 2. In a separate bowl, mix the seafood fry mix and bread crumbs. 3. Take a baking tray and spread some flour on it. 4. Dip the fillets first in the egg wash, then in flour, and at the end coat it with the bread crumbs mixture. 5. Put the fish fillets in thezone 1 basket. 6. Grease the fish fillets with oil spray. 7. Set zone 1 to AIR FRY mode at 400 degrees F/200 degrees C for 14 minutes. 8. Put the potatos in zone 2 basket and lightly grease it with oil spray. 9. Set the zone 2 basket to AIR FRY mode at 400 degrees F/200 degrees C for 22 minutes. 10. Hit the Sync button. 11. Once done, serve and enjoy.

Serving Suggestion: Serve it with mayonnaise

Variation Tip: Use water instead of buttermilk

Nutritional Information Per Serving: Calories 992 | Fat 22.3g | Sodium 1406 mg | Carbs 153.6g | Fiber 10g | Sugar 10g | Protein 40g

Salmon Nuggets

Prep Time: 15 minutes | Cook Time: 15 minutes | Serves: 4

Ingredients:

⅓ cup maple syrup
¼ teaspoon dried chipotle pepper
1 pinch sea salt

1 ½ cups croutons
1 large egg
1 (1 pound) skinless salmon fillet, cut into 1

½-inch chunk
cooking spray

Preparation:

1. Mix chipotle powder, maple syrup, and salt in a saucepan and cook on a simmer for 5 minutes. 2. Crush the croutons in a food processor and transfer to a bowl. 3. Beat egg in another shallow bowl. 4. Season the salmon chunks with sea salt. 5. Dip the salmon in the egg, then coat with breadcrumbs. 6. Divide the coated salmon chunks in the two crisper plates. 7. Return the crisper plate to the Ninja Foodi Dual Zone Air Fryer. 8. Select the Air Fry mode for Zone 1 and set the temperature to 390 degrees F/200 degrees C and the time to 10 minutes. 9. Press the "MATCH" button to copy the settings for Zone 2. 10. Initiate cooking by pressing the START/STOP button. 11. Flip the chunks once cooked halfway through, then resume cooking. 12. Pour the maple syrup on top and serve warm.

Serving Suggestion: Serve with creamy dip and crispy fries.
Variation Tip: Use crushed cornflakes for breading to have extra crispiness.
Nutritional Information Per Serving: Calories 275 | Fat 1.4g | Sodium 582mg | Carbs 31.5g | Fiber 1.1g | Sugar 0.1g | Protein 29.8g

Smoked Salmon

Prep Time: 20 Minutes | Cook Time: 12 Minutes | Serves: 4

Ingredients:

2 pounds salmon fillets, smoked
6 ounces cream cheese
4 tablespoons mayonnaise

2 teaspoons chives, fresh
1 teaspoon lemon zest
Salt and freshly ground black pepper, to taste

2 tablespoons butter

Preparation:

1. Cut the salmon into very small and uniform bite-size pieces. 2. Mix cream cheese, chives, mayonnaise, black pepper, and lemon zest, in a small mixing bowl. 3. Set it aside for further use. 4. Coat the salmon pieces with salt and butter. 5. Divide the bite-size pieces into both zones of the air fryer. 6. Set it on AIR FRY mode at 400 degrees F/200 degrees C for 12 minutes. 7. Select MATCH for zone 2 basket. 8. Once the salmon is done, top it with the cream cheese mixture and serve. 9. Enjoy hot.

Serving Suggestion: Serve it with rice
Variation Tip: Use sour cream instead of cream cheese
Nutritional Information Per Serving: Calories 557 | Fat 15.7g | Sodium 371mg | Carbs 4.8g | Fiber 0g | Sugar 1.1g | Protein 48g

Salmon with Coconut

Prep Time: 10 Minutes | Cook Time: 15 Minutes | Serves: 2

Ingredients:

Oil spray, for greasing
2 salmon fillets, 6 ounces each
Salt and ground black pepper, to taste

1 tablespoon butter, for frying
1 tablespoon red curry paste
1 cup coconut cream

2 tablespoons fresh cilantro, chopped
1 cup cauliflower florets
½ cup Parmesan cheese, hard

Preparation:

1. Mix salt, black pepper, butter, red curry paste, coconut cream in a bowl and marinate the salmon in it. 2. Oil spray the cauliflower florets and then season with salt and freshly ground black pepper. 3. Place the florets in the zone 1 basket. 4. Layer parchment paper over the zone 2 basket, and then place the salmon fillets on it. 5. Set the zone 2 basket to AIR FRY mode at 15 minutes for 400 degrees F/200 degrees C. 6. Hit the Sync button to finish it at the same time. 7. Once the time for cooking is over, serve the salmon with cauliflower florets with Parmesan cheese sprinkled on top.

Serving Suggestion: Serve with rice
Variation Tip: Use Mozzarella cheese instead of Parmesan cheese
Nutritional Information Per Serving: Calories 774 | Fat 59g | Sodium 1223mg | Carbs 12.2g | Fiber 3.9g | Sugar 5.9g | Protein 53.5g

Salmon with Broccoli and Cheese

Prep Time: 15 Minutes | Cook Time: 18 Minutes | Serves: 2

Ingredients:

2 cups broccoli
½ cup butter, melted

Salt and pepper, to taste
Oil spray, for greasing

1 cup grated Cheddar cheese
1 pound salmon, fillets

Preparation:

1. Take a bowl and add broccoli to it. 2. Add salt and black pepper and spray the broccoli with oil. 3. Put the broccoli in the air fryer zone 1 basket. 4. Rub the salmon fillets with salt, black pepper, and butter. 5. Place them into zone 2 basket. 6. Set zone 1 to AIR FRY mode for 5 minters at 400 degrees F/200 degrees C. 7. Set zone 2 to AIR FRY mode for 18 minutes at 390 degrees F/200 degrees C. 8. Sprinkle the grated cheese on top of the salmon and serve.

Serving Suggestion: Serve with rice and baked potato

Variation Tip: Use olive oil instead of butter

Nutritional Information Per Serving: Calories 966 | Fat 79.1g | Sodium 808mg | Carbs 6.8g | Fiber 2.4g | Sugar 1.9g | Protein 61.2g

Frozen Breaded Fish Fillet

Prep Time: 15 Minutes | Cook Time: 12 Minutes | Serves: 2

Ingredients:

4 frozen breaded fish fillets

Oil spray, for greasing

1 cup mayonnaise

Preparation:

1. Take the frozen fish fillets out of the bag and place them in both baskets of the air fryer. 2. Lightly grease them with oil spray. 3. Set the zone 1 basket to 380 degrees F/195 degrees F for 12 minutes. 4. Select the MATCH button for the zone 2 basket. 5. Hit the START/STOP button to start cooking. 6. Once the cooking is done, serve the fish hot with mayonnaise.

Serving Suggestion: Serve it with salad and rice

Variation Tip: Use olive oil instead of butter

Nutritional Information Per Serving: Calories 921 | Fat 61.5g | Sodium 1575mg | Carbs 69g | Fiber 2g | Sugar 9.5g | Protein 29.1g

Spicy Fish Fillet with Onion Rings

Prep Time: 10 Minutes | Cook Time: 12 Minutes | Serves:1

Ingredients:

300 grams onion rings, frozen and packed
1 codfish fillet, 8 ounces

Salt and black pepper, to taste
1 teaspoon lemon juice

Oil spray, for greasing

Preparation:

1. Place the frozen onion rings in zone 1 basket of the air fryer. 2. Pat dry the fish fillets with a paper towel and season them with salt, black pepper, and lemon juice. 3. Grease the fillet with oil spray. 4. Put the fish in the zone 2 basket. 5. Use MAX CRISP for zone 1 at 240 degrees F/115 degrees C for 9 minutes. 6. Set zone 2 to MAX CRISP mode and set it to 210 degrees F/100 degrees C for 12 minutes. 7. Press Sync and press START/STOP button. 8. Once done, serve hot.

Serving Suggestion: Serve with buffalo sauce

Variation Tip: None

Nutritional Information Per Serving: Calories 666 | Fat23.5g | Sodium 911mg | Carbs 82g | Fiber 8.8g | Sugar 17.4g | Protein 30.4g

Salmon with Green Beans

Prep Time: 12 Minutes | Cook Time: 18 Minutes | Serves: 1

Ingredients:

1 salmon fillet, 2 inches thick
2 teaspoons olive oil

2 teaspoons smoked Paprika
Salt and black pepper, to taste

1 cup green beans
Oil spray, for greasing

Preparation:

1. Grease the green beans with oil spray and add them to the zone 1 basket. 2. Rub the salmon fillet with olive oil, smoked Paprika, salt, and black pepper. 3. Put the salmon fillet in the zone 2 basket. 4. Set the zone 1 basket to AIR FRY mode at 350 degrees F/175 degrees C for 18 minutes. 5. Set the zone 2 basket to AIR FRY mode at 390 degrees F/200 degrees C for 16-18 minutes. 6. Hit the Sync button so that they both finish at the same time. 7. Once done, take out the salmon and green beans, transfer them to the serving plates and enjoy.

Serving Suggestion: Serve it with ranch
Variation Tip: Use any other green vegetable of your choice
Nutritional Information Per Serving: Calories 367 | Fat 22 g | Sodium 87mg | Carbs 10.2g | Fiber 5.3g | Sugar 2g | Protein 37.2g

Lemon Pepper Salmon with Asparagus

Prep Time: 20 Minutes | Cook Time: 18 Minutes | Serves: 2

Ingredients:

1 cup green asparagus
2 tablespoons butter
2 fillets salmon, 8 ounces each

Salt and black pepper, to taste
1 teaspoon lemon juice
½ teaspoon lemon zest

Oil spray, for greasing

Preparation:

1. Rinse and trim the asparagus. 2. Rinse and pat dry the salmon fillets. 3. Take a bowl and mix in the lemon juice, lemon zest, salt, and black pepper. 4. Brush the fish fillets with the rub and place them in the zone 1 basket. 5. Place asparagus in the zone 2 basket. 6. Spray the asparagus with oil spray. 7. Set zone 1 to AIR FRY mode for 18 minutes at 390 degrees F/200 degrees C. 8. Set the zone 2 to 5 minutes at 390 degrees F/200 degrees C on AIR FRY mode. 9. Hit the Sync button to finish at the same time. 10. Once done, serve and enjoy.

Serving Suggestion: Serve it with baked potato
Variation Tip: Use olive oil instead of butter
Nutritional Information Per Serving: Calories 482 | Fat 28g | Sodium 209mg | Carbs 2.8g | Fiber 1.5g | Sugar 1.4g | Protein 56.3g

Keto Baked Salmon with Pesto

Prep Time: 15 Minutes | Cook Time: 18 Minutes | Serves: 2

Ingredients:

4 salmon fillets, 2 inches thick
2 ounces green pesto
Salt and black pepper

½ tablespoon canola oil, for greasing
Ingredients: for Green Sauce
1-½ cups mayonnaise

2 tablespoons Greek yogurt
Salt and black pepper, to taste

Preparation:

1. Rub the salmon with pesto, salt, oil, and black pepper. 2. In a small bowl, whisk together all the green sauce ingredients. 3. Divide the fish fillets between both the baskets. 4. Set zone 1 to AIR FRY mode for 18 minutes at 390 degrees F/200 degrees C. 5. Select MATCH button for zone 2 basket. 6. Once the cooking is done, serve it with green sauce drizzled on top. 7. Enjoy.

Serving Suggestion: Serve it with mashed cheesy potatoes
Variation Tip: Use butter instead of canal oil
Nutritional Information Per Serving: Calories 1165 | Fat 80.7g | Sodium 1087mg | Carbs 33.1g | Fiber 0.5g | Sugar 11.5 g | Protein 80.6g

Seafood Shrimp Omelet

Prep Time: 20 Minutes | Cook Time: 15 Minutes | Serves: 2

Ingredients:

6 large shrimp, shells removed and chopped
6 eggs, beaten
½ tablespoon butter, melted

2 tablespoons green onions, sliced
⅓ cup mushrooms, chopped
1 pinch Paprika

Salt and black pepper, to taste
Oil spray, for greasing

Preparation:

1. In a large bowl, whisk the eggs and add the chopped shrimp, butter, green onions, mushrooms, paprika, salt, and black pepper. 2. Take two cake pans that fit inside the air fryer and grease them with oil spray. 3. Pour the egg mixture between the cake pans and place it in the air fryer baskets. 4. Set zone 1 to BAKE mode and set the temperature to 320 degrees F/160 degrees C for 15 minutes. 5. Select the MATCH button to match the cooking time for the zone 2 basket. 6. Once the cooking cycle is complete, take out, and serve hot.

Serving Suggestion: Serve it with rice
Variation Tip: Use olive oil for greasing purposes
Nutritional Information Per Serving: Calories 300 | Fat 17.5g | Sodium 368mg | Carbs 2.9g | Fiber 0.3g | Sugar 1.4 g | Protein 32.2g

Roasted Salmon and Parmesan Asparagus

Prep Time: 10 minutes | Cook Time: 27 minutes | Serves: 4

Ingredients:

2 tablespoons Montreal steak seasoning
3 tablespoons brown sugar
3 uncooked salmon fillets (6 ounces each)

2 tablespoons canola oil, divided
1-pound asparagus, ends trimmed
Kosher salt, as desired

Ground black pepper, as desired
¼ cup shredded parmesan cheese, divided

Preparation:

1. Combine the steak spice and brown sugar in a small bowl. 2. Brush 1 tablespoon of oil over the salmon fillets, then thoroughly coat with the sugar mixture. 3. Toss the asparagus with the remaining 1 tablespoon of oil, salt, and pepper in a mixing bowl. 4. Place a crisper plate in both drawers. Put the fillets skin-side down in the zone 1 drawer, then place the drawer in the unit. Insert the zone 2 drawer into the device after placing the asparagus in it. 5. Select zone 1, then ROAST, then set the temperature to 390 degrees F/200 degrees C with a 17-minute timer. To match the zone 2 settings to zone 1, choose MATCH. To begin cooking, press the START/STOP button. 6. When the zone 2 timer reaches 7 minutes, press START/STOP. Remove the zone 2 drawer from the unit. Flip the asparagus with silicone-tipped tongs. Re-insert the drawer into the unit. Continue cooking by pressing START/STOP. 7. When the zone 2 timer has reached 14 minutes, press START/STOP. Remove the zone 2 drawer from the unit. Sprinkle half the parmesan cheese over the asparagus, and mix lightly. Re-insert the drawer into the unit. Continue cooking by pressing START/STOP. 8. Transfer the fillets and asparagus to a serving plate once they've finished cooking. Serve with the remaining parmesan cheese on top of the asparagus.

Serving Suggestion: Serve with steamed rice.
Variation Tip: Use green beans instead of asparagus.
Nutritional Information Per Serving: Calories 293 | Fat 15.8g | Sodium 203mg | Carbs 11.1g | Fiber 2.4g | Sugar 8.7g | Protein 29g

Honey Teriyaki Tilapia

Prep Time: 5 minutes | Cook Time: 10 minutes | Serves: 4

Ingredients:

8 tablespoons low-sodium teriyaki sauce
3 tablespoons honey

2 garlic cloves, minced
2 tablespoons extra virgin olive oil

3 pieces tilapia (each cut into 2 pieces)

Preparation:

1. Combine all the first 4 ingredients to make the marinade. 2. Pour the marinade over the tilapia and let it sit for 20 minutes. 3. Place a crisper plate in each drawer. Place the tilapia in the drawers. Insert the drawers into the unit. 4. Select zone 1, then AIR FRY, then set the temperature to 360 degrees F/180 degrees C with a 10-minute timer. To match zone 2 settings to zone 1, choose MATCH. To begin, select START/STOP. 5. Remove the tilapia from the drawers after the timer has finished.

Serving Suggestion: Serve over a bed of rice.
Variation Tip: You can use maple syrup instead of honey.
Nutritional Information Per Serving: Calories 350 | Fat 16.4g | Sodium 706mg | Carbs 19.3g | Fiber 0.1g | Sugar 19g | Protein 29.3g

Codfish with Herb Vinaigrette

Prep Time: 15 Minutes | Cook Time: 16 Minutes | Serves: 2

Ingredients:

Vinaigrette Ingredients:

½ cup parsley leaves

1 cup basil leaves

½ cup mint leaves

2 tablespoons thyme leaves

¼ teaspoon red pepper flakes

2 cloves garlic

4 tablespoons red wine vinegar

¼ cup olive oil

Salt, to taste

Other Ingredients:

1.5 pounds fish fillets, codfish

2 tablespoons olive oil

Salt and black pepper, to taste

1 teaspoon Paprika

1 teaspoon Italian seasoning

Preparation:

1. Blend the entire vinaigrette ingredients in a high-speed blender and pulse into a smooth paste. 2. Set aside for drizzling over the cooked fish. 3. Rub the fillets with salt, black pepper, paprika, Italian seasoning, and olive oil. 4. Divide the between two baskets of the air fryer. 5. Set zone 1 to 16 minutes at 390 degrees F/200 degrees C, on AIR FRY mode. 6. Press the MATCH button for zone 2. 7.Once done, serve the fillets with a drizzle of blended vinaigrette on top.

Serving Suggestion: Serve it with rice

Variation Tip: Use sour cream instead of cream cheese

Nutritional Information Per Serving: Calories 1219 | Fat 81.8g | Sodium 1906mg | Carbs 64.4g | Fiber 5.5g | Sugar 0.4g | Protein 52.1g

Two-Way Salmon

Prep Time: 10 Minutes | Cook Time: 18 Minutes | Serves: 2

Ingredients:

2 salmon fillets, 8 ounces each

2 tablespoons Cajun seasoning

2 tablespoons Jerk seasoning

1 lemon cut in half

Oil spray, for greasing

Preparation:

1. First, drizzle lemon juice over the salmon and wash them with tap water. 2. Rinse and pat dry the fillets with a paper towel. 3. Rub the fillets with Cajun seasoning and grease with oil spray. 4. Take the second fillet and rub it with Jerk seasoning. 5. Grease the second fillet of with oil spray. 6. Place the salmon fillets in both the baskets. 7. Set the zone 1 basket to 390 degrees F/200 degrees C for 16-18 minutes. 8. Select MATCH button for zone 2 basket. 9. Hit the START/STOP button to start cooking. 10. Once the cooking is done, serve the fish hot with mayonnaise.

Serving Suggestion: Serve it with ranch

Variation Tip: None

Nutritional Information Per Serving: Calories 238 | Fat 11.8g | Sodium 488mg | Carbs 9g | Fiber 0g | Sugar 8g | Protein 35g

Shrimp With Lemon and Pepper

Prep Time: 5 minutes | Cook Time: 10 minutes | Serves: 4

Ingredients:

1-pound medium raw shrimp, peeled and deveined

½ cup olive oil

2 tablespoons lemon juice

1 teaspoon black pepper

½ teaspoon salt

Preparation:

1. Place the shrimp in a Ziploc bag with the olive oil, lemon juice, salt, and pepper. Carefully combine all the ingredients. 2. Install a crisper plate in both drawers. Divide the shrimp equally into the two drawers. Insert the drawers into the unit. 3. Select zone 1, then AIR FRY, then set the temperature to 360 degrees F/180 degrees C with a 10-minute timer. To match zone 2 settings to zone 1, choose MATCH. To begin, select START/STOP. 4. Remove the shrimp from the drawers after the timer has finished.

Serving Suggestion: Serve the shrimp with pasta.

Variation Tip: You can use lime juice.

Nutritional Information Per Serving: Calories 322 | Fat 28g | Sodium 909mg | Carbs 2g | Fiber 0g | Sugar 0g | Protein 16g

Garlic Butter Salmon

Prep Time: 5 minutes | Cook Time: 10 minutes | Serves: 4

Ingredients:

4 (6-ounce) boneless, skin-on salmon fillets (preferably wild-caught)
4 tablespoons butter, melted

2 teaspoons garlic, minced
2 teaspoons fresh Italian parsley, chopped (or ¼ teaspoon dried)

Salt and pepper to taste

Preparation:

1. Season the fresh salmon with salt and pepper. 2. Mix together the melted butter, garlic, and parsley in a bowl. 3. Baste the salmon fillets with the garlic butter mixture. 4. Place a crisper plate in each drawer. Put 2 fillets in each drawer. Put the drawers inside the unit. 5. Select zone 1, then AIR FRY, then set the temperature to 360 degrees F/180 degrees C with a 10-minute timer. To match zone 2 settings to zone 1, choose MATCH. To begin, select START/STOP. 6. Remove the salmon from the drawers after the timer has finished.

Serving Suggestion: Serve with a side salad.

Variation Tip: You can use tuna instead.

Nutritional Information Per Serving: Calories 338 | Fat 26g | Sodium 309mg | Carbs 1g | Fiber 0g | Sugar 0g | Protein 25g

Flavorful Salmon with Green Beans

Prep Time: 5 minutes | Cook Time: 10 minutes | Serves: 4

Ingredients:

4 ounces green beans
1 tablespoon canola oil

4 (6-ounce) salmon fillets
1/3 cup prepared sesame-ginger sauce

Kosher salt, to taste
Black pepper, to taste

Preparation:

1. Toss the green beans with a teaspoon each of salt and pepper in a large bowl. 2. Place a crisper plate in each drawer. Place the green beans in the zone 1 drawer and insert it into the unit. Place the salmon into the zone 2 drawer and place it into the unit. 3. Select zone 1, then AIR FRY, and set the temperature to 390 degrees F/200 degrees C with a 10-minute timer. 4. Select zone 2, then AIR FRY, and set the temperature to 390 degrees F/200 degrees C with a 15-minute timer. Select SYNC. To begin cooking, press the START/STOP button. 5. Press START/STOP to pause the unit when the zone 2 timer reaches 9 minutes. Remove the salmon from the drawer and toss it in the sesame-ginger sauce. To resume cooking, replace the drawer in the device and press START/STOP. 6. When cooking is complete, serve the salmon and green beans immediately.

Serving Suggestion: Serve with lemon wedges and a side salad.

Variation Tip: You can use cod fillets.

Nutritional Information Per Serving: Calories 305 | Fat 16g | Sodium 535mg | Carbs 8.7g | Fiber 1g | Sugar 6.4g | Protein 34.9g

Honey Sriracha Mahi Mahi

Prep Time: 5 minutes | Cook Time: 7 minutes | Serves: 4

Ingredients:

3 pounds mahi-mahi
6 tablespoons honey

4 tablespoons sriracha
Salt, to taste

Cooking spray

Preparation:

1. In a small bowl, mix the sriracha sauce and honey. Mix well. 2. Season the fish with salt and pour the honey mixture over it. Let it sit at room temperature for 20 minutes. 3. Place a crisper plate in each drawer. Put the fish in a single layer in each. Insert the drawers into the unit. 4. Select zone 1, then AIR FRY, then set the temperature to 400 degrees F/200 degrees C with a 7-minute timer. To match zone 2 settings to zone 1, choose MATCH. To begin, select START/STOP. 5. Remove the fish from the drawers after the timer has finished.

Serving Suggestion: Serve with cauliflower rice.

Variation Tip: You can use cod or salmon instead.

Nutritional Information Per Serving: Calories 581 | Fat 22g | Sodium 495mg | Carbs 26g | Fiber 4g | Sugar 26g | Protein 68g

Scallops

Prep Time: 10 minutes | Cook Time: 5 minutes | Serves: 4

Ingredients:

½ cup Italian breadcrumbs
½ teaspoon garlic powder

¼ teaspoon salt
½ teaspoon black pepper

2 tablespoons butter, melted
1 pound sea scallops, rinsed and pat dry

Preparation:

1. Combine the breadcrumbs, garlic powder, salt, and pepper in a small bowl. Pour the melted butter into another shallow bowl. 2. Dredge each scallop in the melted butter, then roll it in the breadcrumb mixture until well covered. 3. Place a crisper plate in each drawer. Put the scallops in a single layer in each drawer. Insert the drawers into the unit. 4. Select zone 1, then AIR FRY, then set the temperature to 360 degrees F/180 degrees C with a 5-minute timer. To match zone 2 settings to zone 1, choose MATCH. To begin, select START/STOP. 5. Press START/STOP to pause the unit when the timer reaches 3 minutes. Remove the drawers. Use tongs to carefully flip the scallops over. To resume cooking, re-insert the drawers into the unit and press START/STOP. 6. Remove the scallops from the drawers after the timer has finished.

Serving Suggestion: Serve with lemon wedges and a side salad.

Variation Tip: You can add some chopped parsley.

Nutritional Information Per Serving: Calories 81 | Fat 6g | Sodium 145mg | Carbs 3g | Fiber 4g | Sugar 1g | Protein 3g

Tuna Patties

Prep Time: 10 minutes | Cook Time: 10 minutes | Serves: 6

Ingredients:

For the Tuna Patties:

1 tablespoon extra-virgin olive oil
1 tablespoon butter
½ cup chopped onion
½ red bell pepper, chopped
1 teaspoon minced garlic
2 (7-ounce) cans or 3 (5-ounce) cans albacore

tuna fish in water, drained
1 tablespoon lime juice
1 celery stalk, chopped
¼ cup chopped fresh parsley
3 tablespoons grated parmesan cheese
½ teaspoon dried oregano

¼ teaspoon salt
Black pepper, to taste
1 teaspoon sriracha
½ cup panko crumbs
2 whisked eggs

For the Crumb Coating:

½ cup panko crumbs

¼ cup parmesan cheese

Non-stick spray

Preparation:

1. In a skillet, heat the oil and butter over medium-high heat. 2. Sauté the onions, red bell pepper, and garlic for 5 to 7 minutes. 3. Drain the tuna from the cans thoroughly. Put the tuna in a large mixing bowl. Add the lime juice. 4. Add the sautéed vegetables to the mixing bowl. 5. Add the celery, parsley, and cheese. Combine well. 6. Add the oregano, salt, and pepper to taste. Mix well. 7. Add a dash of sriracha for a spicy kick and mix well. 8. Add the panko crumbs and mix well. 9. Mix in the eggs until the mixture is well combined. You can add an extra egg if necessary, but the tuna is usually wet enough that it isn't required. Form 6 patties from the mixture. 10. Refrigerate for 30 to 60 minutes (or even overnight). 11. Remove from refrigerator and coat with a mixture of the ½ cup of panko crumbs and ¼ cup of parmesan cheese. 12. Spray the tops of the coated patties with some non-stick cooking spray. 13. Place a crisper place in each drawer. Put 3 patties in each drawer. Insert the drawers into the unit. 14. Select zone 1, then AIR FRY, then set the temperature to 390 degrees F/200 degrees C with a 10-minute timer. To match zone 2 settings to zone 1, choose MATCH. To begin, select START/STOP. 15. Remove and garnish with chopped parsley.

Serving Suggestion: Serve the patties with a green salad.

Variation Tip: You can use tinned salmon.

Nutritional Information Per Serving: Calories 381 | Fat 16g | Sodium 1007mg | Carbs 23g | Fiber 2g | Sugar 4g | Protein 38g

Fish Tacos

Prep Time: 10 minutes | Cook Time: 30 minutes | Serves: 5

Ingredients:

1 pound firm white fish such as cod, haddock, pollock, halibut, or walleye

¾ cup gluten-free flour blend

3 eggs

1 cup gluten-free panko breadcrumbs

1 teaspoon garlic powder

1 teaspoon onion powder

1 teaspoon cumin

1 teaspoon lemon pepper

1 teaspoon red chili flakes

1 teaspoon kosher salt, divided

1 teaspoon pepper, divided

Cooking oil spray

1 package corn tortillas

Toppings such as tomatoes, avocado, cabbage, radishes, jalapenos, salsa, or hot sauce (optional)

Preparation:

1. Dry the fish with paper towels. (Make sure to thaw the fish if it's frozen.) Depending on the size of the fillets, cut the fish in half or thirds. 2. On both sides of the fish pieces, liberally season with salt and pepper. 3. Put the flour in a dish. 4. In a separate bowl, crack the eggs and whisk them together until well blended. 5. Put the panko breadcrumbs in another bowl. Add the garlic powder, onion powder, cumin, lemon pepper, and red chili flakes. Add salt and pepper to taste. Stir until everything is well blended. 6. Each piece of fish should be dipped in the flour, then the eggs, and finally in the breadcrumb mixture. Make sure that each piece is completely coated. 7. Put a crisper plate in each drawer. Arrange the fish pieces in a single layer in each drawer. Insert the drawers into the unit. 8. Select zone 1, then AIR FRY, then set the temperature to 360 degrees F/180 degrees C with a 20-minute timer. To match zone 2 settings to zone 1, choose MATCH. To begin, select START/STOP. 9. Remove the fish from the drawers after the timer has finished. Place the crispy fish on warmed tortillas.

Serving Suggestion: Serve the fish tacos topped with toppings and sauce of your choice.

Variation Tip: You can use all-purpose flour.

Nutritional Information Per Serving: Calories 534 | Fat 18g | Sodium 679mg | Carbs 63g | Fiber 8g | Sugar 3g | Protein 27g

Bang Bang Shrimp

Prep Time: 15 minutes | Cook Time: 20 minutes | Serves: 4

Ingredients:

For the Shrimp:

1 cup corn starch

Salt and pepper, to taste

2 pounds shrimp, peeled and deveined

½ to 1 cup buttermilk

Cooking oil spray

1 large egg whisked with 1 teaspoon water

For the Sauce:

⅓ cup sweet Thai chili sauce

¼ cup sour cream

¼ cup mayonnaise

2 tablespoons buttermilk

1 tablespoon sriracha, or to taste

Pinch dried dill weed

Preparation:

1. Season the corn starch with salt and pepper in a wide, shallow bowl. 2. In a large mixing bowl, toss the shrimp in the buttermilk to coat them. 3. Dredge the shrimp in the seasoned corn starch. 4. Brush with the egg wash after spraying with cooking oil. 5. Place a crisper plate in each drawer. Place the shrimp in a single layer in each. You may need to cook in batches. 6. Select zone 1, then AIR FRY, then set the temperature to 360 degrees F/180 degrees C with a 5-minute timer. To match zone 2 settings to zone 1, choose MATCH. To begin, select START/STOP. 7. Meanwhile, combine all the sauce ingredients together in a bowl. 8. Remove the shrimp when the cooking time is over.

Serving Suggestion: Serve the shrimp with the sauce on the side.

Variation Tip: You can use potato starch instead of corn starch.

Nutritional Information Per Serving: Calories 415 | Fat 15g | Sodium 1875mg | Carbs 28g | Fiber 1g | Sugar 5g | Protein 38g

Bacon-Wrapped Shrimp

Prep Time: 45 minutes | Cook Time: 10 minutes | Serves: 8

Ingredients:

24 jumbo raw shrimp, deveined with tail on, fresh or thawed from frozen

8 slices bacon, cut into thirds

1 tablespoon olive oil

1 teaspoon paprika

1–2 cloves minced garlic

1 tablespoon finely chopped fresh parsley

Preparation:

1. Combine the olive oil, paprika, garlic, and parsley in a small bowl. 2. If necessary, peel the raw shrimp, leaving the tails on. 3. Add the shrimp to the oil mixture. Toss to coat well. 4. Wrap a piece of bacon around the middle of each shrimp and place seam-side down on a small baking dish. 5. Refrigerate for 30 minutes before cooking. 6. Place a crisper plate in each drawer. Put the shrimp in a single layer in each drawer. Insert the drawers into the unit. 7. Select zone 1, then AIR FRY, then set the temperature to 360 degrees F/180 degrees C with a 10-minute timer. To match zone 2 settings to zone 1, choose MATCH. To begin, select START/STOP. 8. Remove the shrimp from the drawers when the cooking time is over.

Serving Suggestion: Serve with a sauce of your choice.

Variation Tip: You can use ham slices instead of bacon.

Nutritional Information Per Serving: Calories 479 | Fat 15.7g | Sodium 949mg | Carbs 0.6g | Fiber 0.1g | Sugar 0g | Protein 76.1g

Fried Tilapia

Prep Time: 5 minutes | Cook Time: 20 minutes | Serves: 4

Ingredients:

4 fresh tilapia fillets, approximately 6 ounces each

2 teaspoons olive oil

2 teaspoons chopped fresh chives

2 teaspoons chopped fresh parsley

1 teaspoon minced garlic

Freshly ground pepper, to taste

Salt to taste

Preparation:

1. Pat the tilapia fillets dry with a paper towel. 2. Stir together the olive oil, chives, parsley, garlic, salt, and pepper in a small bowl. 3. Brush the mixture over the top of the tilapia fillets. 4. Place a crisper plate in each drawer. Add the fillets in a single layer to each drawer. Insert the drawers into the unit. 5. Select zone 1, then AIR FRY, then set the temperature to 360 degrees F/180 degrees C with a 20-minute timer. To match zone 2 settings to zone 1, choose MATCH. To begin, select START/STOP. 6. Remove the tilapia fillets from the drawers after the timer has finished.

Serving Suggestion: Serve with a sauce of your choice.

Variation Tip: You can use garlic powder instead of fresh garlic.

Nutritional Information Per Serving: Calories 140 | Fat 5.7g | Sodium 125mg | Carbs 1.5g | Fiber 0.4g | Sugar 0g | Protein 21.7g

Chapter 5 Poultry Mains Recipes

Crumbed Chicken Katsu

Prep Time: 15 minutes | Cook Time: 26 minutes | Serves: 4

Ingredients:

1 lb. boneless chicken breast, cut in half	1 ½ cups panko bread crumbs	Cooking spray
2 large eggs, beaten	Salt and black pepper ground to taste	

Sauce:

1 tablespoon sugar	1 tablespoon sherry	2 teaspoons Worcestershire sauce
2 tablespoons soy sauce	½ cup ketchup	1 teaspoon garlic, minced

Preparation:

1. Mix soy sauce, ketchup, sherry, sugar, garlic, and Worcestershire sauce in a mixing bowl. 2. Keep this katsu aside for a while. 3. Rub the chicken pieces with salt and black pepper. 4. Whisk eggs in a shallow dish and spread breadcrumbs in another tray. 5. Dip the chicken in the egg mixture and coat them with breadcrumbs. 6. Place the coated chicken in the two crisper plates and spray them with cooking spray. 7. Return the crisper plate to the Ninja Foodi Dual Zone Air Fryer. 8. Choose the Air Fry mode for Zone 1 and set the temperature to 390 degrees F/200 degrees C and the time to 26 minutes. 9. Select the "MATCH" button to copy the settings for Zone 2. 10. Initiate cooking by pressing the START/STOP button. 11. Flip the chicken once cooked halfway through, then resume cooking. 12. Serve warm with the sauce.

Serving Suggestion: Serve with fried rice and green beans salad.
Variation Tip: Coat the chicken with crushed cornflakes for extra crispiness.
Nutritional Information Per Serving: Calories 220 | Fat 1.7g | Sodium 178mg | Carbs 1.7g | Fiber 0.2g | Sugar 0.2g | Protein 32.9g

Bang-Bang Chicken

Prep Time: 15 minutes | Cook Time: 20 minutes | Serves: 2

Ingredients:

1 cup mayonnaise	⅓ cup flour	2 green onions, chopped
½ cup sweet chili sauce	1 lb. boneless chicken breast, diced	
2 tablespoons Sriracha sauce	1 ½ cups panko bread crumbs	

Preparation:

1. Mix mayonnaise with Sriracha and sweet chili sauce in a large bowl. 2. Keep ¾ cup of the mixture aside. 3. Add flour, chicken, breadcrumbs, and remaining mayo mixture to a resealable plastic bag. 4. Zip the bag and shake well to coat. 5. Divide the chicken in the two crisper plates in a single layer. 6. Return the crisper plate to the Ninja Foodi Dual Zone Air Fryer. 7. Choose the Air Fry mode for Zone 1 and set the temperature to 390 degrees F/200 degrees C and the time to 20 minutes. 8. Select the "MATCH" button to copy the settings for Zone 2. 9. Initiate cooking by pressing the START/STOP button. 10. Flip the chicken once cooked halfway through. 11. Top the chicken with reserved mayo sauce. 12. Garnish with green onions and serve warm.

Serving Suggestion: Serve with tomato ketchup or chili sauce.
Variation Tip: Use crushed cornflakes for breading to have extra crispiness.
Nutritional Information Per Serving: Calories 374 | Fat 13g | Sodium 552mg | Carbs 25g | Fiber 1.2g | Sugar 1.2g | Protein 37.7g

Air Fried Turkey Breast

Prep Time: 10 minutes | Cook Time: 46 minutes | Serves: 4

Ingredients:

2 lbs. turkey breast, on the bone with skin	1 teaspoon salt
½ tablespoon olive oil	¼ tablespoon dry poultry seasoning

Preparation:

1. Rub turkey breast with ½ tablespoons of oil. 2. Season both its sides with turkey seasoning and salt, then rub in the brush half tablespoons of oil over the skin of the turkey. 3. Divide the turkey in half and place each half in each of the crisper plate. 4. Return the crisper plate to the Ninja Foodi Dual Zone Air Fryer. 5. Choose the Air Fry mode for Zone 1 and set the temperature to 390 degrees F/200 degrees C and the time to 46 minutes. 6. Select the "MATCH" button to copy the settings for Zone 2. 7. Initiate cooking by pressing the START/STOP button. 8. Flip the turkey once cooked halfway through, and resume cooking. 9. Slice and serve warm.

Serving Suggestion: Serve with warm corn tortilla and Greek salad.
Variation Tip: Coat and dust the turkey breast with flour after seasoning.
Nutritional Information Per Serving: Calories 502 | Fat 25g | Sodium 230mg | Carbs 1.5g | Fiber 0.2g | Sugar 0.4g | Protein 64.1g

General Tso's Chicken

Prep Time: 20 minutes | Cook Time: 22 minutes | Serves: 4

Ingredients:

1 egg, large

⅓ cup 2 teaspoons cornstarch,

¼ teaspoons salt

¼ teaspoons ground white pepper

7 tablespoons chicken broth

2 tablespoons soy sauce

2 tablespoons ketchup

2 teaspoons sugar

2 teaspoons unseasoned rice vinegar

1 ½ tablespoons canola oil

4 chile de árbol, chopped and seeds discarded

1 tablespoon chopped fresh ginger

1 tablespoon garlic, chopped

2 tablespoons green onion, sliced

1 teaspoon toasted sesame oil

1 lb. boneless chicken thighs, cut into 1 ¼ -inch chunks

½ teaspoon toasted sesame seeds

Preparation:

1. Add egg to a large bowl and beat it with a fork. 2. Add chicken to the egg and coat it well. 3. Whisk ⅓ cup of cornstarch with black pepper and salt in a small bowl. 4. Add chicken to the cornstarch mixture and mix well to coat. 5. Divide the chicken in the two crisper plates and spray them cooking oi. 6. Return the crisper plates to the Ninja Foodi Dual Zone Air Fryer. 7. Choose the Air Fry mode for Zone 1 and set the temperature to 390 degrees F/200 degrees C and the time to 20 minutes. 8. Select the "MATCH" button to copy the settings for Zone 2. 9. Initiate cooking by pressing the START/STOP button. 10. Once done, remove the air fried chicken from the air fryer. 11. Whisk 2 teaspoons of cornstarch with soy sauce, broth, sugar, ketchup, and rice vinegar in a small bowl. 12. Add chilies and canola oil to a skillet and sauté for 1 minute. 13. Add garlic and ginger, then sauté for 30 seconds. 14. Stir in cornstarch sauce and cook until it bubbles and thickens. 15. Toss in cooked chicken and garnish with sesame oil, sesame seeds, and green onion. 16. Enjoy.

Serving Suggestion: Serve with boiled white rice or chow Mein.

Variation Tip: You can use honey instead of sugar to sweeten the sauce.

Nutritional Information Per Serving: Calories 351 | Fat 16g | Sodium 777mg | Carbs 26g | Fiber 4g | Sugar 5g | Protein 28g

Bacon-Wrapped Chicken

Prep Time: 10 minutes | Cook Time: 28 minutes | Serves: 2

Ingredients:

Butter:

½ stick butter softened

½ garlic clove, minced

¼ teaspoon dried thyme

¼ teaspoon dried basil

⅛ teaspoon coarse salt

1 pinch black pepper, ground

⅓ lb. thick-cut bacon

1 ½ lbs. boneless skinless chicken thighs

2 teaspoons garlic, minced

Preparation:

1. Mix garlic softened butter with thyme, salt, basil, and black pepper in a bowl. 2. Add butter mixture on a piece of wax paper and roll it up tightly to make a butter log. 3. Place the log in the refrigerator for 2 hours. 4. Spray one bacon strip on a piece of wax paper. 5. Place each chicken thigh on top of one bacon strip and rub it with garlic. 6. Make a slit in the chicken thigh and add a teaspoon of butter to the chicken. 7. Wrap the bacon around the chicken thigh. 8. Repeat those same steps with all the chicken thighs. 9. Place the bacon-wrapped chicken thighs in the two crisper plates. 10. Return the crisper plates to the Ninja Foodi Dual Zone Air Fryer. 11. Choose the Air Fry mode for Zone 1 and set the temperature to 390 degrees F/200 degrees C and the time to 28 minutes. 12. Select the "MATCH" button to copy the settings for Zone 2. 13. Initiate cooking by pressing the START/STOP button. 14. Flip the chicken once cooked halfway through, and resume cooking. 15. Serve warm.

Serving Suggestion: Serve with tomato ketchup or chili sauce.

Variation Tip: Drizzle mixed dried herbs on top before cooking.

Nutritional Information Per Serving: Calories 380 | Fat 29g | Sodium 821mg | Carbs 34.6g | Fiber 0g | Sugar 0g | Protein 30g

Chicken Drumettes

Prep Time: 15 minutes | Cook Time: 52 minutes | Serves: 5

Ingredients:

10 large chicken drumettes
Cooking spray
¼ cup of rice vinegar
3 tablespoons honey

2 tablespoons unsalted chicken stock
1 tablespoon soy sauce
1 tablespoon toasted sesame oil
⅜ teaspoons crushed red pepper

1 garlic clove, chopped
2 tablespoons chopped unsalted roasted peanuts
1 tablespoon chopped fresh chives

Preparation:

1. Spread the chicken in the two crisper plates in an even layer and spray cooking spray on top. 2. Return the crisper plate to the Ninja Foodi Dual Zone Air Fryer. 3. Choose the Air Fry mode for Zone 1 and set the temperature to 390 degrees F/200 degrees C and the time to 47 minutes. 4. Select the "MATCH" button to copy the settings for Zone 2. 5. Initiate cooking by pressing the START/STOP button. 6. Flip the chicken drumettes once cooked halfway through, then resume cooking. 7. During this time, mix soy sauce, honey, stock, vinegar, garlic, and crushed red pepper in a suitable saucepan and place it over medium-high heat to cook on a simmer. 8. Cook this sauce for 6 minutes with occasional stirring, then pour it into a medium-sized bowl. 9. Add air fried drumettes and toss well to coat with the honey sauce. 10. Garnish with chives and peanuts. 11. Serve warm and fresh.

Serving Suggestion: Serve with tomato ketchup or chili sauce.
Variation Tip: Rub the chicken with lemon juice before seasoning.
Nutritional Information Per Serving: Calories 268 | Fat 10.4g | Sodium 411mg | Carbs 0.4g | Fiber 0.1g | Sugar 0.1g | Protein 40.6g

Crusted Chicken Breast

Prep Time: 15 minutes | Cook Time: 28 minutes | Serves: 4

Ingredients:

2 large eggs, beaten
½ cup all-purpose flour
1 ¼ cups panko bread crumbs
⅔ cup Parmesan, grated

4 teaspoons lemon zest
2 teaspoons dried oregano
Salt, to taste
1 teaspoon cayenne pepper

Freshly black pepper, to taste
4 boneless skinless chicken breasts

Preparation:

1. Beat eggs in one shallow bowl and spread flour in another shallow bowl. 2. Mix panko with oregano, lemon zest, Parmesan, cayenne, oregano, salt, and black pepper in another shallow bowl. 3. First, coat the chicken with flour first, then dip it in the eggs and coat them with panko mixture. 4. Arrange the prepared chicken in the two crisper plates. 5. Return the crisper plate to the Ninja Foodi Dual Zone Air Fryer. 6. Choose the Air Fry mode for Zone 1 and set the temperature to 390 degrees F/200 degrees C and the time to 28 minutes. 7. Select the "MATCH" button to copy the settings for Zone 2. 8. Initiate cooking by pressing the START/STOP button. 9. Flip the half-cooked chicken and continue cooking for 5 minutes until golden. 10. Serve warm.

Serving Suggestion: Serve with fresh-cut tomatoes and sautéed greens.
Variation Tip: Rub the chicken with lemon juice before seasoning.
Nutritional Information Per Serving: Calories 220 | Fat 13g | Sodium 542mg | Carbs 0.9g | Fiber 0.3g | Sugar 0.2g | Protein 25.6g

Brazilian Chicken Drumsticks

Prep Time: 15 minutes | Cook Time: 47 minutes | Serves: 6

Ingredients:

2 teaspoons cumin seeds
2 teaspoons dried parsley
2 teaspoons turmeric powder
2 teaspoons dried oregano leaves

2 teaspoons salt
1 teaspoon coriander seeds
1 teaspoon black peppercorns
1 teaspoon cayenne pepper

½ cup lime juice
4 tablespoons vegetable oil
3 lbs. chicken drumsticks

Preparation:

1. Grind cumin, parsley, salt, coriander seeds, cayenne pepper, peppercorns, oregano, and turmeric in a food processor. 2. Add this mixture to lemon juice and oil in a bowl and mix well. 3. Rub the spice paste over the chicken drumsticks and let them marinate for 30 minutes. 4. Divide the chicken drumsticks in both the crisper plates. 5. Return the crisper plates to the Ninja Foodi Dual Zone Air Fryer. 6. Choose the Air Fry mode for Zone 1 and set the temperature to 390 degrees F/200 degrees C and the time to 47 minutes. 7. Select the "MATCH" button to copy the settings for Zone 2. 8. Initiate cooking by pressing the START/STOP button. 9. Flip the drumsticks when cooked halfway through, then resume cooking. 10. Serve warm.

Serving Suggestion: Serve with tomato ketchup or chili sauce.
Variation Tip: Use buttermilk to soak the drumsticks before seasoning.
Nutritional Information Per Serving: Calories 456 | Fat 16.4g | Sodium 1321mg | Carbs 19.2g | Fiber 2.2g | Sugar 4.2g | Protein 55.2g

Pickled Chicken Fillets

Prep Time: 15 minutes | Cook Time: 28 minutes | Serves: 4

Ingredients:

2 boneless chicken breasts
½ cup dill pickle juice
2 eggs
½ cup milk
1 cup flour, all-purpose
2 tablespoons powdered sugar

2 tablespoons potato starch
1 teaspoon paprika
1 teaspoon of sea salt
½ teaspoon black pepper
½ teaspoon garlic powder
¼ teaspoon ground celery seed ground

1 tablespoon olive oil
Cooking spray
4 hamburger buns, toasted
8 dill pickle chips

Preparation:

1. Set the chicken in a suitable ziplock bag and pound it into ½ thickness with a mallet. 2. Slice the chicken into 2 halves. 3. Add pickle juice and seal the bag. 4. Refrigerate for 30 minutes approximately for marination. Whisk both eggs with milk in a shallow bowl. 5. Thoroughly mix flour with spices and flour in a separate bowl. 6. Dip each chicken slice in egg, then in the flour mixture. 7. Shake off the excess and set the chicken pieces in the crisper plate. 8. Spray the pieces with cooking oil. 9. Place the chicken pieces in the two crisper plate in a single layer and spray the cooking oil. 10. Return the crisper plate to the Ninja Foodi Dual Zone Air Fryer. 11. Choose the Air Fry mode for Zone 1 and set the temperature to 390 degrees F/200 degrees C and the time to 28 minutes. 12. Select the "MATCH" button to copy the settings for Zone 2. 13. Initiate cooking by pressing the START/STOP button. 14. Flip the chicken pieces once cooked halfway through, and resume cooking. 15. Enjoy with pickle chips and a dollop of mayonnaise.

Serving Suggestion: Serve with warm corn tortilla and Greek salad.

Variation Tip: You can use the almond flour breading for low-carb serving.

Nutritional Information Per Serving: Calories 353 | Fat 5g | Sodium 818mg | Carbs 53.2g | Fiber 4.4g | Sugar 8g | Protein 17.3g

Chicken Potatoes

Prep Time: 10 minutes | Cook Time: 22 minutes | Serves: 4

Ingredients:

15 ounces canned potatoes drained
1 teaspoon olive oil
1 teaspoon Lawry's seasoned salt

⅛ teaspoons black pepper optional
8 ounces boneless chicken breast cubed
¼ teaspoon paprika

⅜ cup cheddar, shredded
4 bacon slices, cooked, cut into strips

Preparation:

1. Dice the chicken into small pieces and toss them with olive oil and spices. 2. Drain and dice the potato pieces into smaller cubes. 3. Add potato to the chicken and mix well to coat. 4. Spread the mixture in the two crisper plates in a single layer. 5. Return the crisper plates to the Ninja Foodi Dual Zone Air Fryer. 6. Choose the Air Fry mode for Zone 1 and set the temperature to 390 degrees F/200 degrees C and the time to 22 minutes. 7. Select the "MATCH" button to copy the settings for Zone 2. 8. Initiate cooking by pressing the START/STOP button. 9. Top the chicken and potatoes with cheese and bacon. 10. Return the crisper plates to the Ninja Foodi Dual Zone Air Fryer. 11. Select the Max Crisp mode for Zone 1 and set the temperature to 300 degrees F/150 degrees C and the time to 5 minutes. 12. Initiate cooking by pressing the START/STOP button. 13. Repeat the same step for Zone 2 to broil the potatoes and chicken in the right drawer. 14. Enjoy with dried herbs on top.

Serving Suggestion: Serve with boiled white rice.

Variation Tip: Add sweet potatoes and green beans instead of potatoes.

Nutritional Information Per Serving: Calories 346 | Fat 16.1g | Sodium 882mg | Carbs 1.3g | Fiber 0.5g | Sugar 0.5g | Protein 48.2g

Chili Chicken Wings

Prep Time: 20 minutes | Cook Time: 43 minutes | Serves: 4

Ingredients:

8 chicken wings drumettes
cooking spray

Thai Chili Marinade
1 ½ tablespoons low-sodium soy sauce
½ teaspoon ginger, minced
1 ½ garlic cloves

⅛ cup low-fat buttermilk
¼ cup almond flour

1 green onion
½ teaspoon rice wine vinegar
½ tablespoon Sriracha sauce

McCormick Chicken Seasoning to taste

½ tablespoon sesame oil

Preparation:

1. Put all the ingredients for the marinade in the blender and blend them for 1 minute. 2. Keep this marinade aside. Pat dry the washed chicken and place it in the Ziploc bag. 3. Add buttermilk, chicken seasoning, and zip the bag. 4. Shake the bag well, then refrigerator for 30 minutes for marination. 5. Remove the chicken drumettes from the marinade, then dredge them through dry flour. 6. Spread the drumettes in the two crisper plate and spray them with cooking oil. 7. Return the crisper plate to the Ninja Foodi Dual Zone Air Fryer. 8. Choose the Air Fry mode for Zone 1 and set the temperature to 390 degrees F/200 degrees C and the time to 43 minutes. 9. Select the "MATCH" button to copy the settings for Zone 2. 10. Initiate cooking by pressing the START/STOP button. 11. Toss the drumettes once cooked halfway through. 12. Now brush the chicken pieces with Thai chili sauce and then resume cooking. 13. Serve warm.
Serving Suggestion: Serve with warm corn tortilla and ketchup.
Variation Tip: Rub the wings with lemon or orange juice before cooking.
Nutritional Information Per Serving: Calories 223 | Fat 11.7g | Sodium 721mg | Carbs 13.6g | Fiber 0.7g | Sugar 8g | Protein 15.7g

Balsamic Duck Breast

Prep Time: 15 minutes | Cook Time: 20 minutes | Serves: 2

Ingredients:

2 duck breasts

Marinade:
1 tablespoon olive oil
½ teaspoon French mustard

1 teaspoon parsley

1 teaspoon dried garlic
2 teaspoons honey

Salt and black pepper, to taste

½ teaspoon balsamic vinegar

Preparation:

1. Mix olive oil, mustard, garlic, honey, and balsamic vinegar in a bowl. 2. Add duck breasts to the marinade and rub well. 3. Place one duck breast in each crisper plate. 4. Return the crisper plates to the Ninja Foodi Dual Zone Air Fryer. 5. Choose the Air Fry mode for Zone 1 and set the temperature to 360 degrees F/180 degrees C and the time to 20 minutes. 6. Select the "MATCH" button to copy the settings for Zone 2. 7. Initiate cooking by pressing the START/STOP button. 8. Flip the duck breasts once cooked halfway through, then resume cooking. 9. Serve warm.
Serving Suggestion: Serve with white rice and avocado salad.
Variation Tip: Rub the duck breast with garlic cloves before seasoning.
Nutritional Information Per Serving: Calories 546 | Fat 33.1g | Sodium 1201mg | Carbs 30g | Fiber 2.4g | Sugar 9.7g | Protein 32g

Cheddar-Stuffed Chicken

Prep Time: 10 minutes | Cook Time: 20 minutes | Serves: 4

Ingredients:

3 bacon strips, cooked and crumbled
2 ounces Cheddar cheese, cubed

¼ cup barbeque sauce
2 (4 ounces) boneless chicken breasts

Salt and black pepper to taste

Preparation:

1. Make a 1-inch deep pouch in each chicken breast. 2. Mix cheddar cubes with half of the BBQ sauce, salt, black pepper, and bacon. 3. Divide this filling in the chicken breasts and secure the edges with a toothpick. 4. Brush the remaining BBQ sauce over the chicken breasts. 5. Place the chicken in the crisper plate and spray them with cooking oil. 6. Return the crisper plate to the Ninja Foodi Dual Zone Air Fryer. 7. Choose the Air Fry mode for Zone 1 and set the temperature to 360 degrees F/180 degrees C and the time to 20 minutes. 8. Initiate cooking by pressing the START/STOP button. 9. Serve warm.
Serving Suggestion: Serve with tomato salsa on top.
Variation Tip: Use poultry seasoning for breading.
Nutritional Information Per Serving: Calories 379 | Fat 19g | Sodium 184mg | Carbs 12.3g | Fiber 0.6g | Sugar 2g | Protein 37.7g

Veggie Stuffed Chicken Breasts

Prep Time: 15 minutes | Cook Time: 10 minutes | Serves: 2

Ingredients:

4 teaspoons chili powder
4 teaspoons ground cumin
1 skinless, boneless chicken breast
2 teaspoons chipotle flakes

2 teaspoons Mexican oregano
Salt and black pepper, to taste
½ red bell pepper, julienned
½ onion, julienned

1 fresh jalapeno pepper, julienned
2 teaspoons corn oil
½ lime, juiced

Preparation:

1. Slice the chicken breast in half horizontally. 2. Pound each chicken breast with a mallet into ¼ inch thickness. 3. Rub the pounded chicken breast with black pepper, salt, oregano, chipotle flakes, cumin, and chili powder. 4. Add ½ of bell pepper, jalapeno, and onion on top of each chicken breast piece. 5. Roll the chicken to wrap the filling inside and insert toothpicks to seal. 6. Place the rolls in crisper plate and spray them with cooking oil. 7. Return the crisper plate to the Ninja Foodi Dual Zone Air Fryer. 8. Choose the Air Fry mode for Zone 1 and set the temperature to 360 degrees F/180 degrees C and the time to 10 minutes. 9. Initiate cooking by pressing the START/STOP button. 10. Serve warm.
Serving Suggestion: Serve with tomato ketchup or chili sauce.
Variation Tip: Season the chicken rolls with seasoned parmesan before cooking.
Nutritional Information Per Serving: Calories 351 | Fat 11g | Sodium 150mg | Carbs 3.3g | Fiber 0.2g | Sugar 1g | Protein 33.2g

Cornish Hen with Baked Potatoes

Prep Time: 20 Minutes | Cook Time: 45 Minutes | Serves: 2

Ingredients:

Salt, to taste
1 large potato

1 tablespoon avocado oil
1.5 pounds Cornish hen, skinless and whole

2-3 teaspoons poultry seasoning, dry rub

Preparation:

1. Pierce the large potato with a fork. 2. Rub the potato with avocado oil and salt. 3. Place the potato in the first basket. 4. Coat the Cornish hen thoroughly with poultry seasoning (dry rub) and salt. 5. Place the hen in zone 2 basket. 6. Set zone 1 to AIR FRY mode at 350 degrees F/175 degrees C for 45 minutes. 7. For zone 2 press the MATCH button. 8. Once the cooking cycle is complete, turn off the air fryer and take out the potatoes and Cornish hen from both air fryer baskets. 9.Serve hot and enjoy.
Serving Suggestion: Serve it with coleslaw
Variation Tip: You can use olive oil or canola oil instead of avocado oil
Nutritional Information Per Serving: Calories 612 | Fat 14.3g | Sodium 304mg | Carbs 33.4 g | Fiber 4.5g | Sugar 1.5g | Protein 83.2g

Cornish Hen with Asparagus

Prep Time: 20 Minutes | Cook Time: 45 Minutes | Serves: 2

Ingredients:

10 spears asparagus
Salt and black pepper, to taste
1 Cornish hen

Salt, to taste
Black pepper, to taste
1 teaspoon paprika

Coconut spray, for greasing
2 lemons, sliced

Preparation:

1. Wash and pat dry the asparagus and coat it with coconut oil spray. 2. Sprinkle salt on the asparagus and place them in zone 1 basket. 3. Rub the Cornish hen well with the salt, black pepper, and paprika. 4. Oil spray the Cornish hen and place it in the second air fryer basket. 5. Set zone 1 to AIR FRY mode at 350 degrees F/175 degrees C for 8 minutes. 6. For zone 2, set the time to 45 minutes at 350 degrees F/175 degrees C on ROAST mode. 7. To start cooking, hit the Sync button and press START/STOP button. 8. Serve the chicken with roasted asparagus and slices of lemon. 9. Serve hot and enjoy.
Serving Suggestion: Serve it with ranch dressing
Variation Tip: You can add variation by using chopped cilantro instead of a lemon slice

Chicken Thighs with Brussels sprouts

Prep Time: 20 Minutes | Cook Time: 30 Minutes | Serves: 2

Ingredients:

2 tablespoons honey
4 tablespoons Dijon mustard

Salt and black pepper, to tat
4 tablespoons olive oil

1½ cups Brussels sprouts
8 chicken thighs, skinless

Preparation:

1. Take a bowl and add chicken thighs to it. 2. Add honey, Dijon mustard, salt, pepper, and 2 tablespoons of olive oil to the thighs. 3. Coat the chicken well and marinate it for 1 hour. 4. Season the Brussels sprouts with salt and black pepper along with the remaining olive oil. 5. Place the chicken in the zone 1 basket. 6. Put the Brussels sprouts into the zone 2 basket. 7. Select ROAST mode for chicken and set time to 30 minutes at 390 degrees F/200 degrees C. 8. Select AIR FRY mode for Brussels sprouts and set the timer to 20 minutes at 400 degrees F/200 degrees C. 9. Once done, serve and enjoy.

Serving Suggestion: Serve it with BBQ sauce

Variation Tip: You can use canola oil instead of olive oil

Nutritional Information Per Serving: Calories 1454 | Fat 72.2g | Sodium 869mg | Carbs 23g | Fiber 2.7g | Sugar 19g | Protein 172g

Chicken & Broccoli

Prep Time: 22 Minutes | Cook Time: 35 Minutes | Serves: 2

Ingredients:

1 pound chicken, boneless & bite-size pieces
1½ cups broccoli
2 tablespoons grapeseed oil
⅓ teaspoon garlic powder

1 teaspoon ginger and garlic paste
2 teaspoons soy sauce
1 tablespoon sesame seed oil
2 teaspoons rice vinegar

Salt and black pepper, to taste
Oil spray, for coating

Preparation:

1. Take a small bowl and whisk together the grapeseed oil, ginger and garlic paste, sesame seed oil, rice vinegar, and soy sauce. 2. Take a large bowl and mix the chicken pieces with the prepared marinade. 3. Let it sit for 1 hour. 4. Lightly grease the broccoli with oil spray and season it with salt and black pepper. 5. Put the broccoli into the first basket and grease it with oil spray. 6. Place the chicken into the second basket. 7. Set zone 1 to AIR FRY mode at 350 degrees F/175 degrees C for 8 minutes. 8. For zone 2 set to AIR FRY mode and set the time to 35 minutes at 350 degrees F/175 degrees C. 9. To start cooking, hit the Sync button and press START/STOP button. 10. Once the cooking time is complete, take out and enjoy.

Serving Suggestion: Serve it with lemon wedges

Variation Tip: A light oil alternative can be used as grapeseed oil

Nutritional Information Per Serving: Calories 588 | Fat 32.1g | Sodium 457mg | Carbs 4g | Fiber 1.3 g | Sugar 1g | Protein 67.4 g

Wings with Corn on the Cob

Prep Time: 15 Minutes | Cook Time: 40 Minutes | Serves: 2

Ingredients:

6 chicken wings, skinless
2 tablespoons coconut amino
2 tablespoons brown sugar

1 teaspoon ginger, paste
½ inch garlic, minced
Salt and black pepper to taste

2 corn on cobs, small
Oil spray, for greasing

Preparation:

1. Spray the corns with oil spray and season them with salt. 2. Coat the chicken wings with coconut amino, brown sugar, ginger, garlic, salt, and black pepper. 3. Spray the wings with a good amount of oil spray. 4. Put the chicken wings in the zone 1 basket. 5. Put the corn into the zone 2 basket. 6. Select ROAST mode for the chicken wings and set the time to 23 minutes at 400 degrees F/200 degrees C. 7. Press 2 and select the AIR FRY mode for the corn and set the time to 40 at 300 degrees F/150 degrees C. 8. Once it's done, serve and enjoy.

Serving Suggestion: Serve it with garlic butter sauce

Variation Tip: Use butter instead of oil spray

Nutritional Information Per Serving: Calories 950 | Fat 33.4g | Sodium 592 mg | Carbs 27.4g | Fiber 2.1g | Sugar 11.3 g | Protein 129g

Spiced Chicken and Vegetables

Prep Time: 22 Minutes | Cook Time: 45 Minutes | Serves: 1

Ingredients:

2 large chicken breasts
2 teaspoons olive oil
1 teaspoon chili powder
1 teaspoon Paprika powder
1 teaspoon onion powder

½ teaspoon garlic powder
¼ teaspoon cumin
Salt and black pepper, to taste
Vegetable Ingredients:
2 large potatoes, cubed

4 large carrots cut into bite-size pieces
1 tablespoon olive oil
Salt and black pepper, to taste

Preparation:

1. Take chicken breast pieces and rub them with olive oil, salt, pepper, chili powder, onion powder, cumin, garlic powder, and paprika. 2. Season the vegetables with olive oil, salt, and black pepper. 3. Place the chicken breast pieces in the zone 1 basket. 4. Put the vegetables into the zone 2 basket. 5. Set zone 1 to ROAST at 350 degrees F/175 degrees C for 45 minutes. 6. For zone 2 set the time for 45 minutes on AIR FRY mode at 350 degrees F/175 degrees C. 7. To start cooking hit the Sync button and press START/STOP button. 8. Once the cooking cycle is done, serve, and enjoy.

Serving Suggestion: Serve it with salad or ranch dressing

Variation Tip: Use canola oil instead of olive oil

Nutritional Information Per Serving: Calories 1510 | Fat 51.3g | Sodium 525mg | Carbs 163g | Fiber 24.7 g | Sugar 21.4g | Protein 102.9

Glazed Thighs with French Fries

Prep Time: 22 Minutes | Cook Time: 35 Minutes | Serves: 3

Ingredients:

2 tablespoons soy sauce
Salt, to taste
1 teaspoon Worcestershire sauce

2 teaspoons brown sugar
1 teaspoon ginger paste
1 teaspoon garlic paste

6 boneless chicken thighs
1 pound hand-cut potato fries
2 tablespoons of canola oil

Preparation:

1. Coat the French fries well with canola oil and season with salt. 2. In a small bowl, combine the soy sauce, Worcestershire sauce, brown sugar, ginger, and garlic. 3. Place the chicken in this marinade and let it sit for 40 minutes. 4. Put the chicken thighs into the zone 1 basket and fries into the zone 2 basket. 5. Press button 1 for the first basket, and set it to ROAST mode at 350 degrees F/175 degrees C for 35 minutes. 6. For the second basket hit 2 and set time to 30 minutes at 360 degrees F/180 degrees C on AIR FRY mode. 7. Once the cooking cycle is complete, take out the fries and chicken. Serve it hot.

Serving Suggestion: Serve with ketchup

Variation Tip: You can use honey instead of brown sugar

Nutritional Information Per Serving: Calories 858 | Fat 39g | Sodium 1509mg | Carbs 45.6g | Fiber 4.4g | Sugar 3g | Protein 90g

Dijon Chicken Wings

Prep Time: 15 Minutes | Cook Time: 20 Minutes | Serves: 3

Ingredients:

1 cup chicken batter mix, Louisiana
9 chicken wings
½ teaspoon smoked Paprika

2 tablespoons Dijon mustard
1 tablespoon cayenne pepper
1 teaspoon meat tenderizer, powder

Oil spray, for greasing

Preparation:

1. Pat dry the chicken wings and add mustard, paprika, meat tenderizer, and cayenne pepper. 2. Dredge the wings in the chicken batter mix. 3. Oil spray the chicken wings. 4. Grease both baskets of the air fryer. 5. Divide the wings between the two zones of the air fryer. 6. Set zone 1 to AIR FRY mode at 400 degrees F/200 degrees C for 20 minutes. 7. Select MATCH for zone 2. 8. Hit START/STOP button to begin the cooking. 9. Once the cooking cycle is complete, serve, and enjoy hot.

Serving Suggestion: Serve the wings with salad

Variation Tip: Use American yellow mustard instead of Dijon mustard

Nutritional Information Per Serving: Calories 621 | Fat 32.6g | Sodium 2016mg | Carbs 46.6g | Fiber 1.1g | Sugar 0.2g | Protein 32.1g

Sweet and Spicy Carrots with Chicken Thighs

Prep Time: 15 Minutes | Cook Time: 35 Minutes | Serves: 2

Ingredients:

For Glaze

Cooking spray, for greasing
2 tablespoons butter, melted
1 tablespoon hot honey

1 teaspoon orange zest
1 teaspoon cardamom
½ pound baby carrots

1 tablespoon orange juice
Salt and black pepper, to taste

Other Ingredients:

½ pound carrots, baby carrots

8 chicken thighs

Preparation:

1. Take a bowl and mix all the glaze ingredients in it. 2. Coat the chicken and carrots with the glaze and let them rest for 30 minutes. 3. Place the chicken thighs into zone 1 basket. 4. Put the glazed carrots into the zone 2 basket. 5. Press button 1 for the first basket and set it to ROAST mode at 350 degrees F/175 degrees C for 35 minutes. 6. For the second basket hit 2 and set to AIR FRY mode at 390 degrees F/200 degrees C for 8-10 minutes. 7. Press Sync button so both finish at the same time. 8. Once the cooking cycle is complete, take out the carrots and chicken and serve it hot.

Serving Suggestion: Serve with salad
Variation Tip: Use lime juice instead of orange juice
Nutritional Information Per Serving: Calories 1312 | Fat 55.4g | Sodium 757mg | Carbs 23.3g | Fiber 6.7g | Sugar 12g | Protein 171g

Chicken Breast Strips

Prep Time: 10 Minutes | Cook Time: 22 Minutes | Serves: 2

Ingredients:

2 large organic eggs
1-ounce buttermilk
1 cup cornmeal

¼ cup all-purpose flour
Salt and black pepper, to taste
1 pound chicken breasts, cut into strips

2 tablespoons oil bay seasoning
Oil spray, for greasing

Preparation:

1. Take a medium bowl and whisk the eggs with buttermilk. 2. In a separate large bowl, mix flour, cornmeal, salt, black pepper, and oil bay seasoning. 3. First, dip the chicken breast strip in egg wash and then dredge into the flour mixture. 4. Grease the air fryer baskets and divide the chicken strips into them. 5. Set the zone 1 basket to AIR FRY mode at 400 degrees F/200 degrees C for 22 minutes. 6. Select the MATCH button for zone 2. 7. Hit the START/STOP button to let the cooking start. 8. Once the cooking cycle is done, serve.

Serving Suggestion: Serve it with roasted vegetables
Variation Tip: None
Nutritional Information Per Serving: Calories 788 | Fat 25g | Sodium 835 mg | Carbs60g | Fiber 4.9g | Sugar 1.5g | Protein 79g

Spice-Rubbed Chicken Pieces

Prep Time: 22 Minutes | Cook Time: 40 Minutes | Serves: 6

Ingredients:

3 pounds chicken, pieces
1 teaspoon sweet Paprika
1 teaspoon mustard powder

1 tablespoon dark brown sugar
Salt and black pepper, to taste
1 teaspoon chile powder, New Mexico

1 teaspoon oregano, dried
¼ teaspoon all-spice powder

Preparation:

1. In a bowl and mix in the brown sugar, salt, paprika, mustard powder, oregano, chile powder, black pepper, and All Spice powder. 2. Mix well and rub this spice mixture all over the chicken. 3. Divide the chicken between two air fryer baskets. 4. Oil spray the meat and then add it to the air fryer. 5. Now press button 1 and set the time to 40 minutes at 350 degrees F/175 degrees C. 6. Press MATCH and START/STOP for the cooking process to begin. 7. Once the cooking cycle is complete, press START/STOP for both the zones. 8. Take out the chicken and serve hot.

Serving Suggestion: Serve it with coleslaw, peanut sauce, or ranch
Variation Tip: Use light brown sugar instead of dark brown sugar
Nutritional Information Per Serving: Calories 353 | Fat 7.1g | Sodium 400mg | Carbs 2.2g | Fiber 0.4g | Sugar 1.6g | Protein 66g

Garlic, Buffalo, and Blue Cheese Stuffed Chicken

Prep Time: 15 minutes | Cook Time: 30 minutes | Serves: 2

Ingredients:

¼ teaspoon garlic powder
¼ teaspoon onion powder
¼ teaspoon paprika
2 boneless, skinless chicken breasts

½ tablespoon canola oil
2 ounces softened cream cheese
¼ cup shredded cheddar cheese
¼ cup blue cheese crumbles

¼ cup buffalo sauce
1 tablespoon dry ranch seasoning
2 tablespoons dried chives
1 tablespoon minced garlic

Optional Toppings:
Ranch dressing

Buffalo sauce

Fresh parsley

Preparation:

1. Combine the garlic powder, onion powder, and paprika in a small bowl. 2. Drizzle the chicken breasts with oil and season evenly with the garlic powder mixture on a cutting board. 3. Make a deep pocket in the center of each chicken breast, but be cautious not to cut all the way through. 4. Combine the remaining ingredients in a medium mixing bowl and stir until thoroughly blended. Fill each chicken breast's pocket with the cream cheese mixture. 5. Place the chicken in both drawers and insert both drawers into the unit. Select zone 1, then BAKE, and set the temperature to 375 degrees F/190 degrees C with a 30-minute timer. To match zone 2 and zone 1 settings, select MATCH. To start cooking, use the START/STOP button. 6. Garnish the cooked chicken with ranch dressing, spicy sauce, and parsley on top.
Serving Suggestion: Serve with toppings of your choice.
Variation Tip: You can use red chili flakes.
Nutritional Information Per Serving: Calories 369 | Fat 23.8g | Sodium 568mg | Carbs 4.3g | Fiber 0.4g | Sugar 0.5g | Protein 34.7g

Spicy Chicken

Prep Time: 12 Minutes | Cook Time: 35-40 Minutes | Serves: 4

Ingredients:

4 chicken thighs
2 cups buttermilk
4 chicken legs
2 cups flour

Salt and black pepper, to taste
2 tablespoons garlic powder
½ teaspoon onion powder
1 teaspoon poultry seasoning

1 teaspoon cumin
2 tablespoons Paprika
1 tablespoon olive oil

Preparation:

1. Take a bowl and add the buttermilk to it. 2. Soak the chicken thighs and chicken legs in the buttermilk for 2 hours. 3. Mix the flour, all the seasonings, and olive oil in a small bowl. 4. Take out the chicken pieces from the buttermilk mixture and then dredge them into the flour mixture. 5. Repeat the step for all the pieces and then arrange them in both the air fryer baskets. 6. Set the timer for both the baskets to ROAST mode for 35-40 minutes at 350 degrees F/175 degrees C. 7. Once the cooking cycle is complete take them out and serve hot.
Serving Suggestion: Serve the chicken with garlic dipping sauce
Variation Tip: Use canola oil instead of olive oil
Nutritional Information Per Serving: Calories 624 | Fat 17.6g | Sodium 300mg | Carbs 60g | Fiber 3.5g | Sugar 7.7g | Protein 54.2g

Yummy Chicken Breasts

Prep Time: 15 Minutes | Cook Time: 25 Minutes | Serves: 2

Ingredients:

4 large chicken breasts, 6 ounces each
2 tablespoons oil bay seasoning
1 tablespoon Montreal chicken seasoning

1 teaspoon thyme
½ teaspoon Paprika
Salt, to taste

Oil spray, for greasing

Preparation:

1. Season the chicken breast pieces with the listed seasoning and let them rest for 40 minutes. 2. Grease both sides of the chicken breast pieces with oil spray. 3. Divide the pieces between both baskets. 4. Set zone 1 to AIR FRY mode at 400 degrees F/200 degrees C for 15 minutes. 5. Select the MATCH button for zone 2 basket. 6. Press START/STOP and take out the baskets and flip the chicken breast pieces. 7. Select the zones to 400 degrees F/200 degrees C for 10 more minutes using the MATCH button. 8. Once it's done serve and enjoy.
Serving Suggestion: Serve with baked potato
Variation Tip: None
Nutritional Information Per Serving: Calories 711 | Fat 27.7g | Sodium 895mg | Carbs 1.6g | Fiber 0.4g | Sugar 0.1g | Protein 106.3g

Chicken Ranch Wraps

Prep Time: 5 minutes | Cook Time: 22 minutes | Serves: 4

1½ ounces breaded chicken breast tenders
4 (12-inch) whole-wheat tortilla wraps

2 heads romaine lettuce, chopped
½ cup shredded mozzarella cheese

4 tablespoons ranch dressing

1. Place a crisper plate in each drawer. Place half of the chicken tenders in one drawer and half in the other. Insert the drawers into the unit. 2. Select zone 1, then AIR FRY, and set the temperature to 390 degrees F/200 degrees C with a 22-minute timer. To match zone 2 settings to zone 1, choose MATCH. To begin cooking, press the START/STOP button. 3. To pause the unit, press START/STOP when the timer reaches 11 minutes. Remove the drawers from the unit and flip the tenders over. To resume cooking, re-insert the drawers into the device and press START/STOP. 4. Remove the chicken from the drawers when they're done cooking and chop them up. 5. Divide the chopped chicken between warmed-up wraps. Top with some lettuce, cheese, and ranch dressing. Wrap and serve.

Serving Suggestion: You can add extra toppings of your choice.

Variation Tip: Use any cheese you prefer.

Nutritional Information Per Serving: Calories 212 | Fat 7.8g | Sodium 567mg | Carbs 9.1g | Fiber 34.4g | Sugar 9.7g | Protein 10.6g

Chicken Tenders and Curly Fries

Prep Time: 5 minutes | Cook Time: 35 minutes | Serves: 4

1-pound frozen chicken tenders

1-pound frozen curly French fries

Dipping sauces of your choice

1. Place a crisper plate in each drawer. In the zone 1 drawer, place the chicken tenders, then place the drawer into the unit. 2. Fill the zone 2 drawer with the curly French fries, then place the drawer in the unit. 3. Select zone 1, then AIR FRY, and set the temperature to 390 degrees F/200 degrees C with a 22-minute timer. Select zone 2, then AIR FRY, and set the temperature to 400 degrees F/200 degrees C with a 30-minute timer. Select SYNC. To begin cooking, press the START/STOP button. 4. Press START/STOP to pause the device when the zone 1 and 2 times reach 8 minutes. Shake the drawers for 10 seconds after removing them from the unit. To resume cooking, re-insert the drawers into the unit and press START/STOP. 5. Enjoy!

Serving Suggestion: Serve with dipping sauces of your choice.

Variation Tip: You can use turkey tenders instead of chicken.

Nutritional Information Per Serving: Calories 500 | Fat 19.8g | Sodium 680mg | Carbs 50.1g | Fiber 4.1g | Sugar 0g | Protein 27.9g

Chicken Wings

Prep Time: 10 minutes | Cook Time: 45 minutes | Serves: 4

2 pounds chicken wings
Kosher salt
Freshly ground black pepper

Non-stick cooking spray
¼ cup hot sauce (such as Frank's)
4 tablespoons melted butter

1 teaspoon Worcestershire sauce
½ teaspoon garlic powder

1. Season the wings with salt and pepper. Spray the inside of the drawers with non-stick spray. 2. Place a crisper plate in each drawer. Put half of the chicken wings in the zone 1 drawer and half in the zone 2 drawer, then insert the drawers into the unit. 3. Select zone 1, select AIR FRY, set temperature to 400 degrees F/200 degrees C, and set time to 45 minutes. Select MATCH to match zone 2 settings to zone 1. Press the START/STOP button to begin cooking. 4. When the time reaches 22 minutes, press START/STOP to pause the cooking. Remove the drawers and flip the chicken. Re-insert the drawers into the unit and press START/STOP to resume cooking. 5. When cooking is complete, remove the chicken wings. 6. Meanwhile, combine the hot sauce, butter, Worcestershire sauce, and garlic powder in a large bowl. Add the cooked wings to the mixture and toss gently to coat. Serve hot.

Serving Suggestion: Serve with a side salad.

Variation Tip: You can use fresh garlic.

Nutritional Information Per Serving: Calories 538 | Fat 28.5g | Sodium 710mg | Carbs 0.8g | Fiber 0.1g | Sugar 0.5g | Protein 65.9g

Sesame Ginger Chicken

Prep Time: 10 minutes | Cook Time: 30 minutes | Serves: 4

Ingredients:

4 ounces green beans
1 tablespoon canola oil

1½ pounds boneless, skinless chicken breasts
⅓ cup prepared sesame-ginger sauce

Kosher salt, to taste
Black pepper, to taste

Preparation:

1. Toss the green beans with a teaspoon of salt and pepper in a medium mixing bowl. 2. Place a crisper plate in each drawer. Place the green beans in the zone 1 drawer and insert it into the unit. Place the chicken breasts in the zone 2 drawer and place it inside the unit. 3. Select zone 1, then AIR FRY, and set the temperature to 390 degrees F/200 degrees C with a 10-minute timer. Select zone 2, then AIR FRY, and set the temperature to 390 degrees F/200 degrees C with an 18-minute timer. Select SYNC. To begin cooking, press the START/STOP button. 4. Press START/STOP to pause the unit when the zone 2 timer reaches 9 minutes. Remove the chicken from the drawer and toss it in the sesame ginger sauce. To resume cooking, re-insert the drawer into the unit and press START/STOP. 5. When cooking is complete, serve the chicken breasts and green beans straight away.
Serving Suggestion: Serve with steamed or fried rice.
Variation Tip: You can use asparagus instead of green beans.
Nutritional Information Per Serving: Calories 143 | Fat 7g | Sodium 638mg | Carbs 11.6g | Fiber 1.4g | Sugar 8.5g | Protein 11.1g

Chicken and Broccoli

Prep Time: 10 minutes | Cook Time: 15 minutes | Serves: 4

Ingredients:

1-pound boneless, skinless chicken breast or thighs, cut into 1-inch bite-sized pieces
¼ –½ pound broccoli, cut into florets (1–2 cups)
½ medium onion, cut into thick slices
3 tablespoons olive oil or grape seed oil

½ teaspoon garlic powder
1 tablespoon fresh minced ginger
1 tablespoon low-sodium soy sauce
1 tablespoon rice vinegar
1 teaspoon sesame oil

2 teaspoons hot sauce (optional)
½ teaspoon sea salt, or to taste
Black pepper, to taste
Lemon wedges, for serving (optional)

Preparation:

1. Combine the oil, garlic powder, ginger, soy sauce, rice vinegar, sesame oil, optional spicy sauce, salt, and pepper in a large mixing bowl. 2. Put the chicken in a separate bowl. 3. In a separate bowl, combine the broccoli and onions. 4. Divide the marinade between the two bowls and toss to evenly coat each. 5. Install a crisper plate into both drawers. Place the broccoli in the zone 1 drawer, then insert the drawer into the unit. Place the chicken breasts in the zone 2 drawer, then insert the drawer into the unit. 6. Select zone 1, select AIR FRY, set temperature to 390 degrees F/200 degrees C, and set time to 10 minutes. Select zone 2, select AIR FRY, set temperature to 390 degrees F/200 degrees C, and set time to 20 minutes. Select SYNC. Press the START/STOP button to begin cooking. 7. When zone 2 time reaches 9 minutes, press START/STOP to pause the unit. Remove the drawer and toss the chicken. Re-insert the drawer into the unit and press START/STOP to resume cooking. 8. When cooking is complete, serve the chicken breasts and broccoli while still hot. 9. Add additional salt and pepper to taste. Squeeze optional fresh lemon juice on top and serve warm.
Serving Suggestion: Serve with rice.
Variation Tip: You can use tamari instead of soy sauce.
Nutritional Information Per Serving: Calories 224 | Fat 15.8g | Sodium 203mg | Carbs 4g | Fiber 1g | Sugar 1g | Protein 25g

Chicken Leg Piece

Prep Time: 15 Minutes | Cook Time: 25 Minutes | Serves: 1

Ingredients:

1 teaspoon onion powder
1 teaspoon Paprika powder
1 teaspoon garlic powder
Salt and black pepper, to taste

1 tablespoon Italian seasoning
1 teaspoon celery seeds
2 eggs, whisked
⅓ cup buttermilk

1 cup cornflour
1 pound chicken legs

Preparation:

1. Take a bowl and whisk the eggs along with pepper, salt, and buttermilk and set aside. 2. Mix all the spices in a small separate bowl. 3. Dredge the chicken in the egg wash, then dredge it in the spice seasoning. 4. Coat the chicken legs with oil spray. 5. At the end, dust it with the cornflour. 6. Divide the leg pieces into the two zones. 7. Set zone 1 basket to 400 degrees F/200 degrees C for 25 minutes. 8. Select MATCH for zone 2 basket. 9. Let the air fryer do the magic. 10. Once it's done, serve and enjoy.

Serving Suggestion: Serve it with cooked rice

Variation Tip: Use water instead of buttermilk

Nutritional Information Per Serving: Calories 1511 | Fat 52.3g | Sodium 615 mg | Carbs 100g | Fiber 9.2g | Sugar 8.1g | Protein 154.2g

BBQ Cheddar-Stuffed Chicken Breasts

Prep Time: 10 minutes | Cook Time: 25 minutes | Serves: 2

Ingredients:

3 strips cooked bacon, divided
2 ounces cheddar cheese, cubed, divided

¼ cup BBQ sauce, divided
2 (4-ounces) skinless, boneless chicken breasts

Salt and ground black pepper, to taste

Preparation:

1. In a mixing bowl, combine the cooked bacon, cheddar cheese, and 1 tablespoon BBQ sauce. 2. Make a horizontal 1-inch cut at the top of each chicken breast with a long, sharp knife, producing a little interior pouch. Fill each breast with an equal amount of the bacon-cheese mixture. Wrap the remaining bacon strips around each chicken breast. Coat the chicken breasts with the leftover BBQ sauce and lay them in a baking dish. 3. Install a crisper plate in both drawers. Place half the chicken breasts in zone 1 and half in zone 2, then insert the drawers into the unit. 4. Select zone 1, select AIR FRY, set temperature to 390 degrees F/200 degrees C, and set time to 22 minutes. Select MATCH to match zone 2 settings to zone 1. Press the START/STOP button to begin cooking. 5. When the time reaches 11 minutes, press START/STOP to pause the unit. Remove the drawers and flip the chicken. Re-insert drawers into the unit and press START/STOP to resume cooking. 6. When cooking is complete, remove the chicken breasts.

Serving Suggestion: Serve the chicken with a side salad.

Variation Tip: You can use turkey breasts instead.

Nutritional Information Per Serving: Calories 379 | Fat 12.8g | Sodium 906mg | Carbs 11.1g | Fiber 0.4g | Sugar 8.3g | Protein 37.7g

Buffalo Chicken

Prep Time: 20 minutes | Cook Time: 22 minutes | Serves: 4

Ingredients:

½ cup plain fat-free Greek yogurt
¼ cup egg substitute
1 tablespoon plus 1 teaspoon hot sauce

1 cup panko breadcrumbs
1 tablespoon sweet paprika
1 tablespoon garlic pepper seasoning

1 tablespoon cayenne pepper
1-pound skinless, boneless chicken breasts, cut into 1-inch strips

Preparation:

1. Combine the Greek yogurt, egg substitute, and hot sauce in a mixing bowl. 2. In a separate bowl, combine the panko breadcrumbs, paprika, garlic powder, and cayenne pepper. 3. Dip the chicken strips in the yogurt mixture, then coat them in the breadcrumb mixture. 4. Install a crisper plate in both drawers. Place the chicken strips into the drawers and then insert the drawers into the unit. 5. Select zone 1, select AIR FRY, set temperature to 390 degrees F/200 degrees C, and set time to 22 minutes. Select MATCH to match zone 2 settings to zone 1. Press the START/STOP button to begin cooking. 6. When cooking is complete, serve immediately.

Serving Suggestion: Serve with a dipping sauce of your choice.

Variation Tip: You can use regular breadcrumbs instead of panko.

Nutritional Information Per Serving: Calories 234 | Fat 15.8g | Sodium 696mg | Carbs 22.1g | Fiber 1.1g | Sugar 1.7g | Protein 31.2g

Crispy Ranch Nuggets

Prep Time: 15 minutes | Cook Time: 10 minutes | Serves: 4

Ingredients:

1 pound chicken tenders, cut into 1½–2-inch pieces
1 (1-ounce) sachet dry ranch salad dressing mix

2 tablespoons flour
1 egg
1 cup panko breadcrumbs

Olive oil cooking spray

Preparation:

1. Toss the chicken with the ranch seasoning in a large mixing bowl. Allow for 5–10 minutes of resting time. 2. Fill a resalable bag halfway with the flour. 3. Crack the egg into a small bowl and lightly beat it. 4. Spread the breadcrumbs onto a dish. 5. Toss the chicken in the bag to coat it. Dip the chicken in the egg mixture lightly, allowing excess to drain off. Roll the chicken pieces in the breadcrumbs, pressing them in, so they stick. Lightly spray with the cooking spray. 6. Install a crisper plate in both drawers. Place half the chicken tenders in the zone 1 drawer and half in the zone 2 one, then insert the drawers into the unit. 7. Select zone 1, select AIR FRY, set temperature to 390 degrees F/200 degrees C, and set time to 10 minutes. Select MATCH to match zone 2 settings to zone 1. Press the START/STOP button to begin cooking. 8. When the time reaches 6 minutes, press START/STOP to pause the unit. Remove the drawers and flip the chicken. Re-insert the drawers into the unit and press START/STOP to resume cooking. 9. When cooking is complete, remove the chicken.

Serving Suggestion: Serve with a sauce of your choice.

Variation Tip: You can use almond flour.

Nutritional Information Per Serving: Calories 244 | Fat 3.6g | Sodium 713mg | Carbs 25.3g | Fiber 0.1g | Sugar 0.1g | Protein 31g

Honey-Cajun Chicken Thighs

Prep Time: 10 minutes | Cook Time: 25 minutes | Serves: 6

Ingredients:

½ cup buttermilk
1 teaspoon hot sauce
1½ pounds skinless, boneless chicken thighs
¼ cup all-purpose flour

⅓ cup tapioca flour
2½ teaspoons Cajun seasoning
½ teaspoon garlic salt
½ teaspoon honey powder

¼ teaspoon ground paprika
⅛ teaspoon cayenne pepper
4 teaspoons honey

Preparation:

1. In a resealable plastic bag, combine the buttermilk and hot sauce. Marinate the chicken thighs in the bag for 30 minutes. 2. Combine the flour, tapioca flour, Cajun spice, garlic salt, honey powder, paprika, and cayenne pepper in a small mixing bowl. 3. Remove the thighs from the buttermilk mixture and dredge them in the flour. Remove any excess flour by shaking it off. 4. Install a crisper plate in both drawers. Place half the chicken thighs in the zone 1 drawer and half in zone 2's, then insert the drawers into the unit. 5. Select zone 1, select AIR FRY, set temperature to 390 degrees F/200 degrees C, and set time to 25 minutes. Select MATCH to match zone 2 settings to zone 1. Press the START/STOP button to begin cooking. 6. When the time reaches 11 minutes, press START/STOP to pause the unit. Remove the drawers and flip the chicken. Re-insert the drawers into the unit and press START/STOP to resume cooking. 7. When cooking is complete, remove the chicken and serve.

Serving Suggestion: Serve with a side salad.

Variation Tip: You can use coconut flour.

Nutritional Information Per Serving: Calories 243 | Fat 11.8g | Sodium 203mg | Carbs 16.1g | Fiber 0.4g | Sugar 5.1g | Protein 19g

Buttermilk Fried Chicken

Prep Time: 5 minutes (plus 4 hours for marinating) | Cook Time: 30 minutes | Serves: 6

Ingredients:

1½ pounds boneless, skinless chicken thighs
2 cups buttermilk
1 cup all-purpose flour

1 tablespoon seasoned salt
½ tablespoon ground black pepper
1 cup panko breadcrumbs

Cooking spray

Preparation:

1. Place the chicken thighs in a shallow baking dish. Cover with the buttermilk. Refrigerate for 4 hours or overnight. 2. In a large gallon-sized resealable bag, combine the flour, seasoned salt, and pepper. 3. Remove the chicken from the buttermilk but don't discard the mixture. 4. Add the chicken to the bag and shake well to coat. 5. Dip the thighs in the buttermilk again, then coat in the panko breadcrumbs. 6. Install a crisper plate in each drawer. Place half the chicken thighs in the zone 1 drawer and half in zone 2's, then insert the drawers into the unit. 7. Select zone 1, select AIR FRY, set temperature to 390 degrees F/200 degrees C, and set time to 30 minutes. Select MATCH to match zone 2 settings to zone 1. Press the START/STOP button to begin cooking. 8. When the time reaches 15 minutes, press START/STOP to pause the unit. Remove the drawers and flip the chicken. Re-insert the drawers into the unit and press START/STOP to resume cooking. 9. When cooking is complete, remove the chicken.

Serving Suggestion: Serve with fried rice.

Variation Tip: You can use tofu instead of chicken.

Nutritional Information Per Serving: Calories 335 | Fat 12.8g | Sodium 687mg | Carbs 33.1g | Fiber 0.4g | Sugar 4g | Protein 24.5g

Almond Chicken

Prep Time: 10 minutes | Cook Time: 25 minutes | Serves: 4

Ingredients:

2 large eggs
½ cup buttermilk
2 teaspoons garlic salt

1 teaspoon pepper
2 cups slivered almonds, finely chopped
4 boneless, skinless chicken breast halves (6

ounces each)

Preparation:

1. Whisk together the egg, buttermilk, garlic salt, and pepper in a small bowl. 2. In another small bowl, place the almonds. 3. Dip the chicken in the egg mixture, then roll it in the almonds, patting it down to help the coating stick. 4. Install a crisper plate in both drawers. Place half the chicken breasts in the zone 1 drawer and half in zone 2's, then insert the drawers into the unit. 5. Select zone 1, select AIR FRY, set temperature to 390 degrees F/200 degrees C, and set time to 22 minutes. Select MATCH to match zone 2 settings to zone 1. Press the START/STOP button to begin cooking. 6. When the time reaches 11 minutes, press START/STOP to pause the unit. Remove the drawers and flip the chicken. Re-insert the drawers into the unit and press START/STOP to resume cooking. 7. When cooking is complete, remove the chicken.

Serving Suggestion: Serve with a sauce of your choice.

Variation Tip: You can use walnuts instead.

Nutritional Information Per Serving: Calories 353 | Fat 18g | Sodium 230mg | Carbs 6g | Fiber 2g | Sugar 3g | Protein 41g

Lemon Chicken Thighs

Prep Time: 10 minutes | Cook Time: 25 minutes | Serves: 4

Ingredients:

¼ cup butter, softened
3 garlic cloves, minced
2 teaspoons minced fresh rosemary or ½
teaspoon crushed dried rosemary

1 teaspoon minced fresh thyme or ¼ teaspoon
dried thyme
1 teaspoon grated lemon zest
1 tablespoon lemon juice

4 bone-in chicken thighs (about 1½ pounds)
⅛ teaspoon salt
⅛ teaspoon pepper

Preparation:

1. Combine the butter, garlic, rosemary, thyme, lemon zest, and lemon juice in a small bowl. 2. Under the skin of each chicken thigh, spread 1 teaspoon of the butter mixture. Apply the remaining butter to each thigh's skin. Season to taste with salt and pepper. 3. Install a crisper plate in both drawers. Place half the chicken tenders in the zone 1 drawer and half in zone 2's, then insert the drawers into the unit. 4. Select zone 1, select AIR FRY, set temperature to 390 degrees F/200 degrees C, and set time to 22 minutes. Select MATCH to match zone 2 settings to zone 1. Press the START/STOP button to begin cooking. 5. When the time reaches 11 minutes, press START/STOP to pause the unit. Remove the drawers and flip the chicken. Re-insert the drawers into the unit and press START/STOP to resume cooking. 6. When cooking is complete, remove the chicken and serve.

Serving Suggestion: Serve with a sauce of your choosing.

Variation Tip: You can use garlic powder.

Nutritional Information Per Serving: Calories 329 | Fat 26g | Sodium 253mg | Carbs 1g | Fiber 0g | Sugar 0g | Protein 23g

Whole Chicken

Prep Time: 10 minutes | Cook Time: 20 minutes | Serves: 8

Ingredients:

1 whole chicken (about 2.8 pounds), cut in half
4 tablespoons olive oil

2 teaspoons paprika
1 teaspoon garlic powder

1 teaspoon onion powder
Salt and pepper, to taste

Preparation:

1. Mix the olive oil, paprika, garlic powder, and onion powder together in a bowl. 2. Place the chicken halves, breast side up, on a plate. Spread a teaspoon or two of the oil mix all over the halves using either your hands or a brush. Season with salt and pepper. 3. Flip the chicken halves over and repeat on the other side. You'll want to reserve a little of the oil mix for later, but other than that, use it liberally. 4. Install a crisper plate in both drawers. Place one half of the chicken in the zone 1 drawer and the other half in the zone 2 drawer, then insert the drawers into the unit. 5. Select zone 1, select AIR FRY, set temperature to 390 degrees F/200 degrees C, and set time to 20 minutes. Select MATCH to match zone 2 settings to zone 1. Press the START/STOP button to begin cooking. 6. When cooking is done, check the internal temperature of the chicken. It should read 165°F. If the chicken isn't done, add more cooking time.

Serving Suggestion: Serve with veggies of your choice.

Variation Tip: Use red chili flakes for some kick.

Nutritional Information Per Serving: Calories 131 | Fat 8g | Sodium 51mg | Carbs 0g | Fiber 0g | Sugar 0g | Protein 14g

Chicken Parmesan

Prep Time: 10 minutes | Cook Time: 20 minutes | Serves: 4

Ingredients:

2 large eggs
½ cup seasoned breadcrumbs
⅓ cup grated parmesan cheese

¼ teaspoon pepper
4 boneless, skinless chicken breast halves (6 ounces each)

1 cup pasta sauce
1 cup shredded mozzarella cheese
Chopped fresh basil (optional)

Preparation:

1. Lightly beat the eggs in a small bowl. 2. Combine the breadcrumbs, parmesan cheese, and pepper in a shallow bowl. 3. After dipping the chicken in the egg, coat it in the crumb mixture. 4. Install a crisper plate in both drawers. Place half the chicken breasts in the zone 1 drawer and half in zone 2's, then insert the drawers into the unit. 5. Select zone 1, select AIR FRY, set temperature to 390 degrees F/200 degrees C, and set time to 20 minutes. Select MATCH to match zone 2 settings to zone 1. Press the START/STOP button to begin cooking. 6. When the time reaches 10 minutes, press START/STOP to pause the unit. Remove the drawers and flip the chicken. Re-insert the drawers into the unit and press START/STOP to resume cooking. 7. When cooking is complete, remove the chicken.

Serving Suggestion: Serve with pasta and garnish with fresh basil.

Variation Tip: You can use panko breadcrumbs if you prefer.

Nutritional Information Per Serving: Calories 293 | Fat 15.8g | Sodium 203mg | Carbs 11.1g | Fiber 2.4g | Sugar 8.7g | Protein 29g

Thai Chicken Meatballs

Prep Time: 10 minutes | Cook Time: 10 minutes | Serves: 4

Ingredients:

½ cup sweet chili sauce
2 tablespoons lime juice
2 tablespoons ketchup
1 teaspoon soy sauce

1 large egg, lightly beaten
¾ cup panko breadcrumbs
1 green onion, finely chopped
1 tablespoon minced fresh cilantro

½ teaspoon salt
½ teaspoon garlic powder
1-pound lean ground chicken

Preparation:

1. Combine the chili sauce, lime juice, ketchup, and soy sauce in a small bowl; set aside ½ cup for serving. 2. Combine the egg, breadcrumbs, green onion, cilantro, salt, garlic powder, and the remaining 4 tablespoons chili sauce mixture in a large mixing bowl. Mix in the chicken lightly yet thoroughly. Form into 12 balls. 3. Install a crisper plate in both drawers. Place half the chicken meatballs in the zone 1 drawer and half in zone 2's, then insert the drawers into the unit. 4. Select zone 1, select AIR FRY, set temperature to 390 degrees F/200 degrees C, and set time to 10 minutes. Select MATCH to match zone 2 settings to zone 1. Press the START/STOP button to begin cooking. 5. When the time reaches 5 minutes, press START/STOP to pause the unit. Remove the drawers and flip the chicken. Re-insert the drawers into the unit and press START/STOP to resume cooking. 6. When cooking is complete, remove the chicken meatballs and serve hot.

Serving Suggestion: Serve with fried cauliflower rice.

Variation Tip: You can use ground turkey instead.

Nutritional Information Per Serving: Calories 93 | Fat 3g | Sodium 369mg | Carbs 9g | Fiber 0g | Sugar 6g | Protein 9g

Chicken Cordon Bleu

Prep Time: 10 minutes | Cook Time: 20 minutes | Serves: 4

Ingredients:

4 boneless, skinless chicken breast halves (4 ounces each)
¼ teaspoon salt

¼ teaspoon pepper
4 slices deli ham
2 slices aged Swiss cheese, halved

1 cup panko breadcrumbs
Cooking spray

For the Sauce:

1 tablespoon all-purpose flour
½ cup 2% milk

¼ cup dry white wine
3 tablespoons finely shredded Swiss cheese

⅛ teaspoon salt
Dash pepper

Preparation:

1. Season both sides of the chicken breast halves with salt and pepper. You may need to thin the breasts with a mallet. 2. Place 1 slice of ham and half slice of cheese on top of each chicken breast half. 3. Roll the breast up and use toothpicks to secure it. 4. Sprinkle the breadcrumbs on top and spray lightly with the cooking oil. 5. Insert a crisper plate into each drawer. Divide the chicken between each drawer and insert the drawers into the unit. 6. Select zone 1, select AIR FRY, set temperature to 390 degrees F/200 degrees C, and set time to 7 minutes. Select MATCH to match zone 2 settings to zone 1. Press the START/STOP button to begin cooking. 7. When the time reaches 5 minutes, press START/STOP to pause the unit. Remove the drawers and flip the chicken. Re-insert the drawers into the unit and press START/STOP to resume cooking. 8. To make the sauce, mix the flour, wine, and milk together in a small pot until smooth. Bring to a boil over high heat, stirring frequently, for 1–2 minutes, or until the sauce has thickened. 9. Reduce the heat to medium. Add the cheese. Cook and stir for 2–3 minutes, or until the cheese has melted and the sauce has thickened and bubbled. Add salt and pepper to taste. Keep the sauce heated at a low temperature until ready to serve.

Serving Suggestion: Serve the chicken with the sauce drizzled over the top.

Variation Tip: You can use bacon instead of ham.

Nutritional Information Per Serving: Calories 272 | Fat 8g | Sodium 519mg | Carbs 14g | Fiber 2g | Sugar 1g | Protein 32g

Chapter 6 Beef, Pork, and Lamb Recipes

Pork with Green Beans and Potatoes

Prep Time: 10 minutes | Cook Time: 15 minutes | Serves: 4

Ingredients:

¼ cup Dijon mustard
2 tablespoons brown sugar
1 teaspoon dried parsley flake
½ teaspoon dried thyme

¼ teaspoons salt
¼ teaspoons black pepper
1¼ lbs. pork tenderloin
¾ lb. small potatoes halved

1 (12-oz) package green beans, trimmed
1 tablespoon olive oil
Salt and black pepper ground to taste

Preparation:

1. Preheat your Air Fryer Machine to 400 degrees F/200 degrees C. 2. Add mustard, parsley, brown sugar, salt, black pepper, and thyme in a large bowl, then mix well. 3. Add tenderloin to the spice mixture and coat well. 4. Toss potatoes with olive oil, salt, black pepper, and green beans in another bowl. 5. Place the prepared tenderloin in the crisper plate. 6. Return this crisper plate to the Zone 1 of the Ninja Foodi Dual Zone Air Fryer. 7. Choose the Air Fry mode for Zone 1 and set the temperature to 390 degrees F/200 degrees C and the time to 15 minutes. 8. Add potatoes and green beans to the Zone 2. 9. Choose the Air Fry mode for Zone 2 with 350 degrees F/175 degrees C and the time to 10 minutes. 10. Press the SYNC button to sync the finish time for both Zones. 11. Initiate cooking by pressing the START/STOP button. 12. Serve the tenderloin with Air Fried potatoes
Serving Suggestion: Serve with sautéed leeks or cabbages.
Variation Tip: Rub the tenderloins with garlic cloves before seasoning.
Nutritional Information Per Serving: Calories 400 | Fat 32g | Sodium 721mg | Carbs 2.6g | Fiber 0g | Sugar 0g | Protein 27.4g

Air Fryer Meatloaves

Prep Time: 10 minutes | Cook Time: 22 minutes | Serves: 4

Ingredients:

⅓ cup milk
2 tablespoons basil pesto
1 egg, beaten
1 garlic clove, minced

¼ teaspoons black pepper
1 lb. ground beef
⅓ cup panko bread crumbs
8 pepperoni slices

½ cup marinara sauce, warmed
1 tablespoon fresh basil, chopped

Preparation:

1. Mix pesto, milk, egg, garlic, and black pepper in a medium-sized bowl. 2. Stir in ground beef and bread crumbs, then mix. 3. Make the 4 small-sized loaves with this mixture and top them with 2 pepperoni slices. 4. Press the slices into the meatloaves. 5. Place the meatloaves in the two crisper plates. 6. Return the crisper plate to the Ninja Foodi Dual Zone Air Fryer. 7. Choose the Air Fry mode for Zone 1 and set the temperature to 390 degrees F/200 degrees C and the time to 22 minutes. 8. Select the "MATCH" button to copy the settings for Zone 2. 9. Initiate cooking by pressing the START/STOP button. 10. Top them with marinara sauce and basil to serve. 11. Serve warm.
Serving Suggestion: Serve with avocado dip.
Variation Tip: Add finely chopped carrots and zucchini to the meatloaf.
Nutritional Information Per Serving: Calories 316 | Fat 12.2g | Sodium 587mg | Carbs 12.2g | Fiber 1g | Sugar 1.8g | Protein 25.8g

Beef & Broccoli

Prep Time: 12 Minutes | Cook Time: 12 Minutes | Serves: 4

Ingredients:

12 ounces Teriyaki sauce, divided
½ tablespoon garlic powder
¼ cup soy sauce

1 pound raw sirloin steak, thinly sliced
2 cups broccoli, cut into florets
2 teaspoons olive oil

Salt and black pepper, to taste

Preparation:

1. Mix the Teriyaki sauce, salt, garlic powder, black pepper, soy sauce, and olive oil in a zip-lock bag. 2. Add the beef and let it marinate for 2 hours. 3. Drain the beef from the marinade. 4. Toss the broccoli with oil, teriyaki sauce, and salt and black pepper and place in the zone 1 basket. 5. Place the beef in both baskets and set it to SYNC button. 6. Hit START/STOP button and let the cooking cycle complete. 7. Once it's done, take out the beef and broccoli and serve with the leftover Teriyaki sauce and cooked rice.
Serving Suggestion: Serve it with mashed potatoes
Variation Tip: Use canola oil instead of olive oil
Nutritional Information Per Serving: Calories 344 | Fat 10g | Sodium 4285mg | Carbs 18.2 g | Fiber 1.5g | Sugar 13.3g | Protein 42g

Pork Chops with Brussels Sprouts

Prep Time: 15 minutes | Cook Time: 15 minutes | Serves: 4

Ingredients:

4 bone-in center-cut pork chop
Cooking spray
Salt, to taste

Black pepper, to taste
2 teaspoons olive oil
2 teaspoons pure maple syrup

2 teaspoons Dijon mustard
6 ounces Brussels sprouts, quartered

Preparation:

1. Rub pork chop with salt, ¼ teaspoons black pepper, and cooking spray. 2. Toss Brussels sprouts with mustard, syrup, oil, ¼ teaspoon of black pepper in a medium bowl. 3. Add pork chop to the crisper plate of Zone 1 of the Ninja Foodi Dual Zone Air Fryer. 4. Return the crisper plate to the Ninja Foodi Dual Zone Air Fryer. 5. Choose the Air Fry mode for Zone 1 and set the temperature to 400 degrees F/200 degrees C and the time to 15 minutes. 6. Add the Brussels sprouts to the crisper plate of Zone 2 and return it to the unit. 7. Choose the Air Fry mode for Zone 2 with 350 degrees F/175 degrees C and the time to 13 minutes. 8. Press the SYNC button to sync the finish time for both Zones. 9. Initiate cooking by pressing the START/STOP button. 10. Serve warm and fresh

Serving Suggestion: Serve with Greek salad and crispy bread.

Variation Tip: Rub the pork chops with garlic cloves before seasoning.

Nutritional Information Per Serving: Calories 336 | Fat 27.1g | Sodium 66mg | Carbs 1.1g | Fiber 0.4g | Sugar 0.2g | Protein 19.7g

Turkey and Beef Meatballs

Prep Time: 15 minutes | Cook Time: 24 minutes | Serves: 6

Ingredients:

1 medium shallot, minced
2 tablespoons olive oil
3 garlic cloves, minced
¼ cup panko crumbs
2 tablespoons whole milk

⅔ lb. lean ground beef
⅓ lb. bulk turkey sausage
1 large egg, lightly beaten
¼ cup parsley, chopped
1 tablespoon fresh thyme, chopped

1 tablespoon fresh rosemary, chopped
1 tablespoon Dijon mustard
½ teaspoon salt

Preparation:

1. Preheat your oven to 400 degrees F/200 degrees C. Place a medium non-stick pan over medium-high heat. 2. Add oil and shallot, then sauté for 2 minutes. 3. Toss in the garlic and cook for 1 minute. 4. Remove this pan from the heat. 5. Whisk panko with milk in a large bowl and leave it for 5 minutes. 6. Add cooked shallot mixture and mix well. 7. Stir in egg, parsley, turkey sausage, beef, thyme, rosemary, salt, and mustard. 8. Mix well, then divide the mixture into 1 ½-inch balls. 9. Divide these balls into the two crisper plates and spray them with cooking oil. 10. Return the crisper plates to the Ninja Foodi Dual Zone Air Fryer. 11. Choose the Air Fry mode for Zone 1 and set the temperature to 400 degrees F/200 degrees C and the time to 21 minutes. 12. Select the "MATCH" button to copy the settings for Zone 2. 13. Initiate cooking by pressing the START/STOP button. 14. Serve warm.

Serving Suggestion: Serve with fresh vegetable salad and marinara sauce.

Variation Tip: Add freshly chopped parsley and coriander for change of taste.

Nutritional Information Per Serving: Calories 551 | Fat 31g | Sodium 1329mg | Carbs 1.5g | Fiber 0.8g | Sugar 0.4g | Protein 64g

Steak in Air Fry

Prep Time: 15 Minutes | Cook Time: 20 Minutes | Serves: 1

Ingredients:

2 teaspoons canola oil

1 tablespoon Montreal Steak seasoning

1 pound beef steak

Preparation:

1. Season the steak on both sides with canola oil and then rub a generous amount of steak seasoning all over. 2. Put the steak in the air fryer basket in zone 1and set it to MAX CRISP at 450 degrees F/230 degrees C for 20-22 minutes. 3. After 7 minutes, hit pause, take out the basket to flip the steak and cover it with foil on top for the remaining 14 minutes. 4. Once done, serve the medium-rare steak after it has rested for 10 minutes. 5. Serve by cutting into slices. 6. Enjoy.

Serving Suggestion: Serve it with mashed potatoes

Variation Tip: Use vegetable oil instead of canola oil

Nutritional Information Per Serving: Calories 935 | Fat 37.2g | Sodium 1419mg | Carbs 0g | Fiber 0g | Sugar 0g | Protein 137.5 g

Pork Chops with Broccoli

Prep Time: 15 minutes | Cook Time: 13 minutes | Serves: 2

Ingredients:

2 (5 ounces) bone-in pork chops
2 tablespoons avocado oil
½ teaspoon paprika

½ teaspoon onion powder
½ teaspoon garlic powder
1 teaspoon salt

2 cups broccoli florets
2 garlic cloves, minced

Preparation:

1. Rub the pork chops with avocado oil, garlic, paprika, and spices. 2. Add pork chop to the crisper plate of Zone 1 in the Ninja Foodi Dual Zone Air Fryer. 3. Return the crisper plate to the Air Fryer. 4. Choose the Air Fry mode for Zone 1 and set the temperature to 400 degrees F/200 degrees C and the time to 12 minutes. 5. Add the broccoli to the Zone 2 drawer and return it to the unit. 6. Choose the Air Fry mode for Zone 2 with 375 degrees F/190 degrees C and the time to 13 minutes. 7. Press the SYNC button to sync the finish time for both Zones. 8. Initiate cooking by pressing the START/STOP button. 9. Flip the pork once cooked halfway through. 10. Cut the hardened butter into the cubes and place them on top of the pork chops. 11. Serve warm with crispy broccoli florets
Serving Suggestion: Serve with warm corn tortilla and crouton salad.
Variation Tip: Rub the pork chops with garlic cloves before seasoning.
Nutritional Information Per Serving: Calories 410 | Fat 17.8g | Sodium 619mg | Carbs 21g | Fiber 1.4g | Sugar 1.8g | Protein 38.4g

Beef Cheeseburgers

Prep Time: 15 minutes | Cook Time: 13 minutes | Serves: 4

Ingredients:

1 lb. ground beef
Salt, to taste
2 garlic cloves, minced
1 tablespoon soy sauce

Black pepper, to taste
4 American cheese slices
4 hamburger buns
Mayonnaise, to serve

Lettuce, to serve
Sliced tomatoes, to serve
Sliced red onion, to serve

Preparation:

1. Mix beef with soy sauce and garlic in a large bowl. 2. Make 4 patties of 4 inches in diameter. 3. Rub them with salt and black pepper on both sides. 4. Place the 2 patties in each of the crisper plate. 5. Return the crisper plate to the Ninja Foodi Dual Zone Air Fryer. 6. Choose the Air Fry mode for Zone 1 and set the temperature to 390 degrees F/200 degrees C and the time to 13 minutes. 7. Select the "MATCH" button to copy the settings for Zone 2. 8. Initiate cooking by pressing the START/STOP button. 9. Flip each patty once cooked halfway through, and resume cooking. 10. Add each patty to the hamburger buns along with mayo, tomatoes, onions, and lettuce. 11. Serve.
Serving Suggestion: Serve with tomato ketchup or chili sauce.
Variation Tip: Add breadcrumbs to the beef burger mixture for a crumbly texture.
Nutritional Information Per Serving: Calories 437 | Fat 28g | Sodium 1221mg | Carbs 22.3g | Fiber 0.9g | Sugar 8g | Protein 30.3g

Steak and Mashed Creamy Potatoes

Prep Time: 15 Minutes | Cook Time: 45 Minutes | Serves: 1

Ingredients:

2 Russet potatoes, peeled and cubed
¼ cup butter, divided
⅓ cup heavy cream

½ cup shredded Cheddar cheese
Salt and black pepper, to taste
1 New York strip steak, about a pound

1 teaspoon olive oil
Oil spray, for greasing

Preparation:

1. Rub the potatoes with salt and a teaspoon of olive oil. 2. Next, season the steak with salt and black pepper. 3. Place the potatoes in the zone 1 basket. 4. Oil spray the steak from both sides and then place it in the zone 2 basket. 5. Set Sync button. Once the cooking cycle is complete, take out the steak and potatoes. 6. Mash the potatoes and then add butter, heavy cream, and cheese along with salt and black pepper. 7. Serve the mashed potatoes with the steak. 8. Enjoy.
Serving Suggestion: Serve it with rice
Variation Tip: Use Parmesan instead of Cheddar
Nutritional Information Per Serving: Calories 1932 | Fat 85.2g | Sodium 3069mg | Carbs 82g | Fiber 10.3g | Sugar 5.3g | Protein 22.5g

Lamb Shank with Mushroom Sauce

Prep Time: 15 minutes | Cook Time: 35 minutes | Serves: 4

Ingredients:

20 mushrooms, chopped
2 red bell pepper, chopped
2 red onion, chopped
1 cup red wine

4 leeks, chopped
6 tablespoons balsamic vinegar
2 teaspoons black pepper
2 teaspoons salt

3 tablespoons fresh rosemary
6 garlic cloves
4 lamb shanks
3 tablespoons olive oil

Preparation:

1. Season the lamb shanks with salt, pepper, rosemary, and 1 teaspoon of olive oil. 2. Set half of the shanks in each of the crisper plate. 3. Return the crisper plate to the Ninja Foodi Dual Zone Air Fryer. 4. Choose the Air Fry mode for Zone 1 and set the temperature to 390 degrees F/200 degrees C and the time to 25 minutes. 5. Select the "MATCH" button to copy the settings for Zone 2. 6. Initiate cooking by pressing the START/STOP button. 7. Flip the shanks halfway through, and resume cooking. 8. Meanwhile, add and heat the remaining olive oil in a skillet. 9. Add onion and garlic to sauté for 5 minutes. 10. Add in mushrooms and cook for 5 minutes. 11. Add red wine and cook until it is absorbed 12. Stir all the remaining vegetables along with black pepper and salt. 13. Cook until vegetables are al dente. 14. Serve the air fried shanks with sautéed vegetable fry.
Serving Suggestion: Serve with sautéed zucchini and green beans.
Variation Tip: Rub the lamb shanks with lemon juice before seasoning.
Nutritional Information Per Serving: Calories 352 | Fat 9.1g | Sodium 1294mg | Carbs 3.9g | Fiber 1g | Sugar 1g | Protein 61g

Gochujang Brisket

Prep Time: 20 minutes | Cook Time: 55 minutes | Serves: 6

Ingredients:

½ tablespoons sweet paprika
½ teaspoon toasted sesame oil
2 lbs. beef brisket, cut into 4 pieces
Salt, to taste
⅛ cup Gochujang, Korean chili paste

Black pepper, to taste
1 small onion, diced
2 garlic cloves, minced
1 teaspoon Asian fish sauce
1 ½ tablespoons peanut oil, as needed

½ tablespoon fresh ginger, grated
¼ teaspoon red chili flakes
½ cup of water
1 tablespoon ketchup
1 tablespoon soy sauce

Preparation:

1. Thoroughly rub the beef brisket with olive oil, paprika, chili flakes, black pepper, and salt. 2. Cut the brisket in half, then divide the beef in the two crisper plate. 3. Return the crisper plate to the Ninja Foodi Dual Zone Air Fryer. 4. Choose the Air Fry mode for Zone 1 and set the temperature to 390 degrees F/200 degrees C and the time to 35 minutes. 5. Select the "MATCH" button to copy the settings for Zone 2. 6. Initiate cooking by pressing the START/STOP button. 7. Flip the brisket halfway through, and resume cooking. 8. Meanwhile, heat oil in a skillet and add ginger, onion, and garlic. 9. Sauté for 5 minutes, then add all the remaining ingredients. 10. Cook the mixture for 15 minutes approximately until well thoroughly mixed. 11. Serve the brisket with this sauce on top.
Serving Suggestion: Serve on top of boiled white rice.
Variation Tip: Add Worcestershire sauce and honey to taste.
Nutritional Information Per Serving: Calories 374 | Fat 25g | Sodium 275mg | Carbs 7.3g | Fiber 0g | Sugar 6g | Protein 12.3g

Short Ribs & Root Vegetables

Prep Time: 15 Minutes | Cook Time: 45 Minutes | Serves: 2

Ingredients:

1 pound beef short ribs, bone-in and trimmed
Salt and black pepper, to taste
2 tablespoons canola oil, divided

¼ cup red wine
3 tablespoons brown sugar
2 cloves garlic, peeled, minced

4 carrots, peeled, cut into 1-inch pieces
2 parsnips, peeled, cut into 1-inch pieces
½ cup pearl onions

Preparation:

1. Season the ribs with salt and black pepper and rub a small amount of canola oil on both sides. 2. Place the ribs in zone 1 basket of the air fryer. 3. Next, take a bowl and add the pearl onions, parsnips, carrots, garlic, brown sugar, red wine, salt, and black pepper. 4. Add the vegetable mixture to the zone 2 basket. 5. Press the Sync button. 6. Hit START/STOP button so the cooking cycle begins. 7. Once the cooking is complete, take out and serve. 8. Enjoy it hot.
Serving Suggestion: Serve it with mashed potatoes
Variation Tip: Use olive oil instead of canola oil
Nutritional Information Per Serving: Calories 1262 | Fat 98.6g | Sodium 595mg | Carbs 57g | Fiber 10.1g | Sugar 28.2g | Protein 35.8g

Chipotle Beef

Prep Time: 15 minutes | Cook Time: 18 minutes | Serves: 4

Ingredients:

1 lb. beef steak, cut into chunks
1 large egg

Chipotle Ranch Dip
¼ cup mayonnaise
¼ cup sour cream

½ cup parmesan cheese, grated
½ cup pork panko

1 teaspoon chipotle paste
½ teaspoon ranch dressing mix

½ teaspoon seasoned salt

¼ medium lime, juiced

Preparation:

1. Mix all the ingredients for chipotle ranch dip in a bowl. 2. Keep it in the refrigerator for 30 minutes. 3. Mix pork panko with salt and parmesan. 4. Beat egg in one bowl and spread the panko mixture in another flat bowl. 5. Dip the steak chunks in the egg first, then coat them with panko mixture. 6. Spread them in the two crisper plates and spray them with cooking oil. 7. Return the crisper plate to the Ninja Foodi Dual Zone Air Fryer. 8. Choose the Air Fry mode for Zone 1 and set the temperature to 390 degrees F/200 degrees C and the time to 18 minutes. 9. Select the "MATCH" button to copy the settings for Zone 2. 10. Initiate cooking by pressing the START/STOP button. 11. Serve with chipotle ranch and salt and pepper on top. Enjoy.
Serving Suggestion: Serve with tomato ketchup or chili sauce.
Variation Tip: Add crushed cornflakes for breading to get extra crisp.
Nutritional Information Per Serving: Calories 310 | Fat 17g | Sodium 271mg | Carbs 4.3g | Fiber 0.9g | Sugar 2.1g | Protein 35g

Zucchini Pork Skewers

Prep Time: 15 minutes | Cook Time: 23 minutes | Serves: 4

Ingredients:

1 large zucchini, cut 1" pieces
1 lb. boneless pork belly, cut into cubes
1 onion yellow, diced in squares
1 ½ cups grape tomatoes

1 garlic clove minced
1 lemon, juice only
¼ cup olive oil
2 tablespoons balsamic vinegar

1 teaspoon oregano
olive oil spray

Preparation:

1. Mix together balsamic vinegar, garlic, oregano lemon juice, and ¼ cup of olive oil in a suitable bowl. 2. Then toss in diced pork pieces and mix well to coat. 3. Leave the seasoned pork to marinate for 60 minutes in the refrigerator. 4. Take suitable wooden skewers for your Ninja Foodi Dual Zone Air Fryer's drawer, and then thread marinated pork and vegetables on each skewer in an alternating manner. 5. Place half of the skewers in each of the crisper plate and spray them with cooking oil. 6. Return the crisper plate to the Ninja Foodi Dual Zone Air Fryer. 7. Choose the Air Fry mode for Zone 1 and set the temperature to 390 degrees F/200 degrees C and the time to 23 minutes. 8. Select the "MATCH" button to copy the settings for Zone 2. 9. Initiate cooking by pressing the START/STOP button. 10. Flip the skewers once cooked halfway through, and resume cooking. 11. Serve warm.
Serving Suggestion: Serve with sautéed green beans and cherry tomatoes.
Variation Tip: Use honey glaze to baste the skewers.
Nutritional Information Per Serving: Calories 459 | Fat 17.7g | Sodium 1516mg | Carbs 1.7g | Fiber 0.5g | Sugar 0.4g | Protein 69.2g

Glazed Steak Recipe

Prep Time: 15 Minutes | Cook Time: 25 Minutes | Serves: 2

Ingredients:

1 pound beef steaks
½ cup, soy sauce
Salt and black pepper, to taste

1 tablespoon vegetable oil
1 teaspoon grated ginger
4 cloves garlic, minced

¼ cup brown sugar

Preparation:

1. Whisk together soy sauce, salt, pepper, vegetable oil, garlic, brown sugar, and ginger in a bowl. 2. Once a paste is made from the mixture, rub the steak with it and let it sit for 30 minutes. 3. Add the steak to the air fryer basket and set it to MAX CRISP mode at 400 degrees F/200 degrees C for 18-22 minutes. 4. After 10 minutes, hit START/STOP and take it out to flip and return to the air fryer. 5. Once the time is complete, take out the steak and let it rest. Serve by cutting into slices. 6. Enjoy.
Serving Suggestion: Serve it with mashed potatoes
Variation Tip: Use canola oil instead of vegetable oil
Nutritional Information Per Serving: Calories 563 | Fat 21 g | Sodium 156mg | Carbs 20.6g | Fiber 0.3 g | Sugar 17.8 g | Protein 69.4 g

Mustard Rubbed Lamb Chops

Prep Time: 15 minutes | Cook Time: 31 minutes | Serves: 4

Ingredients:

1 teaspoon Dijon mustard
1 teaspoon olive oil
½ teaspoon soy sauce

½ teaspoon garlic, minced
½ teaspoon cumin powder
½ teaspoon cayenne pepper

½ teaspoon Italian spice blend
⅛ teaspoon salt
4 pieces of lamb chops

Preparation:

1. Mix Dijon mustard, soy sauce, olive oil, garlic, cumin powder, cayenne pepper, Italian spice blend, and salt in a medium bowl and mix well. 2. Place lamb chops into a Ziploc bag and pour in the marinade. 3. Press the air out of the bag and seal tightly. 4. Press the marinade around the lamb chops to coat. 5. Keep then in the fridge and marinate for at least 30 minutes, up to overnight. 6. Place 2 chops in each of the crisper plate and spray them with cooking oil. 7. Return the crisper plate to the Ninja Foodi Dual Zone Air Fryer. 8. Select the Roast mode for Zone 1 and set the temperature to 350 degrees F/175 degrees C and the time to 27 minutes. 9. Select the "MATCH" button to copy the settings for Zone 2. 10. Initiate cooking by pressing the START/STOP button. 11. Flip the chops once cooked halfway through, and resume cooking. 12. Switch the Roast mode to Max Crisp mode and cook for 5 minutes. 13. Serve warm.

Serving Suggestion: Serve the chops with a dollop of cream cheese dip on top.

Variation Tip: Rub the lamb chops with balsamic vinegar or honey before seasoning.

Nutritional Information Per Serving: Calories 264 | Fat 17g | Sodium 129mg | Carbs 0.9g | Fiber 0.3g | Sugar 0g | Protein 27g

Chinese BBQ Pork

Prep Time: 15 Minutes | Cook Time: 25-35 Minutes | Serves: 2

Ingredients:

4 tablespoons soy sauce
¼ cup red wine
2 tablespoons oyster sauce
¼ tablespoon hoisin sauce

¼ cup honey
¼ cup brown sugar
Pinch of salt
Pinch of black pepper

1 teaspoon ginger garlic, paste
1 teaspoon five-spice powder
1.5 pounds pork shoulder, sliced

Preparation:

1. Take a bowl and mix all the sauce ingredients well. 2. Transfer half of it to a sauce pan and cook for 10 minutes, and then set it aside. 3. Let the pork marinate in the remaining sauce for 2 hours. 4. Place the pork slices in the air fryer basket in zone 1 and set it to AIR FRY mode at 450 degrees F/230 degrees C for 25 minutes. 5. Make sure the internal temperature is above 160 degrees F once cooked. 6. If not, add a few more minutes to the overall cooking time. 7. Once done, take it out and baste it with the cooked sauce. 8. Serve and Enjoy.

Serving Suggestion: Serve it with rice

Variation Tip: Skip the wine and add vinegar

Nutritional Information Per Serving: Calories 1239 | Fat 73 g | Sodium 2185 mg | Carbs 57.3 g | Fiber 0.4g | Sugar 53.7 g | Protein 81.5 g

Ham Burger Patties

Prep Time: 15 Minutes | Cook Time: 17 Minutes | Serves: 2

Ingredients:

1 pound ground beef
Salt and pepper, to taste
½ teaspoon red chili powder

¼ teaspoon coriander powder
2 tablespoons chopped onion
1 green chili, chopped

Oil spray for greasing
2 large potato wedges

Preparation:

1. Grease the air fryer baskets with oil. 2. Place the potato wedges into the zone 1 basket. 3. Add the minced beef, salt, pepper, chili powder, coriander powder, green chili, and chopped onion to a bowl and mix well. 4. With wet hands, make two burger patties out of the mixture and place in zone 2 of the air fryer. 5. Set the time for zone 1 to 12 minutes on AIR FRY mode at 400 degrees F/200 degrees C. 6. Select the MATCH button for zone 2. 7. Once the time is up, take the baskets out and flip the patties and shake the potato wedges. 8. Set zone 1 for 4 minutes at 400 degrees F/200 degrees C on AIR FRY. 9. Select the MATCH button for the second basket. 10. Once it's done, serve and enjoy.

Serving Suggestion: Serve with bread slices, cheese, pickles, lettuce, and onions

Variation Tip: None

Nutritional Information Per Serving: Calories 875 | Fat 21.5g | Sodium 622mg | Carbs 88g | Fiber 10.9 g | Sugar 3.4g | Protein 78.8g

Beef Ribs II

Prep Time: 20 Minutes | Cook Time: 1 Hour | Serves: 2

Ingredients:

For Marinade:

¼ cup olive oil

4 garlic cloves, minced

½ cup white wine vinegar

¼ cup soy sauce, reduced-sodium

¼ cup Worcestershire sauce

1 lemon juice

Salt and black pepper, to taste

2 tablespoons Italian seasoning

1 teaspoon smoked Paprika

2 tablespoons mustard

½ cup maple syrup

Meat Ingredients:

Oil spray, for greasing

8 beef ribs lean

Preparation:

1. Take a large bowl and add all the marinade ingredients and mix well then place into a zip lock bag along with the ribs. Let it sit for 4 hours. 2. Grease the air fryer baskets and divide the ribs into them. 3. Set zone 1 to AIR FRY mode at 220 degrees F/105 degrees C for 30 minutes. 4. Select MATCH button for zone 2. 5. After the time is up, select START/STOP and take out the baskets. 6. Flip the ribs and cook for 30 more minutes at 250 degrees F. 7. Once done, serve the juicy and tender ribs. 8. Enjoy.

Serving Suggestion: Serve it with mac and cheese

Variation Tip: Use garlic-infused oil instead of garlic cloves

Nutritional Information Per Serving: Calories 1927 | Fat 116g | Sodium 1394mg | Carbs 35.2g | Fiber 1.3g | Sugar29 g | Protein 172.3g

Pork Chops

Prep Time: 10 Minutes | Cook Time: 17 Minutes | Serves: 2

Ingredients:

1 tablespoon rosemary, chopped

Salt and black pepper, to taste

2 garlic cloves

1-inch ginger

2 tablespoons olive oil

8 pork chops

Preparation:

1. Take a blender and pulse rosemary, salt, pepper, garlic cloves, ginger, and olive oil. 2. Rub this marinade over the pork chops and let it rest for 1 hour. 3. Divide the chops into both the baskets. Set zone 1 to AIR FRY mode for 17 minutes. 4. Select the MATCH button for zone 2. 5. Once done, take out and serve hot.

Serving Suggestion: Serve with salad

Variation Tip: Use canola oil instead of olive oil

Nutritional Information Per Serving: Calories 1154 | Fat 93.8g | Sodium 225mg | Carbs 2.1g | Fiber0.8 g | Sugar 0g | Protein 72.2g

Yogurt Lamb Chops

Prep Time: 10 Minutes | Cook Time: 20 Minutes | Serves: 2

Ingredients:

1½ cups plain Greek yogurt

1 lemon, juice only

1 teaspoon ground cumin

1 teaspoon ground coriander

¾ teaspoon ground turmeric

¼ teaspoon ground allspice

10 rib lamb chops (1–1¼ inches thick cut)

2 tablespoons olive oil, divided

Preparation:

1. In a bowl, add all the ingredients and rub the chops well. Let it marinate for an hour in the refrigerator. 2. After an hour take out the chops and layer the air fryer baskets with parchment paper. 3. Divide the chops between both the baskets. 4. Set the time for zone 1 to 20 minutes at 400 degrees F/200 degrees C on AIR FRY. 5. Select the MATCH button for the zone 2 basket. 6. Hit START/STOP button and then wait for the chops to cook. 7. Once done, serve and enjoy.

Serving Suggestion: Serve over rice

Variation Tip: Use canola oil instead of olive oil

Nutritional Information Per Serving: Calories 1206 | Fat 66.7 g | Sodium 478mg | Carbs 10.6g | Fiber 1.2g | Sugar 6g | Protein 132.8g

Beef Ribs I

Prep Time: 10 Minutes | Cook Time: 15 Minutes | Serves: 2

Ingredients:

4 tablespoons BBQ spice rub
1 tablespoon kosher salt and black pepper

3 tablespoons brown sugar
2 pounds of beef ribs cut in thirds

1 cup BBQ sauce
Oil spray

Preparation:

1. In a small bowl, add salt, pepper, brown sugar, and BBQ spice rub. 2. Grease the ribs with oil spray from both sides and then rub it with BBQ the spice. 3. Divide the ribs into both baskets and set zone 1to AIR FRY mode at 375 degrees F/190 degrees C for 15 minutes. 4. Press MATCH for zone 2. 5. Hit START/STOP button and let the air fryer cook the ribs. 6. Once done, serve with a coating BBQ sauce.

Serving Suggestion: Serve it with salad and baked potato

Variation Tip: Use sea salt instead of kosher salt

Nutritional Information Per Serving: Calories 1081 | Fat 28.6 g | Sodium 1701mg | Carbs 58g | Fiber 0.8g | Sugar 45.7g | Protein 138 g

Spicy Lamb Chops

Prep Time: 15 Minutes | Cook Time: 15 Minutes | Serves: 4

Ingredients:

12 lamb chops, bone-in
Salt and black pepper, to taste
½ teaspoon lemon zest

1 tablespoon lemon juice
1 teaspoon paprika
1 teaspoon garlic powder

½ teaspoon Italian seasoning
¼ teaspoon onion powder

Preparation:

1. Add the lamb chops to the bowl and sprinkle with salt, garlic powder, Italian seasoning, onion powder, black pepper, lemon zest, lemon juice, and paprika. 2. Rub the chops well, and divide them between both the baskets of the air fryer. 3. Set zone 1 basket to 400 degrees F/200 degrees C, for 15 minutes on AIR FRY mode. 4. Select MATCH for zone 2 basket. 5. After 10 minutes, take out the baskets and flip the chops. Cook for the remaining minutes, and then serve.

Serving Suggestion: Serve it over rice

Variation Tip: None

Nutritional Information Per Serving: Calories 787 | Fat 45.3g | Sodium 1mg | Carbs 16.1g | Fiber 0.3g | Sugar 0.4g | Protein 75.3g

Bell Peppers with Sausages

Prep Time: 15 Minutes | Cook Time: 20 Minutes | Serves: 4

Ingredients:

6 beef or pork Italian sausages
4 bell peppers, whole

Oil spray, for greasing
2 cups cooked rice

1 cup sour cream

Preparation:

1. Put the bell peppers in the zone 1 basket and sausages in the zone 2 basket of the air fryer. 2. Set zone 1 to AIR FRY mode for 10 minutes at 400 degrees F/200 degrees C. 3. For zone 2 set it to 20 minutes at 375 degrees F/190 degrees C. 4. Hit the Sync button, so both finish at the same time. 5. After 5 minutes, take out the sausage basket and break or mince it with a plastic spatula and then place it back in. 6. Once done, serve the minced meat with bell peppers and serve over cooked rice with a dollop of sour cream.

Serving Suggestion: Serve it with salad

Variation Tip: Use olive oil instead of oil spray

Nutritional Information Per Serving: Calories 737 | Fat 21.1g | Sodium 124mg | Carbs 85.4g | Fiber 2.8g | Sugar 6.2g | Protein 48.2g

Korean BBQ Beef

Prep Time: 15 minutes | Cook Time: 30 minutes | Serves: 6

Ingredients:

For the Meat:

1 pound flank steak or thinly   sliced steak

¼ cup corn starch

Coconut oil spray

For the Sauce:

½ cup soy sauce or gluten-free soy sauce

½ cup brown sugar

2 tablespoons white wine vinegar

1 clove garlic, crushed

1 tablespoon hot chili sauce

1 teaspoon ground ginger

½ teaspoon sesame seeds

1 tablespoon corn starch

1 tablespoon water

Preparation:

1. To begin, prepare the steak. Thinly slice it in that toss it in the corn starch to be coated thoroughly. Spray the tops with some coconut oil. 2. Spray the crisping plates and drawers with the coconut oil. 3. Place the crisping plates into the drawers. Place the steak strips into each drawer. Insert both drawers into the unit. 4. Select zone 1, Select AIR FRY, set the temperature to 375 degrees F/190 degrees C, and set time to 30 minutes. Select MATCH to match zone 2 settings with zone 1. Press the START/STOP button to begin cooking. 5. While the steak is cooking, add the sauce ingredients EXCEPT for the corn starch and water to a medium saucepan. 6. Warm it up to a low boil, then whisk in the corn starch and water. 7. Carefully remove the steak and pour the sauce over. Mix well.

Serving Suggestion: Serve with rice and steamed veggies.

Variation Tip: You can use potato starch instead of corn starch.

Nutritional Information Per Serving: Calories 500 | Fat 19.8g | Sodium 680mg | Carbs 50.1g | Fiber 4.1g | Sugar 0g | Protein 27.9g

Garlic Butter Steaks

Prep Time: 120 minutes | Cook Time: 25 minutes | Serves: 2

Ingredients:

2 (6 ounces each) sirloin steaks or ribeyes

2 tablespoons unsalted butter

1 clove garlic, crushed

½ teaspoon dried parsley

½ teaspoon dried rosemary

Salt and pepper, to taste

Preparation:

1. Season the steaks with salt and pepper and set them to rest for about 2 hours before cooking. 2. Put the butter in a bowl. Add the garlic, parsley, and rosemary. Allow the butter to soften. 3. Whip together with a fork or spoon once the butter has softened. 4. When you're ready to cook, install a crisper plate in both drawers. Place the sirloin steaks in a single layer in each drawer. Insert the drawers into the unit. 5. Select zone 1, select AIR FRY, set temperature to 360 degrees F/180 degrees C, and set time to 10 minutes. Select MATCH to match zone 2 settings to zone 1. Select START/STOP to begin. 6. Once done, serve with the garlic butter.

Serving Suggestion: Serve with a side salad.

Variation Tip: You can use garlic powder instead of fresh.

Nutritional Information Per Serving: Calories 519 | Fat 36g | Sodium 245mg | Carbs 1g | Fiber 0g | Sugar 0g | Protein 46g

Roast Beef

Prep Time: 5 minutes | Cook Time: 35 minutes | Serves: 4

Ingredients:

2 pounds beef roast

1 tablespoon olive oil

1 medium onion (optional)

1 teaspoon salt

2 teaspoons rosemary and thyme, chopped (fresh or dried)

Preparation:

1. Combine the sea salt, rosemary, and oil in a large, shallow dish. 2. Using paper towels, pat the meat dry. Place it on a dish and turn it to coat the outside with the oil-herb mixture. 3. Peel the onion and split it in half (if using). 4. Install a crisper plate in both drawers. Place half the beef roast and half an onion in the zone 1 drawer and half the beef and half the onion in zone 2's, then insert the drawers into the unit. 5. Select zone 1, select AIR FRY, set temperature to 360 degrees F/180 degrees C, and set time to 22 minutes. Select MATCH to match zone 2 settings to zone 1. Press the START/STOP button to begin cooking. 6. When the time reaches 11 minutes, press START/STOP to pause the unit. Remove the drawers and flip the roast. Re-insert the drawers into the unit and press START/STOP to resume cooking.

Serving Suggestion: Serve with roasted veggies.

Variation Tip: You can use pork instead.

Nutritional Information Per Serving: Calories 463 | Fat 17.8g | Sodium 732mg | Carbs 2.8g | Fiber 0.7g | Sugar 1.2g | Protein 69g

Meatloaf

Prep Time: 10 minutes | Cook Time: 25 minutes | Serves: 6

Ingredients:

For the Meatloaf:

2 pounds ground beef

2 eggs, beaten

2 cups old-fashioned oats, regular or gluten-free

½ cup evaporated milk

½ cup chopped onion

½ teaspoon garlic salt

For the Sauce:

1 cup ketchup

¾ cup brown sugar, packed

¼ cup chopped onion

½ teaspoon liquid smoke

¼ teaspoon garlic powder

Olive oil cooking spray

Preparation:

1. In a large bowl, combine all the meatloaf ingredients. 2. Spray 2 sheets of foil with olive oil cooking spray. 3. Form the meatloaf mixture into a loaf shape, cut in half, and place each half on one piece of foil. 4. Roll the foil up a bit on the sides. Allow it to be slightly open. 5. Put all the sauce ingredients in a saucepan and whisk until combined on medium-low heat. This should only take 1–2 minutes 6. Install a crisper plate in both drawers. Place half the meatloaf in the zone 1 drawer and half in zone 2's, then insert the drawers into the unit. 7. Select zone 1, select AIR FRY, set temperature to 390 degrees F/200 degrees C, and set time to 25 minutes. Select MATCH to match zone 2 settings to zone 1. Press the START/STOP button to begin cooking. 8. When the time reaches 20 minutes, press START/STOP to pause the unit. Remove the drawers and coat the meatloaf with the sauce using a brush. Re-insert the drawers into the unit and press START/STOP to resume cooking. 9. Carefully remove and serve.

Serving Suggestion: Serve with salad or fried quinoa.

Variation Tip: You can use ground pork instead.

Nutritional Information Per Serving: Calories 727 | Fat 34g | Sodium 688mg | Carbs 57g | Fiber 3g | Sugar 34g | Protein 49g

Jerk-Rubbed Pork Loin With Carrots and Sage

Prep Time: 10 minutes | Cook Time: 35 minutes | Serves: 4

Ingredients:

1½ pounds pork loin

3 teaspoons canola oil, divided

2 tablespoons jerk seasoning

1-pound carrots, peeled, cut into 1-inch pieces

1 tablespoon honey

½ teaspoon kosher salt

½ teaspoon chopped fresh sage

Preparation:

1. Place the pork loin in a pan or a dish with a high wall. Using a paper towel, pat the meat dry. 2. Rub 2 teaspoons of canola oil evenly over the pork with your hands. Then spread the jerk seasoning evenly over it with your hands. 3. Allow the pork loin to marinate for at least 10 minutes or up to 8 hours in the refrigerator after wrapping it in plastic wrap or sealing it in a plastic bag. 4. Toss the carrots with the remaining canola oil and ½ teaspoon of salt in a medium mixing bowl. 5. Place a crisper plate in each of the drawers. Put the marinated pork loin in the zone 1 drawer and place it in the unit. Place the carrots in the zone 2 drawer and place the drawer in the unit. 6. Select zone 1 and select AIR FRY. Set the temperature to 390 degrees F/200 degrees C and the time setting to 25 minutes. Select zone 2 and select AIR FRY. Set the temperature to 390 degrees F/200 degrees C and the time setting to 16 minutes. Select SYNC. Press START/STOP to begin cooking. 7. Check the pork loin for doneness after the zones have finished cooking. When the internal temperature of the loin hits 145°F on an instant-read thermometer, the pork is ready. 8. Allow the pork loin to rest for at least 5 minutes on a plate or cutting board. 9. Combine the carrots and sage in a mixing bowl. 10. When the pork loin has rested, slice it into the desired thickness of slices and serve with the carrots.

Serving Suggestion: Serve with a side salad.

Variation Tip: You can use beef instead.

Nutritional Information Per Serving: Calories 500 | Fat 19.8g | Sodium 680mg | Carbs 50.1g | Fiber 4.1g | Sugar 0g | Protein 27.9g

Steak Fajitas With Onions and Peppers

Prep Time: 10 minutes | Cook Time: 15 minutes | Serves: 6

Ingredients:

1 pound steak
1 green bell pepper, sliced
1 yellow bell pepper, sliced

1 red bell pepper, sliced
½ cup sliced white onions
1 packet gluten-free fajita seasoning

Olive oil spray

Preparation:

1. Thinly slice the steak against the grain. These should be about ¼-inch slices. 2. Mix the steak with the peppers and onions. 3. Evenly coat with the fajita seasoning. 4. Install a crisper plate in both drawers. Place half the steak mixture in the zone 1 drawer and half in zone 2's, then insert the drawers into the unit. 5. Select zone 1, select AIR FRY, set temperature to 390 degrees F/200 degrees C, and set time to 15 minutes. Select MATCH to match zone 2 settings to zone 1. Press the START/STOP button to begin cooking. 6. When the time reaches 10 minutes, press START/STOP to pause the unit. Remove the drawers and flip the steak strips. Re-insert the drawers into the unit and press START/STOP to resume cooking. 7. Serve in warm tortillas.
Serving Suggestion: Serve with guacamole and salsa.
Variation Tip: You can use pork strips instead.
Nutritional Information Per Serving: Calories 305 | Fat 17g | Sodium 418mg | Carbs 15g | Fiber 2g | Sugar 4g | Protein 22g

Parmesan Pork Chops

Prep Time: 5 minutes | Cook Time: 20 minutes | Serves: 4

Ingredients:

4 boneless pork chops
2 tablespoons extra-virgin olive oil
½ cup freshly grated parmesan

1 teaspoon kosher salt
1 teaspoon paprika
1 teaspoon garlic powder

1 teaspoon onion powder
½ teaspoon freshly ground black pepper

Preparation:

1. Dry the pork chops with paper towels before brushing both sides with oil. 2. Combine the parmesan and spices in a medium mixing bowl. Coat the pork chops on both sides with the parmesan mixture. 3. Install a crisper plate in both drawers. Place half the pork chops in the zone 1 drawer and half in zone 2's, then insert the drawers into the unit. 4. Select zone 1, select AIR FRY, set temperature to 390 degrees F/200 degrees C, and set time to 20 minutes. Select MATCH to match zone 2 settings to zone 1. Press the START/STOP button to begin cooking. 5. When the time reaches 10 minutes, press START/STOP to pause the unit. Remove the drawers and flip the chicken. Re-insert the drawers into the unit and press START/STOP to resume cooking.
Serving Suggestion: Serve the pork chops with veggies.
Variation Tip: Use any kind of cheese you prefer.
Nutritional Information Per Serving: Calories 199 | Fat 10.8g | Sodium 663mg | Carbs 1.6g | Fiber 0.4g | Sugar 0.4g | Protein 23.9g

Breaded Pork Chops

Prep Time: 10 minutes | Cook Time: 10 minutes | Serves: 4

Ingredients:

4 boneless, center-cut pork chops, 1-inch thick
1 teaspoon Cajun seasoning

1½ cups cheese and garlic-flavored croutons
2 eggs

Cooking spray

Preparation:

1. Season both sides of the pork chops with the Cajun seasoning on a platter. 2. In a small food processor, pulse the croutons until finely chopped; transfer to a shallow plate. 3. In a separate shallow bowl, lightly beat the eggs. 4. Dip the pork chops in the egg, allowing any excess to drip off. Then place the chops in the crouton crumbs. Coat the chops in cooking spray. 5. Install a crisper plate in both drawers. Place half the pork chops in the zone 1 drawer and half in zone 2's, then insert the drawers into the unit. 6. Select zone 1, select ROAST, set temperature to 390 degrees F/200 degrees C, and set time to 10 minutes. Select MATCH to match zone 2 settings to zone 1. Press the START/STOP button to begin cooking. 7. When the time reaches 6 minutes, press START/STOP to pause the unit. Remove the drawers and flip the chops. Reinsert the drawers into the unit and press START/STOP to resume cooking. 8. When cooking is complete, serve and enjoy!
Serving Suggestion: Serve with a sauce of your choice.
Variation Tip: You can use beef chops instead.
Nutritional Information Per Serving: Calories 394 | Fat 18.1g | Sodium 428mg | Carbs 10g | Fiber 0.8g | Sugar 0.9g | Protein 44.7g

Juicy Pork Chops

Prep Time: 5 minutes | Cook Time: 15 minutes | Serves: 4

Ingredients:

4 thick-cut pork chops
Salt and pepper, to taste
2 tablespoons brown sugar

1 teaspoon chili powder
½ teaspoon paprika
1 teaspoon Italian seasoning

1 teaspoon garlic powder

Preparation:

1. Salt and pepper the pork chops. 2. Add the brown sugar, chili powder, paprika, Italian seasoning, and garlic powder to a small bowl. Combine well. Rub the mixture on the pork chops. 3. Install a crisper plate in both drawers. Place half the pork chops in the zone 1 drawer and half in zone 2's. Insert the drawers into the unit. 4. Select zone 1, select AIR FRY, set temperature to 400 degrees F/200 degrees C, and set time to 15 minutes. Select MATCH to match zone 2 settings to zone 1. Press the START/STOP button to begin cooking. 5. When the time reaches 11 minutes, press START/STOP to pause the unit. Remove the drawers and flip the chops. Re-insert the drawers into the unit and press START/STOP to resume cooking. 6. Serve and enjoy!
Serving Suggestion: Serve with a sauce of your choice.
Variation Tip: You can use beef chops instead.
Nutritional Information Per Serving: Calories 265 | Fat 10g | Sodium 86mg | Carbs 14g | Fiber 4.1g | Sugar 0g | Protein 29g

Rosemary and Garlic Lamb Chops

Time: 10 minutes (plus 1 hour for marinating) | Cook Time: 15 minutes | Serves: 4

Ingredients:

8 lamb chops
3 tablespoons olive oil
2 tablespoons chopped fresh rosemary

1 teaspoon garlic powder or 3 cloves garlic, minced
1 teaspoon salt, or to taste

½ teaspoon black pepper, or to taste

Preparation:

1. Dry the lamb chops with a paper towel. 2. Combine the olive oil, rosemary, garlic, salt, and pepper in a large mixing bowl. Toss the lamb in the marinade gently to coat it. Cover and set aside to marinate for 1 hour or up to overnight. 3. Install a crisper plate in both drawers. Place half the lamb chops in the zone 1 drawer and half in zone 2's, then insert the drawers into the unit. 4. Select zone 1, select AIR FRY, set temperature to 390 degrees F/200 degrees C, and set time to 15 minutes. Select MATCH to match zone 2 settings to zone 1. Press the START/STOP button to begin cooking. 5. When the time reaches 10 minutes, press START/STOP to pause the unit. Remove the drawers and flip the chops. Re-insert the drawers into the unit and press START/STOP to resume cooking. 6. Serve and enjoy!
Serving Suggestion: Serve with mashed potatoes.
Variation Tip: You can use other seasonings of your choice.
Nutritional Information Per Serving: Calories 427 | Fat 34g | Sodium 668mg | Carbs 1g | Fiber 1g | Sugar 1g | Protein 31g

Lamb Chops With Dijon Garlic

Prep Time: 10 minutes (plus 30 minutes for marinating) | Cook Time: 22 minutes | Serves: 4

Ingredients:

2 teaspoons Dijon mustard
2 teaspoons olive oil
1 teaspoon soy sauce

1 teaspoon garlic, minced
1 teaspoon cumin powder
1 teaspoon cayenne pepper

1 teaspoon Italian spice blend (optional)
¼ teaspoon salt
8 lamb chops

Preparation:

1. Combine the Dijon mustard, olive oil, soy sauce, garlic, cumin powder, cayenne pepper, Italian spice blend (optional), and salt in a medium mixing bowl. 2. Put the marinade in a large Ziploc bag. Add the lamb chops. Seal the bag tightly after pressing out the air. Coat the lamb in the marinade by shaking the bag and pressing the chops into the mixture. Place in the fridge for at least 30 minutes, or up to overnight, to marinate. 3. Install a crisper plate in both drawers. Place half the lamb chops in the zone 1 drawer and half in zone 2's, then insert the drawers into the unit. 4. Select zone 1, select AIR FRY, set temperature to 390 degrees F/200 degrees C, and set time to 22 minutes. Select MATCH to match zone 2 settings to zone 1. Press the START/STOP button to begin cooking. 5. When the time reaches 11 minutes, press START/STOP to pause the unit. Remove the drawers and flip the lamb chops. Re-insert the drawers into the unit and press START/STOP to resume cooking. 6. Serve and enjoy!
Serving Suggestion: Serve with grilled veggies.
Variation Tip: You can use pork chops.
Nutritional Information Per Serving: Calories 343 | Fat 15.1g | Sodium 380mg | Carbs 0.9 g | Fiber 0.3g | Sugar 0.1g | Protein 48.9g

Paprika Pork Chops

Prep Time: 10 minutes | Cook Time: 12 minutes | Serves: 4

Ingredients:

4 bone-in pork chops (6–8 ounces each)
1½ tablespoons brown sugar
1¼ teaspoons kosher salt
1 teaspoon dried Italian seasoning

1 teaspoon smoked paprika
¼ teaspoon garlic powder
¼ teaspoon onion powder
¼ teaspoon black pepper

1 teaspoon sweet paprika
3 tablespoons butter, melted
2 tablespoons chopped fresh parsley
Cooking spray

Preparation:

1. In a small mixing bowl, combine the brown sugar, salt, Italian seasoning, smoked paprika, garlic powder, onion powder, black pepper, and sweet paprika. Mix thoroughly. 2. Brush the pork chops on both sides with the melted butter. 3. Rub the spice mixture all over the meat on both sides. 4. Install a crisper plate in both drawers. Place half the chops in the zone 1 drawer and half in zone 2's, then insert the drawers into the unit. 5. Select zone 1, select AIR FRY, set temperature to 390 degrees F/200 degrees C, and set time to 12 minutes. Select MATCH to match zone 2 settings to zone 1. Press the START/STOP button to begin cooking. 6. When the time reaches 10 minutes, press START/STOP to pause the unit. Remove the drawers and flip the chops. Re-insert the drawers into the unit and press START/STOP to resume cooking. 7. Serve and enjoy!

Serving Suggestion: Serve with a side salad.

Variation Tip: You can use lamb chops instead.

Nutritional Information Per Serving: Calories 338 | Fat 21.2g | Sodium 1503mg | Carbs 5.1g | Fiber 0.3g | Sugar 4.6g | Protein 29.3g

Tomahawk Steak

Prep Time: 20 minutes | Cook Time: 12 minutes | Serves: 4

Ingredients:

4 tablespoons butter, softened
2 cloves garlic, minced
2 teaspoons chopped fresh parsley

1 teaspoon chopped chives
1 teaspoon chopped fresh thyme
1 teaspoon chopped fresh rosemary

2 (2 pounds each) bone-in ribeye steaks
Kosher salt, to taste
Freshly ground black pepper, to taste

Preparation:

1. In a small bowl, combine the butter and herbs. Place the mixture in the center of a piece of plastic wrap and roll it into a log. Twist the ends together to keep it tight and refrigerate until hardened, about 20 minutes. 2. Season the steaks on both sides with salt and pepper. 3. Install a crisper plate in both drawers. Place one steak in the zone 1 drawer and one in zone 2's, then insert the drawers into the unit. 4. Select zone 1, select AIR FRY, set temperature to 390 degrees F/200 degrees C, and set time to 12 minutes. Select MATCH to match zone 2 settings to zone 1. Press the START/STOP button to begin cooking. 5. When the time reaches 10 minutes, press START/STOP to pause the unit. Remove the drawers and flip the steaks. Add the herb-butter to the tops of the steaks. Re-insert the drawers into the unit and press START/STOP to resume cooking. 6. Serve and enjoy!

Serving Suggestion: Serve with fries and a salad.

Variation Tip: You can add seasonings of your choice.

Nutritional Information Per Serving: Calories 338 | Fat 21.2g | Sodium 1503mg | Carbs 5.1g | Fiber 0.3g | Sugar 4.6g | Protein 29.3g

Chapter 7 Dessert Recipes

Apple Hand Pies

Prep Time: 15 minutes | Cook Time: 21 minutes | Serves: 8

Ingredients:

8 tablespoons butter, softened
12 tablespoons brown sugar
2 teaspoons cinnamon, ground
4 medium Granny Smith apples, diced

2 teaspoons cornstarch
4 teaspoons cold water
1 (14-oz) package pastry, 9-inch crust pie
Cooking spray

1 tablespoon grapeseed oil
½ cup powdered sugar
2 teaspoons milk

Preparation:

1. Toss apples with brown sugar, butter, and cinnamon in a suitable skillet. 2. Place the skillet over medium heat and stir cook for 5 minutes. 3. Mix cornstarch with cold water in a small bowl. 4. Add cornstarch mixture into the apple and cook for 1 minute until it thickens. 5. Remove this filling from the heat and allow it to cool. 6. Unroll the pie crust and spray on a floured surface. 7. Cut the dough into 16 equal rectangles. 8. Wet the edges of the 8 rectangles with water and divide the apple filling at the center of these rectangles. 9. Place the other 8 rectangles on top and crimp the edges with a fork, then make 2-3 slashes on top. 10. Place 4 small pies in each of the crisper plate. 11. Return the crisper plate to the Ninja Foodi Dual Zone Air Fryer. 12. Choose the Air Fry mode for Zone 1 and set the temperature to 390 degrees F/200 degrees C and the time to 17 minutes. 13. Select the "MATCH" button to copy the settings for Zone 2. 14. Initiate cooking by pressing the START/STOP button. 15. Flip the pies once cooked halfway through, and resume cooking. 16. Meanwhile, mix sugar with milk. 17. Pour this mixture over the apple pies. 18. Serve fresh.
Serving Suggestion: Serve with apple sauce.
Variation Tip: Add shredded nuts and coconuts to the filling.
Nutritional Information Per Serving: Calories 284 | Fat 16g | Sodium 252mg | Carbs 31.6g | Fiber 0.9g | Sugar 6.6g | Protein 3.7g

Walnuts Fritters

Prep Time: 15 minutes | Cook Time: 15 minutes | Serves: 6

Ingredients:

1 cup all-purpose flour
½ cup walnuts, chopped
¼ cup white sugar
¼ cup milk

1 egg
1 ½ teaspoons baking powder
1 pinch salt
Cooking spray

2 tablespoons white sugar
½ teaspoon ground cinnamon

Glaze:

½ cup confectioners' sugar
1 tablespoon milk

½ teaspoon caramel extract
¼ teaspoons ground cinnamon

Preparation:

1. Layer both crisper plate with parchment paper. 2. Grease the parchment paper with cooking spray. 3. Whisk flour with milk, ¼ cup of sugar, egg, baking powder, and salt in a small bowl. 4. Separately mix 2 tablespoons of sugar with cinnamon in another bowl, toss in walnuts and mix well to coat. 5. Stir in flour mixture and mix until combined. 6. Drop the fritters mixture using a cookie scoop into the two crisper plate. 7. Return the crisper plate to the Ninja Foodi Dual Zone Air Fryer. 8. Choose the Air Fry mode for Zone 1 and set the temperature to 375 degrees F/190 degrees C and the time to 15 minutes. 9. Select the "MATCH" button to copy the settings for Zone 2. 10. Initiate cooking by pressing the START/STOP button. 11. Flip the fritters once cooked halfway through, then resume cooking. 12. Meanwhile, whisk milk, caramel extract, confectioners' sugar, and cinnamon in a bowl. 13. Transfer fritters to a wire rack and allow them to cool. 14. Drizzle with a glaze over the fritters.
Serving Suggestion: Serve with butter pecan ice cream or strawberry jam.
Variation Tip: Add maple syrup on top.
Nutritional Information Per Serving: Calories 391 | Fat 24g | Sodium 142mg | Carbs 38.5g | Fiber 3.5g | Sugar 21g | Protein 6.6g

Air Fried Bananas

Prep Time: 10 minutes | Cook Time: 13 minutes | Serves: 4

Ingredients:

4 bananas, sliced

1 avocado oil cooking spray

Preparation:

1. Spread the banana slices in the two crisper plates in a single layer. 2. Drizzle avocado oil over the banana slices. 3. Return the crisper plate to the Ninja Foodi Dual Zone Air Fryer. 4. Choose the Air Fry mode for Zone 1 and set the temperature to 350 degrees F/175 degrees C and the time to 13 minutes. 5. Select the "MATCH" button to copy the settings for Zone 2. 6. Initiate cooking by pressing the START/STOP button. 7. Serve.
Serving Suggestion: Serve with a dollop of vanilla ice-cream.
Variation Tip: Drizzle chopped nuts on top of the bananas.
Nutritional Information Per Serving: Calories 149 | Fat 1.2g | Sodium 3mg | Carbs 37.6g | Fiber 5.8g | Sugar 29g | Protein 1.1g

Air Fried Beignets

Prep Time: 15 minutes | Cook Time: 17 minutes | Serves: 6

Ingredients:

Cooking spray
¼ cup white sugar
⅛ cup water
½ cup all-purpose flour

1 large egg, separated
1 ½ teaspoons butter, melted
½ teaspoon baking powder
½ teaspoon vanilla extract

1 pinch salt
2 tablespoons confectioners' sugar, or to taste

Preparation:

1. Beat flour with water, sugar, egg yolk, baking powder, butter, vanilla extract, and salt in a large bowl until lumps-free. 2. Beat egg whites in a separate bowl and beat using an electric hand mixer until it forms soft peaks. 3. Add the egg white to the flour batter and mix gently until fully incorporated. 4. Divide the dough into small beignets and place them in the crisper plate. 5. Return the crisper plate to the Ninja Foodi Dual Zone Air Fryer. 6. Choose the Air Fry mode for Zone 1 and set the temperature to 390 degrees F/200 degrees C and the time to 17 minutes. 7. Select the "MATCH" button to copy the settings for Zone 2. 8. Initiate cooking by pressing the START/STOP button. 9. And cook for another 4 minutes. Dust the cooked beignets with sugar. 10. Serve.

Serving Suggestion: Serve with a dollop of sweet cream dip.

Variation Tip: Add chopped raisins and nuts to the dough.

Nutritional Information Per Serving: Calories 327 | Fat 14.2g | Sodium 672mg | Carbs 47.2g | Fiber 1.7g | Sugar 24.8g | Protein 4.4g

Biscuit Doughnuts

Prep Time: 15 minutes | Cook Time: 15 minutes | Serves: 8

Ingredients:

½ cup white sugar
1 teaspoon cinnamon

½ cup powdered sugar
1 can pre-made biscuit dough

Coconut oil
Melted butter to brush biscuits

Preparation:

1. Place all the biscuits on a cutting board and cut holes in the center of each biscuit using a cookie cutter. 2. Grease the crisper plate with coconut oil. 3. Place the biscuits in the two crisper plates while keeping them 1 inch apart. 4. Return the crisper plates to the Ninja Foodi Dual Zone Air Fryer. 5. Choose the Air Fry mode for Zone 1 and set the temperature to 375 degrees F/190 degrees C and the time to 15 minutes. 6. Select the "MATCH" button to copy the settings for Zone 2. 7. Initiate cooking by pressing the START/STOP button. 8. Brush all the donuts with melted butter and sprinkle cinnamon and sugar on top. 9. Air fry these donuts for one minute more. 10. Enjoy!

Serving Suggestion: Serve the doughnuts with chocolate syrup on top.

Variation Tip: Inject strawberry jam into each doughnut.

Nutritional Information Per Serving: Calories 192 | Fat 9.3g | Sodium 133mg | Carbs 27.1g | Fiber 1.4g | Sugar 19g | Protein 3.2g

Zesty Cranberry Scones

Prep Time: 10 minutes | Cook Time: 16 minutes | Serves: 8

Ingredients:

4 cups of flour
½ cup brown sugar
2 tablespoons baking powder
½ teaspoon ground nutmeg

½ teaspoon salt
½ cup butter, chilled and diced
2 cups fresh cranberry
⅔ cup sugar

2 tablespoons orange zest
1 ¼ cups half and half cream
2 eggs

Preparation:

1. Whisk flour with baking powder, salt, nutmeg, and both the sugars in a bowl. 2. Stir in egg and cream, mix well to form a smooth dough. 3. Fold in cranberries along with the orange zest. 4. Knead this dough well on a work surface. 5. Cut 3-inch circles out of the dough. 6. Divide the scones in the crisper plates and spray them with cooking oil. 7. Return the crisper plates to the Ninja Foodi Dual Zone Air Fryer. 8. Choose the Air Fry mode for Zone 1 and set the temperature to 375 degrees F/190 degrees C and the time to 16 minutes. 9. Select the "MATCH" button to copy the settings for Zone 2. 10. Initiate cooking by pressing the START/STOP button. 11. Flip the scones once cooked halfway and resume cooking. 12. Enjoy!

Serving Suggestion: Serve with cranberry jam on the side.

Variation Tip: Add raisins instead of cranberries to the dough.

Nutritional Information Per Serving: Calories 204 | Fat 9g | Sodium 91mg | Carbs 27g | Fiber 2.4g | Sugar 15g | Protein 1.3g

Apple Nutmeg Flautas

Prep Time: 10 minutes | Cook Time: 8 minutes | Serves: 8

Ingredients:

¼ cup light brown sugar
⅛ cup all-purpose flour
¼ teaspoon ground cinnamon
Nutmeg, to taste

4 apples, peeled, cored & sliced
½ lemon, juice, and zest
6 (10-inch) flour tortillas
Vegetable oil

Caramel sauce
Cinnamon sugar

Preparation:

1. Mix brown sugar with cinnamon, nutmeg, and flour in a large bowl. 2. Toss in apples in lemon juice. Mix well. 3. Place a tortilla at a time on a flat surface and add ½ cup of the apple mixture to the tortilla. 4. Roll the tortilla into a burrito and seal it tightly and hold it in place with a toothpick. 5. Repeat the same steps with the remaining tortillas and apple mixture. 6. Place two apple burritos in each of the crisper plate and spray them with cooking oil. 7. Return the crisper plates to the Ninja Foodi Dual Zone Air Fryer. 8. Choose the Air Fry mode for Zone 1 and set the temperature to 400 degrees F/200 degrees C and the time to 8 minutes. 9. Select the "MATCH" button to copy the settings for Zone 2. 10. Initiate cooking by pressing the START/STOP button. 11. Flip the burritos once cooked halfway through, then resume cooking. 12. Garnish with caramel sauce and cinnamon sugar. 13. Enjoy!

Serving Suggestion: Serve with maple syrup on the side.
Variation Tip: Add orange juice and zest for change of taste.
Nutritional Information Per Serving: Calories 157 | Fat 1.3g | Sodium 27mg | Carbs 1.3g | Fiber 1g | Sugar 2.2g | Protein 8.2g

Apple Crisp

Prep Time: 15 minutes | Cook Time: 14 minutes | Serves: 8

Ingredients:

3 cups apples, chopped
1 tablespoon pure maple syrup
2 teaspoons lemon juice

3 tablespoons all-purpose flour
⅓ cup quick oats
¼ cup brown sugar

2 tablespoons light butter, melted
½ teaspoon cinnamon

Preparation:

1. Toss the chopped apples with 1 tablespoon of all-purpose flour, cinnamon, maple syrup, and lemon juice in a suitable bowl. 2. Divide the apples in the two air fryer baskets with their crisper plates. 3. Whisk oats, brown sugar, and remaining all-purpose flour in a small bowl. 4. Stir in melted butter, then divide this mixture over the apples. 5. Return the crisper plate to the Ninja Foodi Dual Zone Air Fryer. 6. Select the Bake mode for Zone 1 and set the temperature to 375 degrees F/190 degrees C and the time to 14 minutes. 7. Select the "MATCH" button to copy the settings for Zone 2. 8. Initiate cooking by pressing the START/STOP button. 9. Enjoy fresh.

Serving Suggestion: Serve with a warming cup of hot chocolate.
Variation Tip: Use crushed cookies or graham crackers instead of oats.
Nutritional Information Per Serving: Calories 258 | Fat 12.4g | Sodium 79mg | Carbs 34.3g | Fiber 1g | Sugar 17g | Protein 3.2g

Chocolate Chip Muffins

Prep Time: 12 Minutes | Cook Time: 15 Minutes | Serves: 2

Ingredients:

Salt, pinch
2 eggs
⅓ cup brown sugar

⅓ cup butter
4 tablespoons milk
¼ teaspoon vanilla extract

½ teaspoon baking powder
1 cup all-purpose flour
1 pouch chocolate chips, 35 grams

Preparation:

1. Take 4 oven-safe ramekins that are the size of a cup and layer them with muffin papers. 2. In a bowl, with an electric beater mix the eggs, brown sugar, butter, milk, and vanilla extract. 3. In another bowl, mix the flour, baking powder, and salt. 4. Mix the dry ingredients into the wet ingredients slowly. 5. Fold in the chocolate chips and mix them in well. 6. Divide this batter into 4 ramekins and place them into both the baskets. 7. Set the time for zone 1 to 15 minutes at 350 degrees F/175 degrees C on AIR FRY mode. 8. Select the MATCH button for the zone 2 basket. 9. If they are not completely done after 15 minutes, AIR FRY for another minute. 10. Once it is done, serve.

Serving Suggestion: Serve it with chocolate syrup drizzle
Variation Tip: None
Nutritional Information Per Serving: Calories 757 | Fat 40.3g | Sodium 426mg | Carbs 85.4g | Fiber 2.2g | Sugar 30.4g | Protein 14.4g

Oreo Rolls

Prep Time: 10 minutes | Cook Time: 8 minutes | Serves: 9

Ingredients:

1 crescent sheet roll
9 Oreo cookies

Cinnamon powder, to serve
Powdered sugar, to serve

Preparation:

1. Spread the crescent sheet roll and cut it into 9 equal squares. 2. Place one cookie at the center of each square. 3. Wrap each square around the cookies and press the ends to seal. 4. Place half of the wrapped cookies in each crisper plate. 5. Return the crisper plates to the Ninja Foodi Dual Zone Air Fryer. 6. Select the Bake mode for Zone 1 and set the temperature to 360 degrees F/180 degrees C and the time to 4-6 minutes. 7. Select the "MATCH" button to copy the settings for Zone 2. 8. Initiate cooking by pressing the START/STOP button. 9. Check for the doneness of the cookie rolls if they are golden brown, else cook 1-2 minutes more. 10. Garnish the rolls with sugar and cinnamon. 11. Serve.

Serving Suggestion: Serve a cup of spice latte or hot chocolate.

Variation Tip: Dip the rolls in melted chocolate for a change of taste.

Nutritional Information Per Serving: Calories 175 | Fat 13.1g | Sodium 154mg | Carbs 14g | Fiber 0.8g | Sugar 8.9g | Protein 0.7g

Chocolate Chip Cake

Prep Time: 12 Minutes | Cook Time: 15 Minutes | Serves: 4

Ingredients:

Salt, pinch
2 eggs, whisked
½ cup brown sugar
½ cup butter, melted

10 tablespoons almond milk
¼ teaspoon vanilla extract
½ teaspoon baking powder
1 cup all-purpose flour

1 cup chocolate chips
½ cup cocoa powder

Preparation:

1. Take 2 round baking pans that fit inside the baskets of the air fryer and line them with baking paper. 2. In a bowl with an electric beater, mix the eggs, brown sugar, butter, almond milk, and vanilla extract. 3. In a second bowl, mix the flour, cocoa powder, baking powder, and salt. 4. Slowly add the dry ingredients to the wet ingredients. 5. Fold in the chocolate chips and mix well with a spoon or spatula. 6. Divide this batter into the round baking pans. 7. Set the time for zone 1 to 16 minutes at 350 degrees F/175 degrees C on AIR FRY mode. 8. Select the MATCH button for the zone 2 basket. 9. After the time is up, check. 10. If they're not done, let them AIR FRY for one more minute. 11. Once it is done, serve.

Serving Suggestion: Serve it with chocolate syrup drizzle

Variation Tip: Use baking soda instead of baking powder

Nutritional Information Per Serving: Calories 736 | Fat 45.5g | Sodium 356mg | Carbs 78.2g | Fiber 6.1g | Sugar 32.7g | Protein 11.5 g

Bread Pudding

Prep Time: 12 Minutes | Cook Time: 8-12 Minutes | Serves: 2

Ingredients:

Nonstick spray, for greasing ramekins
2 slices of white bread, crumbled
4 tablespoons white sugar

5 large eggs
½ cup cream
Salt, pinch

⅓ teaspoon cinnamon powder

Preparation:

1. Take a bowl and whisk eggs in it. 2. Add sugar and salt to the eggs and whisk it all well. 3. Then add cream and use a hand beater to incorporate the ingredients. 4. Next add cinnamon, and the crumbled white bread. 5. Mix it well and add into two round shaped baking pans. 6. Place each baking pan in the air fryer basket. 7. Set zone 1 to AIR FRY mode at 350 degrees F/175 degrees C for 8-12 minutes. 8. Press MATCH button for zone 2. 9. Once it's cooked, serve.

Serving Suggestion: Serve it with coffee

Variation Tip: Use brown sugar instead of white sugar

Nutritional Information Per Serving: Calories 331 | Fat 16.1g | Sodium 331mg | Carbs 31g | Fiber 0.2g | Sugar 26.2g | Protein 16.2g

Mini Strawberry and Cream Pies

Prep Time: 12 Minutes | Cook Time: 10 Minutes | Serves: 2

Ingredients:

1 box store-bought pie dough, Trader Joe's
1 cup strawberries, cubed

3 tablespoons cream, heavy
2 tablespoons almonds

1 egg white, for brushing

Preparation:

1. Take the store-bought pie dough and flatten it on a surface. 2. Use a round cutter to cut it into 3-inch circles. 3. Brush the dough with egg white all around the edges. 4. Now add almonds, strawberries, and cream in a tiny amount in the center of the dough, and top it with another dough circle. 5. Press the edges with a fork to seal it. 6. Make a slit in the middle of the pie and divide them into the baskets. 7. Set zone 1 to AIR FRY mode 360 degrees F/180 degrees C for 10 minutes. 8. Select MATCH for zone 2 basket. 9. Once done, serve.

Serving Suggestion: Serve it with vanilla ice-cream
Variation Tip: Use orange zest instead of lemon zest
Nutritional Information Per Serving: Calories 203 | Fat 12.7g | Sodium 193mg | Carbs 20g | Fiber 2.2g | Sugar 5.8g | Protein 3.7g

Mini Blueberry Pies

Prep Time: 12 Minutes | Cook Time: 10 Minutes | Serves: 2

Ingredients:

1 box store-bought pie dough, Trader Joe's
¼ cup blueberry jam

1 teaspoon lemon zest
1 egg white, for brushing

Preparation:

1. Take the store-bought pie dough and cut it into 3-inch circles. 2. Brush the dough with egg white all around the edges. 3. Now add blueberry jam and zest in the middle and top it with another circle. 4. Press the edges with a fork to seal it. 5. Make a slit in the middle of each pie and divide them between the baskets. 6. Set zone 1 to AIR FRY mode 360 degrees F/180 degrees C for 10 minutes. 7. Select the MATCH button for zone 2. 8. Once cooked, serve.

Serving Suggestion: Serve it with vanilla ice-cream
Variation Tip: Use orange zest instead of lemon zest
Nutritional Information Per Serving: Calories 234 | Fa t8.6g | Sodium 187 mg | Carbs 38.2 g | Fiber 0.1g | Sugar 13.7g | Protein 2g

Lemony Sweet Twists

Prep Time: 15 Minutes | Cook Time: 9 Minutes | Serves: 2

Ingredients:

1 box store-bought puff pastry
½ teaspoon lemon zest

1 tablespoon lemon juice
2 teaspoons brown sugar

Salt, pinch
2 tablespoons Parmesan cheese, freshly grated

Preparation:

1. Put the puff pastry dough on a clean work surface. 2. In a bowl, combine Parmesan cheese, brown sugar, salt, lemon zest, and lemon juice. 3. Press this mixture into both sides of the dough. 4. Now, cut the pastry into 1" x 4" strips. 5. Twist 2 times from each end. 6. Place the strips into the air fryer baskets. 7. Select zone 1 to AIR FRY mode at 400 degrees F/200 degrees C for 9-10 minutes. 8. Select MATCH for zone 2 basket. 9. Once cooked, serve and enjoy.

Serving Suggestion: Serve them with champagne
Variation Tip: None
Nutritional Information Per Serving: Calories 156 | Fat 10g | Sodium 215mg | Carbs 14g | Fiber 0.4g | Sugar 3.3g | Protein 2.8g

Air Fryer Sweet Twists

Prep Time: 15 Minutes | Cook Time: 9 Minutes | Serves: 2

Ingredients:

1 box store-bought puff pastry
½ teaspoon cinnamon

½ teaspoon sugar
½ teaspoon black sesame seeds

Salt, pinch
2 tablespoons Parmesan cheese, freshly grated

Preparation:

1. Place the dough on a work surface. 2. Take a small bowl and mix in cheese, sugar, salt, sesame seeds, and cinnamon. 3. Press this mixture on both sides of the dough. 4. Now, cut the pastry into 1" x 3" strips. 5. Twist each of the strips twice from each end. 6. Transfer them to both the air fryer baskets. 7. Select zone 1 to AIR FRY mode at 400 degrees F/200 degrees C for 9-10 minutes. 8. Select the MATCH button for the zone 2 basket. 9. Once cooked, serve.

Serving Suggestion: Serve it with champagne
Variation Tip: None
Nutritional Information Per Serving: Calories 140 | Fat9.4g | Sodium 142mg | Carbs 12.3g | Fiber 0.8 g | Sugar 1.2g | Protein 2g

Fudge Brownies

Prep Time: 20 Minutes | Cook Time: 16 Minutes | Serves: 4

Ingredients:

½ cup all-purpose flour
¼ cup unsweetened cocoa powder
¾ teaspoon kosher salt
2 large eggs, whisked

1 tablespoon almond milk
½ cup brown sugar
½ cup packed white sugar
½ tablespoon vanilla extract

8 ounces semisweet chocolate chips, melted
½ cup unsalted butter, melted

Preparation:

1. Take a medium bowl, and use a hand beater to whisk together eggs, milk, both the sugars and vanilla. 2. In a separate microwave-safe bowl, mix the melted butter and chocolate and microwave it for 30 seconds to melt the chocolate. 3. Add all the dry ingredients to the chocolate mixture. 4. Slowly add the egg mixture to the bowl. 5. Spray a reasonable round baking pan and pour the batter into the pan. 6. Select the AIR FRY mode and adjust the setting the temperature to 300 degrees F/150 degrees C, for 30 minutes. 7. Check it after 30 minutes and if not done, cook for 10 more minutes. 8. Once it's done, take it out and let it cool before serving. 9. Enjoy.

Serving Suggestion: Serve it with a dollop of the vanilla ice cream
Variation Tip: Use dairy milk instead of almond milk
Nutritional Information Per Serving: Calories 760 | Fat 43.3 g | Sodium 644mg | Carbs 93.2g | Fiber 5.3g | Sugar 70.2g | Protein 6.2g

Churros

Prep Time: 10 minutes | Cook Time: 10 minutes | Serves: 8

Ingredients:

1 cup water
⅓ cup unsalted butter, cut into cubes
2 tablespoons granulated sugar

¼ teaspoon salt
1 cup all-purpose flour
2 large eggs

1 teaspoon vanilla extract
Cooking oil spray

For the Cinnamon-Sugar Coating:

½ cup granulated sugar

¾ teaspoon ground cinnamon

Preparation:

1. Add the water, butter, sugar, and salt to a medium pot. Bring to a boil over medium-high heat. 2. Reduce the heat to medium-low and stir in the flour. Cook, stirring constantly with a rubber spatula until the dough is smooth and comes together. 3. Remove the dough from the heat and place it in a mixing bowl. Allow 4 minutes for cooling. 4. In a mixing bowl, beat the eggs and vanilla extract with an electric hand mixer or stand mixer until the dough comes together. The finished product will resemble gluey mashed potatoes. Press the lumps together into a ball with your hands, then transfer to a large piping bag with a large star-shaped tip. Pipe out the churros. 5. Install a crisper plate in both drawers. Place half the churros in the zone 1 drawer and half in zone 2's, then insert the drawers into the unit. 6. Select zone 1, select AIR FRY, set temperature to 390 degrees F/200 degrees C, and set time to 12 minutes. Select MATCH to match zone 2 settings to zone 1. Press the START/STOP button to begin cooking. 7. In a shallow bowl, combine the granulated sugar and cinnamon. 8. Immediately transfer the baked churros to the bowl with the sugar mixture and toss to coat.

Serving Suggestion: Serve warm with Nutella or chocolate dipping sauce.
Variation Tip: You can use coconut flour instead.
Nutritional Information Per Serving: Calories 204 | Fat 9g | Sodium 91mg | Carbs 27g | Fiber 0.3g | Sugar 15g | Protein 3g

Apple Fritters

Prep Time: 10 minutes | Cook Time: 10 minutes | Serves: 14

Ingredients:

2 large apples
2 cups all-purpose flour
½ cup granulated sugar
1 tablespoon baking powder

1 teaspoon salt
1 teaspoon ground cinnamon
½ teaspoon ground nutmeg
¼ teaspoon ground cloves

¾ cup apple cider or apple juice
2 eggs
3 tablespoons butter, melted
1 teaspoon vanilla extract

For the Apple Cider Glaze:
2 cups powdered sugar
¼ cup apple cider or apple juice

½ teaspoon ground cinnamon
¼ teaspoon ground nutmeg

Preparation:

1. Peel and core the apples, then cut them into ¼-inch cubes. Spread the apple chunks out on a kitchen towel to absorb any excess moisture. 2. In a mixing bowl, combine the flour, sugar, baking powder, salt, and spices. 3. Add the apple chunks and combine well. 4. Whisk together the apple cider, eggs, melted butter, and vanilla in a small bowl. 5. Combine the wet and dry ingredients in a large mixing bowl. 6. Install a crisper plate in both drawers. Use an ice cream scoop to scoop 3 to 4 dollops of fritter dough into the zone 1 drawer and 3 to 4 dollops into the zone 2 drawer. Insert the drawers into the unit. You may need to cook in batches. 7. Select zone 1, select BAKE, set temperature to 390 degrees F/200 degrees C, and set time to 10 minutes. Select MATCH to match zone 2 settings to zone 1. Press the START/STOP button to begin cooking. 8. Meanwhile, make the glaze: Whisk the powdered sugar, apple cider, and spices together until smooth. 9. When the fritters are cooked, drizzle the glaze over them. Let sit for 10 minutes until the glaze sets.

Serving Suggestion: Serve with your favorite hot beverage.

Variation Tip: You can use pears instead.

Nutritional Information Per Serving: Calories 221 | Fat 3g | Sodium 288mg | Carbs 46g | Fiber 2g | Sugar 29g | Protein 3g

Pumpkin Muffins with Cinnamon

Prep Time: 20 Minutes | Cook Time: 20 Minutes | Serves: 4

Ingredients:

1 and ½ cups all-purpose flour
½ teaspoon baking soda
½ teaspoon baking powder
1 and ¼ teaspoons cinnamon, groaned

¼ teaspoon ground nutmeg, grated
2 large eggs
Salt, pinch
¾ cup granulated sugar

½ cup dark brown sugar
1 and ½ cups pumpkin puree
¼ cup coconut milk

Preparation:

1. Take 4 ramekins and layer them with muffin paper. 2. In a bowl, add the eggs, brown sugar, baking soda, baking powder, cinnamon, nutmeg, and sugar and whisk well with an electric mixer. 3. In a second bowl, mix the flour, and salt. 4. Slowly add the dry ingredients to the wet ingredients. 5. Fold in the pumpkin puree and milk and mix it in well. 6. Divide this batter into 4 ramekins. 7. Place two ramekins in each air fryer basket. 8. Set the time for zone 1 to 18 minutes at 360 degrees F/180 degrees C on AIR FRY mode. 9. Select the MATCH button for the zone 2 basket. 10. Check after the time is up and if not done, and let it AIR FRY for one more minute. 11. Once it is done, serve.

Serving Suggestion: Serve it with a glass of milk

Variation Tip: Use almond milk instead of coconut milk

Nutritional Information Per Serving: Calories 291 | Fat 6.4g | Sodium 241mg | Carbs 57.1g | Fiber 4.4g | Sugar 42g | Protein 5.9g

Fried Oreos

Prep Time: 2 minutes | Cook Time: 8 minutes | Serves: 8

Ingredients:

1 can Pillsbury Crescent Dough (or equivalent)   8 Oreo cookies

1–2 tablespoons powdered sugar

Preparation:

1. Open the crescent dough up and cut it into the right-size pieces to completely wrap each cookie. 2. Wrap each Oreo in dough. Make sure that there are no air bubbles and that the cookies are completely covered. 3. Install a crisper plate in both drawers. Place half the Oreo cookies in the zone 1 drawer and half in zone 2's. Sprinkle the tops with the powdered sugar, then insert the drawers into the unit. 4. Select zone 1, select AIR FRY, set temperature to 390 degrees F/200 degrees C, and set time to 8 minutes. Select MATCH to match zone 2 settings to zone 1. Press the START/STOP button to begin cooking. 5. Serve warm and enjoy!

Serving Suggestion: Serve warm with vanilla ice cream and a dusting of powdered sugar.

Variation Tip: You can use brown sugar.

Nutritional Information Per Serving: Calories 338 | Fat 21.2g | Sodium 1503mg | Carbs 5.1g | Fiber 0.3g | Sugar 4.6g | Protein 29.3g

Grilled Peaches

Prep Time: 5minutes | Cook Time: 10 minutes | Serves: 4

Ingredients:

2 yellow peaches
¼ cup graham cracker crumbs

¼ cup brown sugar
¼ cup butter, diced into tiny cubes

Whipped cream or ice cream, for serving.

Preparation:

1. Cut the peaches into wedges and pull out their pits. 2. Install a crisper plate in both drawers. Put half of the peach wedges into the drawer in zone 1 and half in zone 2's. Sprinkle the tops of the wedges with the crumbs, sugar, and butter. Insert the drawers into the unit. 3. Select zone 1, select AIR FRY, set the temperature to 390 degrees F/200 degrees C, and set the time to 10 minutes. Select MATCH to match zone 2 settings to zone 1. Press the START/STOP button to begin cooking.

Serving Suggestion: Serve the peaches with whipped cream or ice cream.

Variation Tip: You can use apples if you prefer.

Nutritional Information Per Serving: Calories 200 | Fat 13.2g | Sodium 132mg | Carbs 20.1g | Fiber 1.3g | Sugar 16.8g | Protein 1.3g

Strawberry Nutella Hand Pies

Prep Time: 20 minutes | Cook Time: 10 minutes | Serves: 8

Ingredients:

1 tube pie crust dough
3–4 strawberries, finely chopped

Nutella
Sugar

Coconut oil cooking spray

Preparation:

1. Roll out the pie dough and place it on a baking sheet. Cut out hearts using a 3-inch heart-shaped cookie cutter as precisely as possible. 2. Gather the leftover dough into a ball and roll it out thinly to make a few more heart shapes. For 8 hand pies, I was able to get 16 hearts from one tube of pie crust. 3. Set aside a baking tray lined with parchment paper. 4. Spread a dollop of Nutella (approximately 1 teaspoon) on one of the hearts. Add a few strawberry pieces to the mix. Add a pinch of sugar to the top. 5. Place another heart on top and use a fork to tightly crimp the edges. Gently poke holes in the top of the pie with a fork. Place on a baking sheet. Repeat for all the pies. 6. All of the pies on the tray should be sprayed with coconut oil. 7. Install a crisper plate in both drawers. Place half the pies in the zone 1 drawer and half in zone 2's, then insert the drawers into the unit. 8. Select zone 1, select BAKE, set temperature to 390 degrees F/200 degrees C, and set time to 10 minutes. Select MATCH to match zone 2 settings to zone 1. Press the START/STOP button to begin cooking.

Serving Suggestion: Serve with ice cream.

Variation Tip: You can use your choice of berries.

Nutritional Information Per Serving: Calories 41 | Fat 2.1g | Sodium 18mg | Carbs 5.5g | Fiber 0.4g | Sugar 4.1g | Protein 0.4g

Baked Apples

Prep Time: 5 minutes | Cook Time: 20 minutes | Serves: 4

Ingredients:

4 granny smith apples, halved and cored
¼ cup old-fashioned oats (not the instant kind)

1 tablespoon butter, melted
2 tablespoon brown sugar

½ teaspoon ground cinnamon
Whipped cream, for topping (optional)

Preparation:

1. Insert the crisper plates into the drawers. Lay the cored apple halves in a single layer into each of the drawers (the apple's flesh should be pointing up). Insert the drawers into the unit. 2. Select zone 1, select AIR FRY, set temperature to 350 degrees F/175 degrees C, and set time to 10 minutes. Select MATCH to match zone 2 settings to zone 1. Press the START/STOP button to begin cooking. 3. Meanwhile, mix the oats, melted butter, brown sugar, and cinnamon to form the topping. 4. Add the topping to the apple halves when they've cooked for 10 minutes. 5. Select zone 1, select BAKE, set temperature to 390 degrees F/200 degrees C, and set time to 22 minutes. Select MATCH to match zone 2 settings to zone 1. Press the START/STOP button to begin cooking. 6. Serve warm and enjoy!

Serving Suggestion: Serve with whipped cream or vanilla ice cream.

Variation Tip: You can use pears instead.

Nutritional Information Per Serving: Calories 98 | Fat 3g | Sodium 25mg | Carbs 17g | Fiber 2g | Sugar 11g | Protein 1g

Cinnamon Sugar Dessert Fries

Prep Time: 5 minutes | Cook Time: 15 minutes | Serves: 4

Ingredients:

2 sweet potatoes
1 tablespoon butter, melted

1 teaspoon butter, melted
2 tablespoons sugar

½ teaspoon ground cinnamon

Preparation:

1. Peel and cut the sweet potatoes into skinny fries. 2. Coat the fries with 1 tablespoon of butter. 3. Install a crisper plate into each drawer. Place half the sweet potatoes in the zone 1 drawer and half in zone 2's, then insert the drawers into the unit. 4. Select zone 1, select AIR FRY, set temperature to 390 degrees F/200 degrees C, and set time to 15 minutes. Select MATCH to match zone 2 settings to zone 1. Press the START/STOP button to begin cooking. 5. When the time reaches 11 minutes, press START/STOP to pause the unit. Remove the drawers and flip the fries. Re-insert the drawers into the unit and press START/STOP to resume cooking. 6. Meanwhile, mix the 1 teaspoon of butter, the sugar, and the cinnamon in a large bowl. 7. When the fries are done, add them to the bowl, and toss them to coat. 8. Serve and enjoy!

Serving Suggestion: Serve with chocolate dipping sauce.

Variation Tip: You can add a pinch of ground nutmeg.

Nutritional Information Per Serving: Calories 110 | Fat 4g | Sodium 51mg | Carbs 18g | Fiber 2g | Sugar 10g | Protein 1g

Lava Cake

Prep Time: 10 minutes | Cook Time: 10 minutes | Serves: 4

Ingredients:

1 cup semi-sweet chocolate chips
8 tablespoons butter
4 eggs

2 teaspoons vanilla extract
½ teaspoon salt
6 tablespoons all-purpose flour

1 cup powdered sugar

For the Chocolate Filling:

2 tablespoons Nutella

1 tablespoon butter, softened

1 tablespoon powdered sugar

Preparation:

1. Heat the chocolate chips and butter in a medium-sized microwave-safe bowl in 30-second intervals until thoroughly melted and smooth, stirring after each interval. 2. Whisk together the eggs, vanilla, salt, flour, and powdered sugar in a mixing bowl. 3. Combine the Nutella, softened butter, and powdered sugar in a separate bowl. 4. Spray 4 ramekins with oil and fill them halfway with the chocolate chip mixture. Fill each ramekin halfway with Nutella, then top with the remaining chocolate chip mixture, making sure the Nutella is well covered. 5. Install a crisper plate in both drawers. Place 2 ramekins in each drawer and insert the drawers into the unit. 6. Select zone 1, select AIR FRY, set temperature to 390 degrees F/200 degrees C, and set time to 22 minutes. Select MATCH to match zone 2 settings to zone 1. Press the START/STOP button to begin cooking. 7. Serve hot.

Serving Suggestion: Serve with a sprinkling of powdered sugar and a scoop of vanilla ice cream.

Variation Tip: You can use a mixture of semi-sweet and dark chocolate.

Nutritional Information Per Serving: Calories 338 | Fat 21.2g | Sodium 1503mg | Carbs 5.1g | Fiber 0.3g | Sugar 4.6g | Protein 29.3g

Jelly Donuts

Prep Time: 5 minutes | Cook Time: 5 minutes | Serves: 4

Ingredients:

1 package Pillsbury Grands (Homestyle)
½ cup seedless raspberry jelly

1 tablespoon butter, melted
½ cup sugar

Preparation:

1. Install a crisper plate in both drawers. Place half of the biscuits in the zone 1 drawer and half in zone 2's, then insert the drawers into the unit. You may need to cook in batches. 2. Select zone 1, select AIR FRY, set temperature to 390 degrees F/200 degrees C, and set time to 22 minutes. Select MATCH to match zone 2 settings to zone 1. Press the START/STOP button to begin cooking. 3. Place the sugar into a wide bowl with a flat bottom. 4. Baste all sides of the cooked biscuits with the melted butter and roll in the sugar to cover completely. 5. Using a long cake tip, pipe 1–2 tablespoons of raspberry jelly into each biscuit. You've now got raspberry-filled donuts!

Serving Suggestion: Serve with your favorite hot beverage.

Variation Tip: You can use brown sugar instead.

Nutritional Information Per Serving: Calories 252 | Fat 7g | Sodium 503mg | Carbs 45g | Fiber 0g | Sugar 23g | Protein 3g

Conclusion

If you plan to purchase the Ninja Foodi 2-Basket Air Fryer, then this book is a perfect choice. I hope you will understand all features and cooking methods of this appliance. You can prepare recipes from this book with the Ninja Foodi 2-Basket Air Fryer. Whether serving a large family gathering or cooking for your small family, the Ninja Foodi 2-Basket Air Fryer fulfills all your cooking needs. You don't need to buy a separate oven or dehydrator to bake or dehydrate food. This appliance offers all the useful functions that you need. You can prepare all types of food using this appliance. Thank you for choosing us!

Appendix 1 Measurement Conversion Chart

WEIGHT EQUIVALENTS

US STANDARD	METRIC (APPROXINATE)
1 ounce	28 g
2 ounces	57 g
5 ounces	142 g
10 ounces	284 g
15 ounces	425 g
16 ounces (1 pound)	455 g
1.5pounds	680 g
2pounds	907 g

VOLUME EQUIVALENTS (LIQUID)

US STANDARD	US STANDARD (OUNCES)	METRIC (APPROXIMATE)
2 tablespoons	1 fl.oz	30 mL
¼ cup	2 fl.oz	60 mL
½ cup	4 fl.oz	120 mL
1 cup	8 fl.oz	240 mL
1½ cup	12 fl.oz	355 mL
2 cups or 1 pint	16 fl.oz	475 mL
4 cups or 1 quart	32 fl.oz	1 L
1 gallon	128 fl.oz	4 L

VOLUME EQUIVALENTS (DRY)

US STANDARD	METRIC (APPROXIMATE)
⅛ teaspoon	0.5 mL
¼ teaspoon	1 mL
½ teaspoon	2 mL
¾ teaspoon	4 mL
1 teaspoon	5 mL
1 tablespoon	15 mL
¼ cup	59 mL
½ cup	118 mL
¾ cup	177 mL
1 cup	235 mL
2 cups	475 mL
3 cups	700 mL
4 cups	1 L

TEMPERATURES EQUIVALENTS

FAHRENHEIT (F)	CELSIUS (C) (APPROXIMATE)
225 ℉	107℃
250 ℉	120℃
275 ℉	135℃
300 ℉	150℃
325 ℉	160℃
350 ℉	180℃
375 ℉	190℃
400 ℉	205℃
425 ℉	220℃
450 ℉	235℃
475 ℉	245℃
500 ℉	260℃

Appendix 2 Air Fryer Cooking Chart

Chicken	Temp (℉)	Time (min)
Chicken Whole (3.5 lbs)	350	45-60
Chicken Breast (boneless)	380	12-15
Chicken Breast (bone-in)	350	22-25
Chicken Drumsticks	380	23-25
Chicken Thighs (bone-in)	380	23-25
Chicken Tenders	350	8-12
Chicken Wings	380	22-25

Beef	Temp (℉)	Time (min)
Burgers (1/4 Pound)	350	8-12
Filet Mignon (4 oz.)	370	15-20
Flank Steak (1.5 lbs)	400	10-14
Meatballs (1 inch)	380	7-10
London Broil (2.5 lbs.)	400	22-28
Round Roast (4 lbs)	390	45-55
Sirloin Steak (12oz)	390	9-14

Pork & Lamb	Temp (℉)	Time
Bacon	350	8-12
Lamb Chops	400	8-12
Pork Chops (1" boneless)	400	8-10
Pork Loin (2 lbs.)	360	18-21
Rack of Lamb (24-32 oz.)	375	22-25
Ribs	400	10-15
Sausages	380	10-15

Fish & Seafood	Temp (℉)	Time
Calamari	400	4-5
Fish Fillets	400	10-12
Salmon Fillets	350	8-12
Scallops	400	5-7
Shrimp	370	5-7
Lobster Tails	370	5-7
Tuna Steaks	400	7-10

Vegetables	Temp (℉)	Time
Asparagus (1" slices)	400	5
Beets (whole)	400	40
Broccoli Florets	400	6
Brussel Sprouts (halved)	380	12-15
Carrots (1/2" slices)	360	12-15
Cauliflower Florets	400	10-12
Corn on the Cob	390	6-7
Eggplant (1 1/2" cubes)	400	12-15
Green Beans	400	4-6
Kale Leaves	250	12
Mushrooms (1/4" slices)	400	4-5
Onions (pearl)	400	10
Peppers (1" chunks)	380	8-15
Potatoes (whole)	400	30-40
Potatoes (wedges)	390	15-18
Potatoes (1" cubes)	390	12-15
Potatoes (baby, 1.5 lbs.)	400	15
Squash (1" cubes)	390	15
Sweet Potato (whole)	380	30-35
Tomatoes (cherry)	400	5
Zucchini (1/2" sticks)	400	10-12

Frozen Foods	Temp (℉)	Time
Breaded Shrimp	400	8-9
Chicken Burger	360	12
Chicken Nuggets	370	10-12
Chicken Strips	380	12-15
Corn Dogs	400	7-9
Fish Fillets (1-2 lbs.)	400	10-12
Fish Sticks	390	12-15
French Fries	380	12-17
Hash Brown Patties	380	10-12
Meatballs (1-inch)	350	10-12
Mozzarella Sticks (11 oz.)	400	8
Meat Pies (1-2 pies)	370	23-25
Mozzarella Sticks	390	7-9
Onion Rings	400	10-12
Pizza	390	5-10
Tater Tots	380	15-17

Made in the USA
Las Vegas, NV
09 November 2023

80457717R10062